Desaparición

Hispanic Studies: Culture and Ideas

Volume **53**

Edited by
Claudio Canaparo

PETER LANG
Oxford · Bern · Berlin · Bruxelles · Frankfurt am Main · New York · Wien

Gabriele Andreozzi (ed.)

Desaparición

Argentina's Human Rights Trials

PETER LANG
Oxford · Bern · Berlin · Bruxelles · Frankfurt am Main · New York · Wien

Bibliographic information published by Die Deutsche Nationalbibliothek.
Die Deutsche Nationalbibliothek lists this publication in the Deutsche Nationalbibliografie; detailed bibliographic data is available on the Internet at http://dnb.d-nb.de.

A catalogue record for this book is available from the British Library.

Library of Congress Cataloging-in-Publication Data:

Andreozzi, Gabriele.
Desaparición : Argentina's human rights trials / Gabriele Andreozzi.
pages cm. -- (Hispanic Studies : Culture and Ideas ; 53)
Includes bibliographical references and index.
ISBN 978-3-0343-0857-1 (alk. paper)
1. Human rights--Argentina--History. 2. Crimes against humanity--Argentina--History. 3. Trials (crimes against humanity)--Argentina--History. 4. Disappeared persons--Argentina--History. 5. Argentina--Politics and government. I. Title.
KHA3003.A95 2013
342.8208'5--dc23

2013024565

Cover image: Ysa Casse, *Chaos II*. Mixed media on canvas, 24cm × 30cm

ISSN 1661-4720
ISBN 978-3-0343-0857-1

Hochfeldstrasse 32, CH-3012 Bern, Switzerland
info@peterlang.com, www.peterlang.com, www.peterlang.net

This publication has been peer reviewed.

Contents

To my grandmothers who taught me to listen to the stories of each person.

To Carolina and Tosca

GABRIELE ANDREOZZI

Introduction

Memory allows us to communicate: through it we can recover the meaning of words; it permits us to move around in our environment and recognize ourselves; memory gives us a past and a future.

Past events must be addressed through a process of redefining perspectives in understanding a society and in the ability to re-elaborate the present.

The 1970s represents, on a global level, a period of cultural ferment which created alternative political models, but it is also thought of as a period during which states institutionalized, at different levels and with different modalities, the use of violence so as to suppress aspirations for social justice.

Governments monopolize the "legitimacy" of the use of violence through the method of the exclusion of the *other*, who is stigmatized as an enemy of society. Prisons, centres for the identification and expulsion of immigrants in Europe, Guantánamo, Abu Ghraib, secret detention centres in Argentina, the Nazi concentration camps, represent – each one with its own distinctions and peculiarities – structured and disciplined punitive forms of the perennial dialectic of "discipline and punish" in the constant establishment of public order. It is the perfect realization of a two-faced state, or dual state, together with the advanced realization of a regime of "authoritarian democracy" in which dehumanization is raised to legality with the consequent separation of formal and substantive law.

The book raises the question of the dialectic between history and memory in which memory enters explosively into the field of history through the courtrooms, and is not limited to them. The period of the Argentinean trials marks an indispensable moment in the rebuilding of a society traumatized by a history of grave crimes against humanity.

For a person born in Italy after the 1970s but who has suffered its burdens and its consequences, to speak of Argentina has different meanings. These range from not forgetting the tragedy of an atrocity, to understanding the present socio-political evolution – not only in Argentina – of the dialectic which arises between impunity, denied and forgotten memory, and continuous regressions to an unsuperseded past.

This is why I believe that only through an analysis of the years of the dictatorship and the transition to democracy can the behaviours of today's society, the democratic credibility of the institutions, the sense of belonging to the community and the reconstruction of the lost identity be understood. Such an analysis is necessarily composed of different substrata and has multiple nuances.

There are many different ways of approaching the facts: documents, stories which create a past, and the methods of truth formation. The choice of a multidisciplinary project of reflection has been dictated not only by the need to give a true picture of the complexity of the social and institutional dynamics in relation to the subject of memory, but above all because of the firm conviction that the instruments of the composition of the truth will and be should be numerous in a debate about a past which is both permanent and contemporary.

Both a society and a human being who have been deprived of memory, find their intrinsic path of evolution irreparably jeopardized. Error without memory – not only as reminiscence but above all as reflection – implies being condemned to repetition, to an infinite present, because it does not permit the creation of antidotes such as the deviations innate both to a society and to the human being. Memory, therefore, represents one of the fundamental pillars of the social structure, without which the latter is put at risk.

Argentina's history is marked by recurrent coups which have sadly conditioned the country's moments of democratic development. Currently, the state is distancing itself from an atavistic impunity, thus freeing itself from the social obsession of being a nation without memory.

The current "judicial season"[1] is creating the preconditions for the consolidation of those democratic institutions in which citizens can recognize the object of a complex process of discussion about the role of the state. Truth, justice and memory have been, and are, hallmarks of an Argentinean dynamics around which a strong collective identity is being created, beyond the all too high a risk of a new social breakdown. It is enough to think about the legal discourse. This is founded on the reception of the dictates of international conventions for the protection of Human Rights which are at the core of this democratic renewal. Precisely because they are universal, they can be related to a *"rational being"* outside of time and space.

In the trial of the unconstitutionality of the amnesty laws, the *Corte Suprema* (Supreme Court) made reference to international law in order to strengthen the national legal system, transforming the fundamental rights from mere "noble affirmations" into true and proper, effective and exercisable, rights. The actual scope of the semantics of the universality of rights is thus established. These are no longer universals treated as a dead letter because the world is becoming globalized, but are proper to the human being as such, regardless of political action (compliance or lack of compliance with the various international conventions), and a collective perspective which takes account of peoples, their history and identity. They are rights inscribed in the *Constitución Nacional* (National Constitution), the constitutive moment of every nation, and taken up by international law as the result of a globally accepted ethic in which the action of the individual and the right to live a decent life are preserved. With this summary the aim is to demonstrate that, in the context of a history of serious crimes against humanity, the indivisibility and interconnectedness of human rights cannot renounce the judicial moment because of the turn of society in a truly democratic direction.

1 The trial has been defined by Luigi Ferrajoli, as "the only case of historiographical experiment". The judge who guides the interrogation of the accused and the witnesses ("the sources ... events performing live") behaves like a historian who calls them into question in order to analyse different documents. But the documents (the accused and the witnesses) do not speak by themselves C. Ginzburg, *Il giudice e lo storico*, Milan, Universale Economica Feltrinelli, 1991, p. 33.

The present account, whether developed inside or outside of the courtroom, is a tortuous passage which serves both to condemn the violent past of the state and to rethink social, economic, institutional, trade union and political relations. In its rational and collective signification, its high foundational value should be understood as belonging to everyone, not tainted by any political affiliation, so as to avoid influencing history with a partisan vision or colouring. Without justice, the minimum conditions for democracy do not exist and without democracy nor do the conditions to decode, and thus decipher, the social fracture.

It is necessary to recognize the political support which one part of Argentina's ruling class has given to the exercise of legal action against the military, the capacity of having illuminated the power and beauty of the law as the receiver of demands arising from below and as of the stories told so far. The trials affirm a judicial truth and legitimate a new story of the Argentinean past, to be shared by the majority of society, and at the same they time react against this, because of the high symbolic value such a story assumes. The criminal charges for crimes against humanity are the offspring of international visions of law, of the conviction that the right to truth is an essential tool for the creation and strengthening of institutions in which the citizen is recognized, believes and feels himself to be represented and protected as an active member of a community. Today, involved in restoring dignity to the thousands of victims of state terrorism is just one of the three state powers: the judiciary. The State must regain credibility, weakened by years of coups, by not neglecting the law's capacity to act, which "is the premise of happiness".[2]

The active exercise and substantial recognition of law represent the nodal turning point of a new constituent moment. It is with the law and in the law that the condemnation of State violence, torture and betrayal is executed, as a fundamental means of orientation of political action.

2 R. Saviano, quoted in Raitre's transmission, "*Vieni via con me*", to the Italian judge Giovanni Falcone, murdered in an attack by the Mafia in 1992 because of the institutionalization of the maxi-trials.

Therefore, the criminal process delineates a renewed confidence in the institutions, but includes a moment of *reconciliation* with the past itself.[3]

The pursuit of justice, collective memory and history, although they are considered to be distinct, do not contradict each other but nourish each other in the fight against the snares of oblivion.[4] The methods of investigation of the judge[5] and the historian[6] are both oriented by the reality principle, to the obtaining of evidence, and are united in a very close relationship. The historian is credited with a privileged investigative

3 A reconciliation understood not in the religious-ethical sense in relation to the military – which in any case cannot take place given that it demands the sacrament of penitence while the military have never wanted to look back at the history experienced, even less disown it – but a reconciliation with oneself and the community. At the core of the religious concept of reconciliation is the idea that, being themselves victims and perpetrators, it is useless blame or apologize. Better to recognize the evil thereof.

4 "Renan argued that forgetting is an 'essential factor in creating a nation', while adding that historical research can be a danger, 'because it brings to light the violence that accompanied the origin of all political formations' even those considered beneficial. To make use of forgetting as a factor unifying the Italians, it will be necessary to tame historical research. An appropriate fee for Oblivion could tell historians what things can be recorded and which should be forgotten, continually adapting the past to the need for a common history. Even if, obviously, Days of Forgetting cannot be instituted instead of Days of Memory, because all days are moments to be remembered. It may be more practical and effective to do without history and get the Italians used to, if the Italian government survives, living like animals. That man is envious – according to Nietzsche – because animals forget immediately and wander in a present without history".

5 "The relationship between history and law have always been very narrow: ever since, 2,500 years ago, when the literary genre we call 'history' appears in Greece. If the word 'storia' (history) is derived from medical language, the argumentative capacity it implies comes in turn from the legal field. History as an intellectual activity is constituted (as Arnaldo Momigliano reminded us some years ago) at the intersection between medicine and rhetoric: it examines cases and situations, seeking natural causes according to the example of the first and exposes them following the rules of the second – an art of born in the courts". C. Ginzburg, *Il Giudice and what storico*, Milan, Feltrinelli Universale Economica, March 2006, pp. 16–17.

6 A historian is entitled to notice a problem where a judge would say "there are no grounds to proceed". It is a significant discrepancy, which presupposes an element that unites historians and judges: the use of proof. Idem, p. 20.

position which allows him to assume procedural acts not only as sources of knowledge of events or situations which are the subject of trials – of which traces are also found in the trial – but also as a parameter for evaluating the correctness or incorrectness of the research procedures and the conclusions reached by the judges. It is also through the criminal trial that the reconstruction of the process of cultural control over the use of the discourses is achieved.

The Argentinean dictatorship has reacted at the cultural level by enacting a process of the emancipation of language, thus reducing society to aphasia. The society has been, and is, nothing other than the freezing of words, an extirpation, but at the same time a state of alarm in relation to external stimuli. It is as if an entire nation had been affected by this disease, and that recovering the internal disposition to cure itself has cost it much. The human rights organizations have been the remedies, and throughout their trajectory have been able to make themselves heard and to this day have been a symbol of the cure of the disease. Therefore, through recently launched cultural actions, a new generation of Argentineans exists, engaged in different fields of political activity, and this generation is rebuilding the interrupted semantic field. We are witnessing the resumption of the principles of social struggle and of the consequent commitment to dispelling fear, which is the symbol of despotism, not of democracy. The recovery of memory is even taking place through the recovery of lost language skills and the restoration of the different centres involved in the functioning of language.

Calling things by their name, thus giving them an identity, is an action directed toward the future and represents a democratic legacy for generations to come in the perpetual journey of the consolidation of institutions.

Replacing one word by another with a different meaning, or from the same family, or using the wrong word, but with a similar sound to that of the right one, or even a word completely different and without any apparent connection with the correct one, completely misrepresents the content, the actual image we want to represent with the word.[7]

7 "There is no word in any human language, able to comfort those guinea pigs who do not know the reason for their deaths. A survivor of Hiroshima". Quoted in E. Morante, *Storia, Uno scandalo che dura dieci mila anni*, Turin, Einaudi, 1974.

Consider the reality enclosed and summarized in the word *disappearance*. The official military phrase suppresses the action in favour of the fate of the person who becomes a non-person. The disappeared is that which "... while it is gone, can not have any special treatment, is unknown, is a disappeared, has no significance, is neither alive nor dead, it is disappeared".[8]

How do you explain to future generations the aberrant sense of *disappearance?* How will it be recounted when there are no more direct testimonies of what has happened?

The relatives of the victims, the grandmothers, mothers and children, experience this absence on a continual basis. They are only ones able to describe the full meaning and magnitude of intimate and emotional emptiness. On the other hand, it is much more complex to illustrate and decipher the social reach of the forced disappearance of an entire generation either for society or for history. Meanwhile, on the social plane, the reconstruction of history is enriched by the discussion between signifiers and signifieds in the reconquest of those semantic cultural and political spaces which were removed by the military, in search of a socialization of justice and the specification of the manifold identity of which a group is constituted.

The disappeared are *present* in the courtrooms, in the acts of commemoration, in the demonstrations. Their names resonate throughout the country through the narrative which serves to take revenge on the desire for their complete elimination. The *disappearance* is the power which hides itself and at the same time the power which hides concealment.[9] The lack of a body, and therefore of mourning, is one of the most lacerating wounds a human being can endure. The intention of the military was to truncate the evolution of a different political activity, as a prolonged extirpation in order to cure a disease. It is a torture in time, with devastating effects on families and society. The ideas and the alternative political message were annihilation, transformation and subjection. Today the opposition is no

8 R. Videla, *Clarín*, 14 January 1979.

9 Consider, for example, the physical and cultural elimination of the indigenous peoples in the Desert Campaign or the disappearance of Eva Perón's body, which for fourteen years had been stolen and buried far from her land and the person who wanted to honour her.

longer considered a *cancer to be removed*,[10] but rather represents a way of vindicating the rights themselves, a form of active participation. Democracy needs active citizens, while authoritarian regimes prefer the apathy and indifference which make people easier to control. For this reason the current debate about reform of the law – coveted by the last dictatorship – which disciplines the media should not be underestimated.[11]

At this point in time, after certain memorable elections, and using the tools proper to the criminal law, Argentina is experiencing a season of the rediscovery of her own story, a story different from the "official" story of the dictatorship. This story has taken place at the international level over a period of three decades, beginning with the social and political euphoria of the renewal which comes from the below in the second half of the 1960s, through the violence of the 1970s, to the rejection of politics and the triumph of neoliberalism in the 1980s and 1990s.

10 It suffices to consider that one of the torture chambers of the ESMA was called the *operating room*. Cels, *Los niños desaparecidos*, Buenos Aires, 1982, p. 21.

11 The role of collusion of the journalists with the military who today see them as the absolute owners of the national information and as being influential at the international level. The evolution of a case such as that of Papel Prensa, which even today generates so many unresolved questions that still are present in society and its fundamental mechanisms. The articles read in Europe are taken from the daily *Clarín*, obviously demonstrating that information is power. In Italy, either because of our will to eliminate, or as a result of the truly shoddy nature of the journalism which refers to international issues, we have a completely distorted perception of phenomena in South America, and among these is the present-day Argentina: http://www.ilfattoquotidiano.it/2010/09/10/argentina-la-riforma-dei-media-che-dividestop-al-monopolio-o-silenziatore-alla-stampa/58662/ http://www.ilfattoquotidiano.it/2010/08/29/guerra-di-carta-in-argentina-tra-il-governo-e-i-giornali/54074/. Throughout the year 2009, *Repubblica* wrote only one article on the presidency of Cristina Kirchner. The picturesque tone, omitting mention of Argentinean politics and qualitative comments about the personal behaviour of the President: http://www.repubblica.it/2009/01/sezioni/persone/cristina-kirchner/cristina-kirchner/cristina-kirchner.html?ref=search. By contrast, the Grupo Prisa, of which *El País* is part, is the leading media group in the market for news in the Spanish and Portuguese languages. It is a leader in information, present in twenty-two countries with fifty million users through the different products issued, and presents a varied and constant analysis in relation to Argentina.

The 1970s have been an unusual decade in the evolution of society in a large part of the world: characterized both by mass civil participation and reformist zeal, but also by widespread political violence on the part of the state. From *Berkeley* to the *Sorbonne*, students, together with workers and committed intellectuals, invoked "all power to the imagination"[12] so as to defeat the Vietnam war and injustice in the world. They became enraptured by the Cuban revolution and the redemption of the African colonies. In the continent of South America the ideas of revolt encountered the strong opposition of bloody dictatorships.

The 1970s appear to be a still somehow unresolved period. They are an open space for reflection, especially with regard to the use of violence as a political instrument. There was everyday violence – in language, in public demonstrations in the squares, in addition to a series of serious incidents – in Europe. Organized and systematic violence on the part of the police and military was experienced in Latin America through Plan Condor, a sort of joint coordination of the various security forces, trained at the famous school of the Americas in the United States and in France by the Foreign Legion.

The aim of these reflections is not intended only to describe what has happened, but above all, to offer understanding of whether, to what extent and how the recent past is present in public life today.

Globally, the 1970s, with their arcane beauty, exercise a state of fascination and concern, designating the new syntax of the "regulation" of violence.

I consider that the tension between criticism and counter-criticism, between memory and forgetting, can help boost the socialization of memory even in a country like Italy, where a past which is considered too heavy an inheritance has been carefully obscured in a deeply entrenched cultural and political process. Otherwise, in Italy, as in Spain and in other countries, an analysis has been lacking of the influence which the use of terror and the state of emergency have had on successive social, economic and political transformations. The desire has been to convey only a collective memory attached to the spiral of violence, removing the forms and content of social vindication, confining discourse to the presence of *dos demonios* ("two demons").

12 A slogan written on the walls of Paris during 1968.

The *demonio* has more of an ethical than a political dimension, summoning up an almost pathological symbology of madness, without adding anything about the reasons for the evolution of political confrontation. In terms of political science, the need to control and suppress social and work-based conflict and preserve political unity and identity, implies a continuous polarization of the conflict, justified by the identification of an internal and / or external enemy. If in Argentina this manipulation has been transformed into the establishment of a violent autocratic regime, in Italy the repressive response of the state has taken place in only apparently less clamorous terms, acquiesced to by the democratic state and the Constitution,[13] which does not imply that a profound social upheaval is not possible today.[14]

I think the social shock of the 1970s has felt the consequences of the lack of a route of judicial conviction for the crimes committed during the Civil War (1943–1945) between *repubblichini*[15] and *partisanos* (partisans).[16]

13 The discretionary nature of police intervention was amplified, the terms of preventive detention prolonged. To give an idea of the violence of those years in numbers: between 1969 and 1980 there were 12,960 bombings in which 362 people died, 150 of them in massacres carried out by the state. Cf. A. Silj, *Malpaese. Criminalità, corruzione e politica nell'Italia della prima Repubblica 1943–1994*, Rome, Donzelli, p. 113. For these reasons I consider inappropriate – because they are incomplete – the eulogistic reference to Italy made by Ernesto Sabato in the prologue to *Nunca Más*. Sabato, citing the words of General Carlo Alberto Dalla Chiesa: "... better to lose to Moro than to implement torture in Italy ..." – omits to say that there was a negotiation under way between the State and the Red Brigades, that the emergency laws were passed, arresting many militants for only a hypothetical and supposed ideological closeness to the Red Brigades.

14 Consider the presence of fragments diverted from the State, the role of the subversive right, or the many unsolved killings by the State: Piazza Fontana, 12 December 1969; the Massacre of Gioia Tauro, 22 July 1970; Piazza della Loggia 28 May 1974; the Massacre on the express train Rome–Brenner (Italicus), 16 March 1978; the kidnapping of Aldo Moro; 2 August 1980, the explosion of a bomb in Bologna station.

15 *Repubblichino*: Member or adherent of the Italian Social Republic which was created by Fascism in the centre-north of Italy during the Nazi occupation (December 1953 to April 1945).

16 On 8 December 1943 the Armistice was signed between Italy and the Allies. This sanctioned irretrievably the fracturing of Italian society. The country was pierced by

Not only has Italy never condemned the crimes committed by the fascists, but it has conducted some trials against the partisans. These are trials of protagonists who, at the collective level, have been lost from memory.[17]

The unsuccessful criminal charges brought against fascist crimes has had as it consequence the sense of dissatisfaction and frustration produced by the fact of seeing at liberty those who had caused so much intolerance in the years of fascism. It is a case of a freedom and an impunity which threatened the possibility of recreating a fascist coup only a few years after the fall of the regime. The state, in part exalted, has wanted to create a strong polarization, leading to the continuity of confrontation in the period prior to the 1970s, reflected even in the symbolism of period.[18] The armed struggle has had as a matrix the partisan resistance to fascism, whether as a resumption of a direct experience or as a collective heritage.

Italy today, with its anomalies, social fragmentation and the inflexibility of its ruling class, is partially the daughter of an ignorance of history

---

a civil war which pitted the partisan movement against those who chose to continue fighting for Mussolini and joined the ranks of the newly born Italian Social Republic. More than 600,000 Italian soldiers were captured by the German army, and sent to different concentration camps with the qualification IMI (Italian military internees). At the same time, the united commitment of different political persuasions (Catholics, communists, liberals, actionists, anarchists) opposed the Nazi-fascism in the context of the liberation of Italy. The period of resistance ends with call for armed insurrection in the city of Milan on 25 April.

17 F. Focardi, *Criminali di guerra in libertà, un accordo segreto tra Italia e Germania federale 1949–1955*, Bari and Rome, Carocci, 2008.

18 The Red Brigades: the name would have been chosen at random at the end of a walk through the streets of Milan. Piazzale Loreto, where the bodies of Mussolini and other fascists had been exposed after the execution, would have awakened the memory of partisan brigades. De Volante Rossa would have become transformed into the Red Brigades thanks to Margherita Cagol, who had in mind the *Rote Armee Fraktion* (RAF), so admired for having implemented the first urban guerrilla action in Europe. With respect to the symbol, it is, for Curcio, an allusion to the Tupamaros. M. Lazar, *Il libro deli anni di piombo, storia e memoria del terrorismo italiano*, Milan, Rizzoli, 2010, p. 9. The Italian Social Movement was founded by survivors of the Italian Social Republic and former representatives of the fascist regime. The symbol of the party took up the emblem of the troops of the Assault Corps of the First World War.

itself. As a contribution to the historical reconstruction and the socialization of memory as well as a reparation, the battle to achieve true justice has more a private value – that of the relatives of the victims and a few more – than the character of a collective heritage. The lack of an institutional commitment to fulfilling the right to truth runs the risk of rhetoric, the instrumentalization of memory, and thus of the anomalies of democratic life which are obviously dramatic.

The bad mannered way in which we look at those years is one of the reasons why our memory is tendentious. So far, historical reconstruction has been entrusted to the memorials of the protagonists of the armed struggle and the politicians. This results in partial and sometimes idealized stories which lack a necessary contextualization which would avoid over-polarizing the present. Even public celebrations in remembrance of the victims have always been the prerogative of one political coalition against another, in a pernicious perpetuation of polemic to the detriment of the consolidation of the historical facts and democratic principles.

The 1980s were the time of the transition to harmony and social cohesion: this was something desired from the top and accepted hierarchically. The impulses towards reform have been archived quickly and everything which had anything to do with politics has been perceived negatively. Those who started the armed struggle have not yet reconsidered the past itself by analysing it self-critically, either for internal reasons or lack of the will to listen on the part of the institutions.

Apparent recognition absolves a key role in the plan, whether individual or collective, whether it is the need to know oneself, or to know who we are and what we are destined to be. And therefore to retrieve a collective social perception through the verification of the political process itself, within the limits and weaknesses which this entails. Italy, unlike Argentina,[19] has lacked a great movement of cultural reworking of those

19 In addition to the trials and the flowering of a historiographical literature about the years of the dictatorship and even about the errors committed by the opposing party, we want to recall here, by way of example, the commitment of civic theatre, the cinematographic reworkings, in addition to controversial Open Letter of Oscar del Barco. Cited by *Revista Intemperie*, Issue 17 (October 2004) *Memoria(s)*

years, which would have been capable of complementing the historiographical and judicial contributions, even if there remained gaps. Collective memory has a central role in the evolution of the social self, representing the backbone of a people and their country. "*We are what we remember*".

In this sense the juridical sentence, especially in the case of serious crimes against humanity, is indispensable for understanding what has been experienced. This is so because it is the limit of the human being, defining it and reactivating the dialectic between ethics and politics. And since the individual memory is labile and physiologically selective, it is the task of the state to safeguard the value of memory, ensuring the continuation of the stories as part of the right even to collective reparation and as an antidote against the risk of persisting in a condition of permanent rupture.

In this sense, the Argentinean road to truth is a crucial and innovative example of the processes of the resolution of a violent and traumatic past through full compliance with the rule of law, and even through the actions of the national court. It is the Argentinean justice system which, exercising its own prerogatives in the establishment and verification of the responsibilities for a massacre which at a social and academic level is defined as genocide, has made itself responsible for the recovery of the prospects for the future. From the perspective of democratic reconstruction, the innovation lies in the fact that the trials are being carried out by the ordinary national authorities, without the aid of special and international courts, and that they are doing so in the context of renewed confidence and a reacquisition of the sense of justice on the part of the population.

---

y política, M. del Carmen de la Peza, *Experiencia, poéticas y construcciones de nación*. The political and literary works of Luis Mattini, of Feinmann, Osvaldo Bayer, and Juan Gelman. Luis Mattini: *Los perros, Memorias de un combatiente revolucionario*, 2006, Peña lillo / continente, *Los Perros 2, Memorias de la rebeldía femenina en los '70*, Peña lillo / continente 2007, *El secreto de Lisboa*, Peña lillo / continente, *Cartas profanas, Novela de la correspondencia entre Santucho y Gombrowicz*, Peña lillo / continente, 2008. Osvaldo Bayer, *Exilio con Juan Gelman*, Buenos Aires, Legasa, 1984. José Juan Feinmann, *Ultimo días de la victimas*, Seix barral, 1978, *Timote*, Planeta, 2009. Juan Gelman, *Ni el flaco perdón de Dios/Hijos de desaparecidos*, Planeta, 1997; *Valer la pena*, Seix barral, 2001, *País que fue será*, Rustica, 2004.

The effectiveness of these trials causes me much perplexity, as it is also a justice of the victors or of international powers over the vanquished and over governments which do not have international support.

I am extremely sceptical of the reparatory capacity of other extra-judicial instruments, such as the long-studied and exalted Commission for Truth and Reconciliation through which South Africa has gambled on the possibility of a peaceful transition to democracy. The basic idea behind this Commission was to build a mechanism which would permit understanding of what had happened, without provoking actions of revenge, as if fighting a crime, and indeed one which was recognized internationally as a crime against humanity, was to carry out a humiliation. While the work of the Commission had satisfied the right to truth, because there is no amnesty without truth, I believe that a reflection about the past itself, which starts from a commitment to belittle a part of law, commits a grave sin which will inevitably impact on the ability of the community to adapt to the new social democracy: "When everyone is guilty, nobody is, the confessions of guilt are the best possible guarantee against the discovery of the real culprits, and the very magnitude of the crime is the best excuse for doing nothing. In this particular case it is, moreover, a dangerous and tendentious rise in racism toward higher, less tangible, zones".[20] In the face of the current situation in South Africa it would be necessary to rethink whether the Commission has failed in its most important goal: that of substituting itself for the right of the victims to criminal and civil proceedings against the perpetrators of the crimes, who have achieved and received the amnesty with other rights, obviously recognizing that each situation and each country must provide itself with its own way of reviewing the past. It would be relevant to give the same weight and importance to the international relevance of the Argentinean case. In fact, I believe that justice has the power, if properly exercised, to break and therefore, to resolve positively the relationship with the "guilty" time. This perception has been confirmed by my attending a series of hearings in open trials in Argentina. The experience has helped me to understand better a country with so many

20 H. Arendt, *Sulla violenza*, Parma, Guanda, 2008, p. 69.

nuances and contradictions, which, in its struggle for justice, demonstrates a willingness to give back credit to those institutions, including the judiciary, which had not fulfilled their proper role during the dictatorship.

Every day, in many venues scattered throughout the country, you can participate in the ritual meeting between state and society, in which *reparation* is celebrated through the painful testimonies of the survivors, creatures of the return which make present the absence of those who are no longer here.[21]

The witness preserves the memory of the terror, of the places of detention, of the faces of both victims and torturers. Witnessing has a cathartic function, whether for family members and survivors who are freed from an anguish contained in time, or for the whole community which participates in empathy and is obliged to become aware of the traumatic impact which the conflict has had on the person. It means giving form to a horror, finding effective words to describe the irrationality of *organized evil* and, at the same time, regaining their own dignity on seeing themselves accorded the opportunity to speak publicly about their suffering.

The struggle of the human rights organizations, which have adapted themselves over the years to the historical and legal contingencies of the moment, has always firmly sustained the very vindication of the claim for the right to the truth. Human history is ambiguous for anyone who tries to give it a meaning. Violence is a dominant category of history and politics, taken for granted even when no one "[...] dares to deny that evil has always prevailed over good, joy over pain, unhappiness over happiness, death over life".[22] Good and evil are blurred. That response is provided by the joy of family members, who have transformed pain into responsibility and power – such as the capacity to react concretely – and death into experienced life. What has happened has been an organized and planned "horror".

21 "The mothers of the partisans shot, or killed in the searches, crying, showed photographs of children. I remember the faces of youths, with their eyes turned forever into nothingness. The only ones at peace within that troubled sea, full of anger and pleading for justice". G. Pansa, *Il sangue dei vinti, Quello che accadde in Italia dopo il 25 aprile*, Milan, Sperling & Kupfer, 2003, p. 9.

22 N. Bobbio, *L'età dei diritti*, Turin, Einaudi, 1997, p. 51.

I have often wondered what things captivated me when hearing the stories populated with death or attending a hearing in front of the loftiest exponent of the regime Jorge Rafael Videla. What impelled me to take photographs? Specifically, the will to represent evil concretely, as if we could understand and measure its amplitude. I did so in order to represent through the vehicle of photography the symbol of violence. As if for the post-1970s generation evil and violence were incomprehensible, but in reality ever present in society and therefore something still to be codified. There is something morbid in the continuing search for understanding of the *banality of evil*, represented in those rooms by the pyramid of command which stretches from the responsible intellectual to the executor. Man has evil in himself and it is therefore very difficult to listen to the stories with the distance and impartiality which should accompany rational understanding.

In this sense, perhaps, the law, with its sober and austere language, develops an adjunct role, necessary in times of upheaval and a propaedeutic to sanity.[23]

Even with its limitations,[24] the judicial episode is, therefore, one of the moments of differentiation from the traditional language and the previous conceptual political cadre, in which the State is also required to answer

23 "To be able to react in a reasonable way it is necessary first of all be 'moved', and the opposite of emotion is not the 'rational', whatever that means, but the inability permit oneself to be moved, which is usually a pathological phenomenon, or sentimentality, which is a perversion of feeling". H. Arendt, *Sulla violenza*, Parma, Guanda, 2001, p. 69.

24 Without trying to discuss the issue thoroughly, consider for example the fact that, the way the trials are organized means that the victims are at risk of continued re-victimization, to the extent that they are required to repeat the same testimony, and therefore to relive the trauma, as many times as, for example, the number of the secret detention centres through which they have passed, or for the number of disappeared with whom they were in contact during the period of detention. This occurs because the trials are created to judge the guilt of a defendant for limited individual acts, instead of unifying the different cases in "hyper-trials", for example, one for each detention facility. The amount of work which falls upon the ordinary judge complicates the activity of the courts and, in the face of the imprescriptibility of the crimes is also the subject of a completion date, and to this day their completion is not foreseeable.

for its own responsibilities. It is a physiological aspect of the transition to democracy that there is a moment, such as the present one, of judicial leadership. It is also indisputable that, in historical terms, this phase does not exhaust the path of memory, which is the instrument the human being uses to comprehend history. It would be reasonable to ask the criminal process to generate or produce a rigorous analytic truth about the phenomenon of state terrorism and its historical context. This is so not least because it is still necessary to understand the motivations which led the military to carry out the most detestable tortures: violations, electric shocks, introducing elements into the anus, torture in front of children, forced isolation with the permanent use of hoods for days at a time, forced imposition of silence, physical and moral denigration, leaving detainees in inhumane physical and unhygienic conditions, and the intention to imprison them in the conditions of the *Muslim* described by Levi in the concentration camps.

It should be explained why it is a question of turning a man into a *Muslim*[25] in the idea of absolute power, why this is taken to the point of the complete loss of humanity and to reduction to the condition of an animal And through the jailers the state executed a total power over the prisoners, the absolute despotism of the government over its own citizens in an attempt to re-educate the above-mentioned social deviation, the carrier of political unrest, crime and abnormality. One of the most commonly implemented forms of violence has been against the woman, the embodiment of life over death, who represents exactly what the man cannot have: the ability to give life. The politicized woman arouses more fear, because she threatens to undermine the *status quo* of the centuries old dominant power of the man; for this reason she becomes the object of the worst abuses. At

25 "We, the survivors, are not the true witnesses [...], it is them, the 'Muslims' [i.e., in the jargon of the field, those who, from exhaustion, have lost all resilience, are reduced to a handful of ruined organic functions] who are the comprehensive witnesses; but no one who has seen the Gorgon [who has hit the bottom] has returned to tell the story; or has returned mute. They are the rule; we are the exception. Touched by fate [...] we have tried to recount not only our own destiny but also that of others, that of the sunken ones, to be precise; but it has been a speech by "third parties", the story of things seen up close, not experienced personally". G. Agamben, *Quel che resta di Auschwitz, l'archivio e il testimone*, Turin, Bollati Boringhieri, Gennaio 2010, p. 31.

the same time, women have shown a higher level of resistance to that of men in the face of physical and mental pain during torture. True, but who else apart you thinks about it? How do you justify it?

In the ongoing trials an important element to consider as a crime against humanity is precisely the rape of minors,[26] committed systematically in relation to women as a methodological form of subjection repeated over time. The silence of the survivors is understandable and it is still difficult to give testimony to it publicly. In these cases too the court has been a sort of psychic catharsis for some women who have related for the first time the abuses they have suffered. It is as if the criminal trial has managed to interrupt the lack of rights and the constant feeling of fear which had been created by the clandestine centre. The way of *truth* will not stop at the courtroom, risking emptying the leading role of thousands of individuals of its meaning, victimizing them and not restoring their historical dignity. It is necessary to put the various facts into historical context so as to be able to deliver to future generations not only fragments, but the complexity of the case. Repression has thrashed an alternative model of the political process. The forced disappearance of persons and the exile of huge numbers of people means, not only eliminating their ideas and projects, but also marking indelibly the development of a country. The notion of the "subversive" has been sufficiently broad to include in the persecution almost anyone who acted by showing any form of political affiliation or empathy.

Today it is necessary to undertake much work beyond historiographical and judicial reconstruction. This is the work of the recovery of the correct use of the terms through which citizens might feel themselves to be an active part in public affairs, inasmuch as the semantics are understood as a matter of historical perspective.

26 Rape is an act of death, the reduction of the woman to mere object which is used and discarded by male desire. It is annihilation, the destruction of the female identity, the stripping of individuality *de jure*, that is to say, as the bearer of rights. With the rape of a minor, they would like to sanction, at the individual level, the non-existence of woman as a subject who disposes of her own body and mind, and from a collective perspective, her exclusion from participation in the social group, precisely because she is regarded as an individual in fact, a mere "good", and therefore violated in her the dignity of being human. C. Forneris; *El Salvador, 1983: Marianela Garcia Villas n. 43,337 nell'elenco delle vittime civili*, Storia delle donne, University of Florence, p. 4.

Society is neither the evil genius which produces the dictatorship nor its victim.[27] The battle for the affirmation of a collective memory has begun with the recognition of the human rights organizations and relatives of the disappeared: Abuelas, Madres de Plaza de Mayo, Familiares, HIJOS (Grandmothers, Mothers of Plaza de Mayo, Relatives, Children for Identity and Justice and Against Forgetting and Silence). Memory has become the basis of the considerations of the past and today has a political charge and a significant effect on the governmental agenda. It has developed over the years through various reflections, according to the contingency and evolution of political events. There are many social actors – above all the institutions – which would have preferred to have closed the past through a *caesura neta* between "before" and "after": an absolute "refounding" through an commission of institutional investigation or an amnesty.

The ruling classes[28] tend to have an univocal vision of the past – because of the complexity of intra-political relations, of the responsibilities and moral and political agreements – and as such, would like to preserve it by means of official truths.

27 The 1970s saw the social movements distance themselves from the historic parties which were unable to interpret their demands. The collapse of the Peronist movement has led to the explosion of violence which had not been channelled in any democratic way, either by the State or by the parties and unions which failed to collect and *constitutionalise* – in other words, take responsibility for translating into rights – the demands of the social movements. The *increase* in violence cannot be understood without going back in the history of a country that has seen the democratic path interrupted since 1955 (when the main square of Buenos Aires was bombed and three hundred and fifty people killed) at the hands of the military with endorsement of a part of society and some party coalitions.

28 Think for instance of one of the symbols of modern democracies: political parties. The weakness and endemic inconsistency of the parties have been one of the causes of the rise of the military and has enabled it to conquer power as a result. In addition, the opposition parties have always attempted to do deals with the military so as to achieve a non-violent and unpunished passage to democracy. Historically there is no political party which has not given support to or participated in at least one of the numerous coups which have taken place between 1930 and 1976. Radicals, conservatives, Peronists, Socialists and Communists have all been associated with the military caste on different occasions. With the return of democracy, there still has been neither a deep analysis nor a political debate about the role of these institutions, nor of that of the unions.

After the fall of the regime the reflection of state policy has been based on the balance between the claims of human rights protection and reasons of state. Subsequently, the democratic government of Raúl Alfonsín, in order to justify impunity, introduces the *theory of two demons*, thus putting state terrorism on the same level as the crimes of the guerrillas. With the trial of the military junta, the victims appear for the first time in the public arena as such, stripped of any real or presumed political identity. In this way society frees itself from the responsibility of indifference, for not having acted in a timely manner, for not having understood the signs and symptoms and even for having been in part a participant in the events. It can also reclaim the fallen, all the more so if they are innocent, uncommitted victims, who were not resisting that model, uncontaminated and non-political figures such as those newly born in captivity in the ESMA or other clandestine centres and given to families close to the military.

From the thesis of Marc Bloch, according to which each generation has the right and duty to write history in first person,[29] is born the association of children born of disappeared: HIJOS. It is a – still controversial – body of unquestionable moral and political value, which has had a significant impact on society. The never violent vehemence of youth, together with demands for truth mixed with the continued pain felt for the loss, have been one of the signs of the renewal of Argentinean society. The battle for political memory is identified with the generation of the 1970s. There exists a "symbolic" capital, bequeathed to the recovery of politics and militancy which feeds itself from public recognition by the state and from which institutionalized power removes some of its legitimacy. It should be stressed that, in relation to what has just been affirmed, an academic literature has recently flowered which tends to define Argentina's last dictatorship as both military and civilian. And with this it becomes evident how the structure – the factor of the commitment of the military in power – specifies a greater degree of responsibility (economic, political, religious, but even international) in the commission the abuses falling under the so-called third level.

29 Cf. M. Bloch, *Apologia della storia o Mestiere di Storico*, Turin, Piccola Biblioteca Einaudi, 2009.

This civics lesson of constructive memory can be represented on a symbolic level in the choice of 24 March, the day of the coup, as the day of memory. I do not think it is accidental that the choice has been made, not to commemorate the end of the dictatorship, but to evoke each year the loss of the innocence of a nation. Looking carefully, when the law is bound and belittled in a *reductio ad Hitlerum*[30] in support of the military regime, emptying and thus disrupting the meaning of civil obedience, and mentoring a phantom public order and reasons of state, nothing is more effective in restoring dignity and credibility than a State which consents to the exercise of recognition of a universal culture of protection, and therefore promotion of Fundamental Rights.

The essays presented here are therefore explorations of this objective which revolves around a break which is renewed in every moment of our existence and at every latitude, looking ahead to an intertwining of opportunities for the involvement of memory.

The topics discussed are even more interesting when understood as incentives for some European states – I mean above all Italy and Spain – to themselves face up to those periods and unresolved memories, to their own forgettings, of the violent events of the recent past. The peculiarities of the Argentine case provide a new contribution of knowledge to the sensitive issue of the relationship between memory and history and between the public and private uses of history and memory.

An answer to the paradox of generations who, educated in history, forget the motivations of those who have gone before, may be found the strengthening of the historical ties between Italy and Argentina – as a country which many Italians helped to establish, with the desire not to forget the economic, cultural and political collusion with the dictatorship[31]

30 An ironic expression coined by Leo Strauss, *Natural Right and History*, Chicago, University of Chicago Press, 1965.

31 There are many examples of agreements between Italy and the Argentine military regime. Consider, for example, the sinister figure of Licio Gelli (a Francoite volunteer in Spain, and a collaborator with the American and British secret services), head of the P2 Masonic Lodge in which twenty-one Argentineans were enrolled, including Admiral Emilio Massera and General Suárez Mason. Gelli, who had been awarded

– but especially in a joint reflection on the universal values of the search for truth, the construction of an present memory inserted in a common history, but not forcibly shared.

Bibliography

Agamben, Giorgio, *Quel che remainder di Auschwitz, l'il archivio and Testimonials*, Turin, Bollati Boringhieri, 1998.
Bloch, Marc, *Apologia della storia di storico or mestiere*, Turin, Einaudi, 1998.
Bobbio, Norberto, *L'eta dei diritti*, Turin, Einaudi, 1997.

---

the highest national prize by Alberto Vignes, the foreign minister of the government of Juan Domingo Perón, was arrested in Switzerland under a false identity using a passport forged by Victor Basterra during his detention at the ESMA. "In Argentina Gelli established close relations with the head of the national oil agency, launched an import-export activity according to the testimony of Elia Valori – negotiated with the Argentinean bankers on behalf of the Banca Nazionale del Lavoro. Through López Rega, Gelli had very important political and commercial links to Perón and the entire government sector, which, I believe, no other Italian citizen has ever had. Along with Ortolani and Calvi, also in Argentina, Gelli also takes care of the printing industry and the press in Argentina, eventually assuming control of 23 newspapers". See S. Flamini, *Trame Atlantiche, Storia della Loggia P2 Segreta masson*, Milan, Kaos, 1996, p. 93. The FIAT presence in Córdoba, from which thirty-two people disappeared during the dictatorship, the deal between the Macri family (of Italian origin), the P2 and the Italian Socialist Party under the protection of Bettino Craxi, with the aim of selling weapons, which was illegal at that time because of the embargo on Argentina. In that period the two Macri brothers, Antonio and Franco, are accused by an Italian investigation of having interwoven business with the Italian Socialist Party with regard to the issue of the manufacture of helicopters and illegal arms trafficking. By means of their holding company, the Macris controlled more than fifty companies, acquiring control of the subsidiary Fiat Argentina with heavy losses, building roads and highways, making a public tender for the cleaning of Buenos Aires and representing the Techint (an Italian company with a support role in the extermination plan, which affected some of its employees. http://www.fondazionecipriani.it/Writings/palermo.html).

Boatti, Giorgio, *Piazza Fontana, 12 Dicembre 1969: il giorno dell'innocenza Perduto*, Turin, Einaudi, 2009.
Focardi, Filippo, *Criminali di Guerra in libertà. Un accordo segreto tra Italia* e *Germania federale, 1949–1955*, Rome, Carocci, 2008.
Foucault, Michel, *Sorvegliare and punire*, Nascita della Prigione, Turin, Einaudi, 1976.
Gentile, Emilio, *Né né stato Nazione, senza italiani goal*, Rome and Bari, Laterza Luglio, 2010.
Ginzburg, Carlo, *Il Giudice and what storico*, Turin, Einaudi, 1991.
Levi, Primo, *I sommersi ei Salvati*, Turin, Einaudi, 1986.
Morante, Elsa, *La Storia, One last sixteen mila scandalo anni che*, Turin, Einaudi, 1974.
Pansa, Giampaolo, *Il sangue dei Vinti Gianpaolo, Quello che il dopo accadde in Italy 25 April*, Milan, Sperling & Kupfer, 2003.
Ranzato, Gabriele, *di Bronzo Il passato, L'Eredità della democratic civil war nella Spagna*, Rome and Bari, Laterza.

PART I

Argentina, 1983–2010: Democratization

HORACIO VERBITSKY

Argentinean Society Today: Between Memory and Forgetting

Between 1930 and 1990 Argentina experienced more governments chosen by soldiers' boots than by votes cast in free elections. During those sixty years the country suffered no fewer than one military coup per decade and in some cases up to five. Each dictatorship was bloodier than the previous one. The last one, which lasted from 1976 to 1983 and in whose presidency four Army generals took turns, did all it could to decree that its crimes be forgotten. In 1979, it offered to negotiate a political opening for the proscribed parties in exchange for the validation of everything it had done. In 1980, when the *Comisión Interamericana de Derechos Humanos* (CIDH: Interamerican Commission of Human Rights) published its report on its visit of the previous year, in which it confirmed widespread and systematic violations of human rights and concluded that all the disappeared detainees had been assassinated, the Interior Minister, General Albano Harguindeguy, said that Argentina knelt down only before God. The Commander in Chief of the Army and dictator Roberto Viola called the disappeared *ausentes para siempre* ("absent forever") and his successor Leopoldo Galtieri warned not to ask for explanations because they would not give them, as they had saved the country.

The Self-Amnesty

After the military disaster in the war against Great Britain over the Malvinas, the Armed Forces had to convene elections urgently. But first they tried once more to impose conditions on the political parties, warning them that they would not permit investigations into the dirty war against Argentinean society. Moreover, they issued a so-called *Documento Final de la Junta Militar* (Final Document of the Military Junta) in which they proclaimed that in order to face the future it would be necessary to confront with Christian spirit the stage which was beginning. "In this almost apocalyptic context errors were made which, as happens in every military conflict, could sometimes cross the limits of respect for fundamental rights", they conceded. Such errors ought to be subject to the judgment of God and the understanding of men. The document maintained that in every armed conflict it is difficult to give complete details, and in a war in which the enemy did not wear uniform and whose documents of identification were spurious, the number of unidentified deaths increased significantly. This deliberate inversion of the terms (relatives demanding to know the fate of identified persons who were arrested alive, and the document responding about unidentified deaths), introduced the central paragraph of the military report. This denied the existence of secret places of detention and considered dead those disappeared who were not found in exile or in hiding. As was inevitable in the military prose of the era, it added the desire that the dead enemies received the pardon of God. The key which the document did not reveal was exactly what had happened in this transition between the detention of a living person, with a name and surname, and their conversion into an anonymous death. The data which the Human Rights organizations had even in those days indicate that 80 per cent of the disappeared had been abducted from their homes, in the street or in workplaces, in front of witnesses.

When there were only five weeks left before the presidential elections, the final dictator, Benito Bignone, signed a decree of self-amnesty in order to lay the foundations of the definitive pacification of the country, national reconciliation and the supersession of past tragedies. The Catholic Bishopric followed Bignone's diktat with a so-called *servicio de reconciliación* ("service of reconciliation"), in which he pressed for all the political and social forces to accept this decree of forgetting. The decree's conclusions stated that the armed forces had fought for the dignity of man while the terrorist subversion had posed battle in a cruel and cunning form, which could have had the result that, in the course of the struggle, things were done which were inconsistent with the army's purpose. In the battles people were killed and wounded and the supreme values which were being defended were also damaged, it said. The amnesty included the military and its civilian collaborators who, in potential, as usual, "may have resorted to the use of procedures which passed the legal limit"; naturally they would not have done so of their own will, but because of the usual "imposition of the unprecedented and extreme conditions in which these took place". On the other hand, it excluded the partisans who, it asserted, "attacked the nation".

During the electoral campaign of 1983, the candidate of the Unión Cívica Radical, Raúl Alfonsín, promised that there would be no impunity for the crimes of State terrorism, while the candidate of the Partido Justicialista (Peronist), Italo Lúder, pronounced the validity of the self-amnesty dictated by the Armed Forces themselves.

The CONADEP and the Trial of the Juntas

Alfonsín devised a complicated mechanism whose practical application escaped his control. On one hand there was the *Comisión de Notables*, which ought only to have drawn up the list of those detained or disappeared; on the other, the inclusion in the *Código de Justicia Militar* (Military Justice Code) of a clause of *Obediencia Debida* (Due Obedience). This permitted the armed forces themselves to judge a few senior officers and acquit those who followed orders, except for those who had committed excesses in pursuance of the plan. Nothing turned out as he imagined. the human rights organizations which had documented the criminal actions of the dictatorship as they occurred worked in the secretariat of the CONADEP. To Alfonsín's annoyance, the latter not only identified the disappeared but also those who had made them disappear. Without an absolute majority in the *Senado* (Senate), the government saw that its legal project was being modified in such a way that the duty of obedience did not cover the authors of aberrant and atrocious crimes – that is to say none of them, given the method of sequestration, torture and clandestine murder.

Alfonsín calculated that putting the leadership on trial would put the Armed Forces on the defensive and thus act to deter future coups. This has been his greatest contribution to Argentinean democracy, although he never showed respect for the victims of the dictatorship and even said that the *Madres de Plaza de Mayo* (Mothers of the Plaza de Mayo) were financed by shady international interests. Thus, in 1985, after a trial whose public hearings threw into a state of suspense a country which was waking up from a dark nightmare, various ex commanders in chief, amongst them the First Military Junta (Jorge Videla, Emilio Massera y Orlando Agosti) were condemned to prison; they were so condemned by a tribunal which gave them every right of defence which their victims had not had during the dictatorship. The trial also culminated with another judgment against two former chiefs of police and several officers of the Province of Buenos Aires.

Punto Final and *Obediencia Debida*

When the judges went beyond what the government had sketched out and also ordered the prosecution of the heads of both the *Cuerpo de Ejército* (Army Corps) and of the areas of repression, Alfonsín tried to restrain them. He did so, first with instructions to the public prosecutors, and later with the laws of *Obediencia Debida* (Due Obedience) and *Punto Final* (Full Stop). With barely 24 hours of difference between them, the *Punto Final* law was voted for in Argentina and a Law of the *Caducidad de la Pretensión Punitiva del Estado* (Expiry of the Punitive Claims of the State) was passed in the neighbouring Uruguay. This coincidence has to do with agreements between the governments of both countries and the close relationship between the presidents Alfonsín and Julio Sanguinetti. Nor can the recommendations of the US State Department be dismissed, of which there are no proofs but rather strong indications. At that point, the government of the United States was extremely concerned that these proceedings should not advance beyond what they considered prudent, and raised the need for agreements between the democratic political parties so as to support institutionalization and impede abuses of justice.

In 1987 court proceedings against officers of the First Army Corps and of the *Escuela de Mecánica de la Armada* (ESMA: School of Naval Mechanics) began. Then the military *carapintada* insurrections took place (named after the camouflage paint used by the army commandoes). Under this pressure, Alfonsín's government persuaded Congress to vote for the law of *Obediencia Debida*. There were still more military insurrections because, in spite of this law, a couple of hundred officers of the armed forces remained on trial.

The Amnesties

The families of the victims and the human rights organizations continued to protest against immunity; this was a dimension the government had not contemplated, because at first it saw only the political convenience of the trials, and later only that of interrupting them, as if human values and ethics were not involved. The law of *Obediencia Debida* implied setting hundreds of defendants at liberty; but many others still remained in prison, and with the aim of rescuing them, Alfonsín devised a change in the number of members of the *Corte Suprema de Justicia* (Supreme Court of Justice). He negotiated with the Peronists the designation of two new ministers of the Court, one proposed by each party but both committed to a restrictive interpretation of the law, which left at liberty every officer lower than former commanders and heads of army corps. But he did not see this happen, because he had to leave the government before completing his term, driven out by the hyperinflation and the lootings.

As soon as Carlos Menem assumed the presidency he disowned the pact he had made with Alfonsín. Instead of increasing by two the number of members of the *Corte Suprema de Justicia*, he designated four, without discussing their names with anyone. Moreover, he obtained the resignation of the previous ones in such a way that he could now count on six out of nine ministers. But, unlike Alfonsín, he did not need the judges in order to put an end to the prosecutions, but rather to protect members of his government in the cases of corruption which soon began to accumulate in the federal courts. He solved the military question at a stroke, with the amnesties of 1989 of those who were on trial, and in 1990, of those already condemned.

When he closed the judicial road by means of the laws of impunity, the popular struggles had already been ebbing for several years. With the government of Menem there was also a great sense of economic relief caused by his containing of the hyperinflation which had been experienced during the previous government. The auction at a ridiculously low price of the social capital accumulated by generations of Argentineans in public enterprises, plus the uncontrolled external indebtedness, brought several years of calm, in which social discontent abated. It seemed that the question of human rights had been forgotten, that Argentinean society no longer wanted to demand justice for the crimes of the dictatorship. However, every time it was consulted with political sociology surveys, never less than 60 per cent, and on several occasions more than 80 per cent of the population, pronounced themselves against impunity and in favour of justice. And the human rights organizations maintained a permanent mobilization, although at that point it seemed that the road had been closed once and for all. Both Alfonsín's laws and Menem's decrees excluded from impunity the crimes of the abduction of the children of the detained-disappeared and the looting of their goods. However, few trials for these crimes advanced and at an uncertain pace.

The Confession

In March 1995 Adolfo Scilingo, a naval officer, the captain of a frigate, confessed that he had thrown 30 people live into the sea from naval aircraft, a story which I have narrated in my book *El vuelo*. This confession provoked an unprecedented uproar, not because it was not known that the armed forces had used this method, which according to Scilingo the Christian hierarchy had approved of as "a Christian form of death", but because this time it was not a survivor who was recounting the story but rather one of the perpetrators. There followed hasty self-criticisms by the three chiefs of the General Staff and the trial was reopened. The founding president of the *Centro de Estudios Legales y Sociales* (Centre for Legal and Social Studies: CELS), Emilio Mignone, maintained that the laws which impeded the judgment of those responsible did not revoke the right of each family to the truth. The *Cámara Federal de la Capital* (Federal Chamber of the Capital) agreed and opened an investigation in order to determine what had happened to the daughter of the accuser, the Catechist Catholic Mónica Candelaria Mignone. In next to no time there were trials for the truth all over the country. Menem tried to stop them, using the *Corte Suprema de Justicia*, but after an accusation by Carmen Lapacó before the *Comisión Interamericana de Derechos Humanos* (Interamerican Commission of Human Rights), he had no choice but to permit their continuation. The confession also produced an unexpected effect in the children of disappeared detainees, who ceased to feel like pariahs and guilty of something and made themselves known through a new organization for identify and justice and against silence and forgetting, HIJOS. A new generation appeared on the national scene and on 24 March 1996 a rally bigger than any previously known filled the Plaza de Mayo in demand of memory, truth and justice.

The External Factor

The Spanish public prosecutor Carlos Castresana saw images of that demonstration on television and asked himself if he could do something to help those people. He turned to old codes, constitutions and treaties, in which he found a form of action possible for the Spanish judiciary. Although the crimes had been committed against Argentineans, by Argentineans and in Argentina, they injured the whole of humanity and could be judged wherever there was the will to do so. The judge Baltasar Garzón accepted this argument and, invoking *jurisdicción universal* (universal jurisdiction), demanded from Argentina the extradition of more than 100 military and naval personnel to be judged in Madrid. Menem and the president who succeeded him, Fernando De la Rúa, refused, invoking national sovereignty. But a mechanism had been set in motion which could not now be halted.

In France, Alfredo Astiz had been condemned for the sequestration of the French nuns of the Church of Santa Cruz; in the United States, General Carlos Suárez Mason was ordered to compensate his victims, Horacio Martínez Baca, Alfredo Forti and Debora Benchoam, to the amount of twenty million dollars; in Italy, Suárez Mason and General Santiago Riveros were condemned for the disappearance of Italian citizens. Chileans resident in Spain asked Judge Garzón to proceed in cases in his country and in 1998 this led to the detention in London of the former Chilean dictator Augusto Pinochet. I had the privilege to take part in one of the court hearings for his extradition in the seat of the British Parliament in Westminster. When the Chilean dictator's defence attorney said before the robed and bewigged judges that Pinochet enjoyed the sovereign immunity that Hitler would have had if he had survived the Second World War, I thought I had misunderstood. But they confirmed that this is what she had said and I felt certain that he would lose his case. Only a few days remained until the half centenary of the Universal Declaration of Human Rights and the wars of the dissolution of former Yugoslavia had shown the world via satellite concentration camps that had not been believed possible after the Second World War. The universal consciousness no longer permitted that kind of boast.

The Vespers

The day after the arrest of Pinochet, the Argentine judge Adolfo Bagnasco detained the former admiral Emilio Massera in Buenos Aires for the appropriation of babies, a crime for which, from the end of June, Videla was also detained. Congress revoked the laws of *Punto Final* and *Obedencia Debida*, but did not gain sufficient votes to declare them null and void. These investigations continued throughout 1999 and by the start of the third millennium several dozen high-ranking military chiefs had been arrested. We believe that there remained no ethical, political, juridical, national or international reasons underpinning the survival of the impunity laws. The following year it would be a quarter century since the coup and the predictable popular demonstrations of repudiation would balance the pressure of the entrenched powers and would permit justice to de declared in accordance with the facts of the case if chosen and the applicable law. The request to annul the laws of impunity was made in a case particularly suitable to showing their lack of viability. These repressors, Julio Simón, known as Turco Julián (Julian the Turk) and Juan Del Cerro, known as "Colores" (Colours), were arrested and prosecuted for the appropriation of a newborn baby assigned to a sterile military family, who registered her as their own, but could not be brought under indictment for the kidnapping, torture and enforced disappearance of the parents of the newborn – José Poblete and Gertrudis Hlaczik – a crime of the utmost gravity.

The *Abuelas de Plaza de Mayo* (Grandmothers of the Plaza de Mayo), who from the start had accompanied these searches, took up the cause of the baby and CELS accused for crimes against the parents. In March 2001 the federal judge Gabriel Cavallo declared null and void the laws of *Punto Final* and of*Obediencia Debida* and extended the proceedings also to the forced disappearance of the couple. Barely two weeks later, the *Corte Interamericana de Derechos Humanos* gave its verdict in the Barrios Altos case in Peru, to the same effect as that of Cavallo. Those grave violations of human rights cannot be amnestied nor can their penal prosecution cease because of the mere passing of time. Cavallo's decision was confirmed by the Federal Chamber and different judges took on other similar cases all over the country.

The government of De la Rúa, however, attempted to hinder the progress of these trials and even attempted to assign missions in affairs of internal security to the Armed Forces, which the basic laws sanctioned by multiparty agreements in the 1980s and 1990s prohibited. In the final months of his term (which because of the president's resignation was completed by the senator Eduardo Duhalde, who was in charge of the Executive Power on an interim basis), the attempts to frustrate the work of justice intensified. Participating in these were Ricardo Brinzoni, the head of the army (accused of participation in the massacre of Margarita Belén), Julio Nazareno, the head of the Court, and Senator Duhalde himself. The then Army Bishop, Antonio Baseotto, appeared before the Court and demanded in person that it annul the proceedings and ratify the validity of the laws of impunity. This bartering operation included the withdrawal of any attempt to impeach the ministers of the *Corte Suprema*. Joining in these manoeuvres was the person who it was considered would be the justice minister of Néstor Kirchner, Rafael Bielsa. He was the author of a work entitled "That war is over", published in the newspaper *La Nación* in August 2001, in which he urged "healing the wounds" and spurned *jurisdicción universal* (universal jurisdiction) with ironies about African countries and concluded that "time passes and nothing can be the same".

The Annulment

The new president, Néstor Kirchner, had another idea. He asked Duhalde to leave to him the benefits which the protagonists of the combination expected to derive from closure of the trials, sent Bielsa to another ministry without interference in the field and in the first two weeks of his administration carried out by surprise two decisive acts which distinguished his presidency. In the first week he decapitated the leadership of the reborn *Partido Militar* (Military Party); in the second he promoted judicial proceedings against the automatic majority of the *Corte Suprema*. He also called for the ratification of the international convention which determines the imprescriptibility of statutory limitations to the forced disappearances of persons. Congress ratified it and also declared null and void the laws of *Punto Final* and *Obediencia Debida*.

In March 2004 Kirchner took two other highly symbolic decisions, proposed by the human rights organizations: the eviction of the *Escuela de Mecánica de la Armada* (School of Naval Engineers) so as to establish there the Museum of Memory which the legislature of the City of Buenos Aires had ordered, and the removal of the portraits of the former dictators Videla and Bignone from the Military College. Finally, in May 1995, the *Corte Suprema*, now composed of respected judges without spurious links to the Executive Power, confirmed the judgment of Cavallo in the Poblete/Simón case. The laws of *Punto Final* and *Obediencia Debida* could not be interposed in the judgment of crimes against humanity committed by the organized apparatus of power of state terrorism. A later judgment extended this nullity to the pardons granted by Menem.

The Trials

Since then the tribunals have advanced slowly and in such as way as to impede demonstration of the gravity and magnitude of the acts submitted for their consideration. In Buenos Aires in December 2007 the first sentence against military personnel was pronounced after the reopening of two cases. Those condemned in the case known as *Batallón de Inteligencia 601* (Intelligence Battalion 601) were no less than the former Army Chief Cristino Nicolaides and seven colonels of the 601st Intelligence Battalion of the Army. Later in Tucumán, General Bussi, in Córdoba, General Luciano Menéndez, and in La Plata, the former chief of operations in the Buenos Aires police, Commissioner Miguel Etchecolatz, and the Catholic chaplain, the priest Christian von Wernich, were condemned. In Ciudad Federal an oral tribunal condemned the brigadiers who, during the dictatorship, were in charge of the principal units of the Armed Forces involved in the repression, and the second-in-command of the Army Corps. In 2010, the year of the trials, the super trials of the repression by the Campo de Mayo Military Garrison, near the capital, the School of Navy Mechanics and the First Army Corps have been carried out. This is not a question of small pieces, but of the principal people responsible for what happened in Argentina thirty years ago. A number of human rights organizations have objected to the dispersion of the cases as a result of which the same witnesses have to repeat time and time again their painful stories in order to incriminate one repressor at a time, when there were tens or even hundreds in the same concentration camp. Their organization according to centre of detention and their distribution in different oral tribunals, so as to avoid the log jam which would occur if they were concentrated in a few, are undeferable measures.

MARCOS NOVARO

The Politics of Human Rights in Argentina, from Alfonsín to Menem

Introduction

The fact that the military dictatorship ended with the collapse of military power meant that it was unable to impose greater conditions on the civilian actors. There was thus opened a window of opportunity for the institutions of democracy to investigate what had happened to the thousands of the *desparecidos* (disappeared) which had been caused by the implementation of state terrorism from the mid-1970s. Raúl Alfonsín and his party, the *Unión Cívica Radical*, made an explicit promise in this regard as part of their electoral campaign during the transition to democracy in 1983. This undertaking was important, although how important it was is difficult to measure, not least in ensuring Alfonsín's triumph over the Peronists, whose candidate endorsed the self-amnesty issued shortly before by the Military Junta. Hence, once in government they devoted themselves with some care to fulfilling this promise.

The human rights policy of the government of Alfonsín has frequently been used as a privileged interpretive key for understanding the period which stretches from the military collapse of 1983 to the hyperinflation of 1989. And its shortcomings and the its somewhat frustrating results have been considered as the origin of the decisions which came to be taken by his successor, the Peronist Carlos Menem, who after 1989 moved towards guaranteeing the impunity of the crimes of the dictatorship. This is so because the policy of Alfonsín brings together some features which permit their classification as the flagship or paradigm of a wider project, the promise of change which the first democratic government would have encouraged.

In the end this promise was largely frustrated and because of its frustration there would later be imposed a more definitive "solution" to the civil–military conflict, that of Menem and the Peronist movement. This solution was highly restrictive with regard to access to justice but nonetheless more effective than the "ambiguous" initiatives which preceded it.

At least two features of Alfonsín's policies are easy to recognize. The first consists in its direct and explicit involvement in the subject on which it was based and its proposal of a project of transformation as its major innovation: that is to say, the legitimacy and efficacy of the rule of law as the moral basis of a republican order. The second is its engagement, also in a direct and substantive way, of the morally motivated will of its main protagonists, a president and a party identified with the task of creating robust and powerful institutions for representative democracy in the country; this was a will which in the course of the implementation of this policy would reveal its limitations, owing to which it would be weakened and eventually consumed.

We do not deny the importance of the policy in question, neither for understanding the general trend which the democratization of Argentina followed until the late 1980s (and also the one which would have to be followed subsequently), nor the fate of the Alfonsín government in particular. We will try, however, to question some of the assumptions behind a broadly shared common sense view about what was at stake. The first of these is that it is possible to understand this policy in and of itself, isolated, first, from other equally or more relevant policies which Alfonsín tried to implement, and, second, from the broader processes of change taking place during his term of office, processes which largely escaped his control and strongly conditioned it. The second assumption is that the policy was carried out by actors who remained homogeneous over time, actors which would share the same preferences and develop among themselves the same strategic game at the beginning, during and at the end of the period. These actors include the president himself and his party, the military, the judges, the human rights organizations, and public opinion and other political forces,

Challenging these premises will allow us to problematize a judgment which, on a regular basis, explicitly or implicitly, has marked the analysis thereof: that in essence the policy of Alfonsín in this area consisted of an exercise of the will, and that its development can be reconstructed in terms of a journey which starts from the initial "push", through a process of gradual moderation, the result of the obstacles encountered as well as of the mistakes made, and concludes, at the end of his term, with his resignation in the face the "immutability" of the situations inherited. Alfonsín has himself explicitly aired and given sustenance to this story, both during and after the events. But rather than a disclosure of a particularly acute retrospective understanding of the vicissitudes his time in government, it is a question of the very particular way in which he already understood them during his tenure. For the exaltation of the will is not merely the fruit of an analytical exercise which has been performed on our recent political history; it is born of the very system of legitimization which Alfonsín and other players in our democratic life have built for themselves. It is now time to subject it to critical analysis.

Questions

How can we account for and assess the achievements and failures of Alfonsín's human rights policy? Why did he make progress in some goals but could not achieve many others which were proposed in this field, and why do some of those which were achieved later show an unexpected regression? These objectives were, in any case, more than extensive: the disciplining of the military by civil power; the drawing of a line of demarcation between *procesistas* (supporters of the so-called *Proceso de Reorganización Nacion*: Process of National Reorganisation) and the democratic professionals among the military officers, the security and intelligence forces and associated sectors of other actors; the broadest subjection of force to the rule of law as a way of achieving the rapid moral victory of democracy over the traditionally predominant authoritarianism and corporatism; the demonstration of the effectiveness of the division of powers and the rule of law in resolving conflicts; the reparation of a particularly intolerable and unforgivable harm, among the many which the dictatorship had imposed on society; the purging of political violence and crime as tolerated mechanisms of political competition; the consolidation of a consensus based on citizens' rights and on the liberal-republican tradition as the basis of the new political order and new political actors; the deactivation of tensions and conflicts encouraged by decades of dominance of praetorianism, populism, and counter-revolutionary projects; the return of Argentina to the concert of civilized nations.

It is usually affirmed, first, that several of these goals were contradictory, and therefore a policy aimed at achieving them all simultaneously could not but fail. In addition, it is alleged that the Radical government made too many mistakes in trying to implement them and adapt them to the reactions aroused in others. In the first case, that is to day, if the goals were contradictory, these errors do not matter much, since the policy as such was doomed from the start. Interestingly, this perspective would serve to explain the "impossibility" of Alfonsín's project for quite different, even diametrically opposed, reasons. It is said both that Alfonsín should have not have judged any military officer, at least none then in active service, so to ensure the support of the barracks, and that he should have judged many more, to avoid their challenging him. In both versions, the use of not very precise counterfactual arguments results in increasingly biased considerations; these are politically or morally motivated and are not very useful for explanations in terms of history or political science. In the second case, it is usually a question of arriving at equally specious conclusions when it comes to concretely identifying the specific errors which would have damaged a policy which, in principle, had chances of fruition. Did he want to carry out too many prosecutions or too few? Did he want to centralize the trials too much or did he fail to centralize sufficiently? Did he concede too much to the division of powers and to a notion (which, for simplicity, we can call "liberal Republican"), of the rights in question, or was he not consistent with them?

As can be easily seen, moreover, the choice between an explanation based on the lack of viability of the policy itself and another focused on errors of implementation is not necessarily exclusive: it depends on which side is stressed. If we value above all the progress of justice or the fencing in of the political power of the military, for example, we will identify one or other error or problem as impossibilities. In particular, it is important to stress this last point, because of the contradictory results of this policy. These included, on the one hand, initiatives which were only partly effective for punishing the crimes committed under the previous military regime and for disciplining the armed forces, and also, on the other, a social consensus and civil actors who, in their preferences and strategies, largely diverged from the moral premises and institutional principles endorsed by Alfonsín with the aim of consolidating democracy.

If we focus attention on the social consensus on human rights, we will see that the divorce between it and Alfonsinism, although not complete, is in itself significant and followed a peculiar course. After an initial period (which runs from 1983 to 1985) in which the harmony between the two appears to be considerable, we move to a stage of decline which towards the end of his term gives rise to two views equally opposed to those promoted by the government. According to the first view, the trials had not been implemented firmly enough to undo the damage and to subject the military to civil authority; the second claims that they had been excessive and had damaged the possibility of achieving this submission. If we consider the preferences and inclinations of the organized and institutional actors, the divorce from the premises of the Alfonsínist consensus on the subject is even more marked. This is particularly, and most significantly, the case with the human rights movement, which was becoming ever more impervious to liberal-republican notions of rights and the political choices made by the radical government. The decline of the institution initially closest to them and most influential in the movement, the *Asamblea Permanente por los Derechos Humanos* (APDH: Permanent Assembly for Human Rights), can be considered sufficient proof of that frustration and divorce.

This point leads us to ask another question, which this work can not fully address, but which can not be ignored when analysing the experience of the 1980s in light of the perspective offered by the passage of time. Why has a human rights movement developed in Argentina which is largely indifferent, and in its most influential sectors frankly negative, to liberal-republican ideas? If we accept that political liberalism and republicanism are components, perhaps necessary but not sufficient, of every struggle posed in terms of human rights, then we must accept that this is a paradoxical phenomenon. The collapse of the Alfonsinist consensus on this issue has much to say about this paradox. This consensus was forged around certain policy initiatives, grew out of their implementation and sank when these were exhausted. Did it leave in its wake a positive political balance? Absolutely. But it failed to become flesh in the preferences and strategies of sufficiently representative actors, it failed to impose sufficiently legitimate principles on public opinion, and did not give rise to a sufficiently effective institutional order and rules. Adding this consideration gives us a good measure of the frustration with which the cycle closed.

The question which links these different aspects of the problem is one which aims to locate the consideration of the impracticality and errors in the diagnosis, design and implementation of this Alfonsinist policy in the broader context of the political conflicts which dominated the transition and the first stage of democracy in Argentina in the 1980s. This will enable us to distinguish, we hope, what ought to be attributed to failed courses of action, from that which, being a consequence of more structural and unchangeable factors, cannot be blamed on that administration. It will also enable the bracketing off of morally or politically motivated judgments, particularly in the consideration of an issue as sensitive as the violations of human rights, which strongly influence the consideration of the solutions proposed in this regard. These moral and political considerations have, openly or covertly, coloured to this day the discussions of what Alfonsinism intended to do, actually did and should have done in this area.

There is much evidence of this "contamination", both in academic studies and in investigations of a journalistic nature or in sectoral and party discourses. These include, but are not limited to, those who adopt a perspective which privileges the demands of the human rights movement. A key step in the analysis shall identify and criticize these arguments. In summary: in what follows we will identify a vision which we will call the "conventional criticism" of the human rights policy of Alfonsín[1] and

1 In order to form the basic thesis of this vision, we have consulted the following works: ACUÑA, Carlos y SMULOVITZ, Catalina (1991): *¿Ni olvido ni perdón? Derechos*

which we will subject to two types of objection. The first is that the pursuit of "moderate means" to reconcile the different and even contradictory objectives which this politics sought to achieve was doomed to failure in principle. The second is that the errors usually identified as complementary or alternative reasons for that failure, and which in general terms are related to an alleged "lack of will" or "firmness", are in fact those which were actually committed and affected its results. On this basis, it will be possible to identify more precisely what can be considered more fundamental, their mistakes or failures.

---

humanos y tensiones cívico-militares en la transición argentina (Buenos Aires: CEDES); BRYSK, Alison (1994): *The Politics of Human Rights in Argentina. Protest, Change and Democratization* (Stanford: Stanford University Press); DÍAZ COLODRERO, José Luis & ABELLA, M. (1987): *Punto Final. Amnistía o voluntad popular* (Buenos Aires: Puntosur); FELD, Claudia (2002): *Del estrado a la pantalla: las imágenes del juicio a los ex comandantes en Argentina* (Madrid: Siglo Veintiuno); GONZÁLEZ BOMBAL, Inés & SONDEREGUER, M. (1987): "Derechos humanos y democracia" (in JELIN, Elizabeth, *Movimientos sociales y democracia emergente.* Buenos Aires: CEAL); JELIN, Elizabeth (1995): "La política de la memoria: el movimiento de derechos humanos y la construcción democrática en la Argentina" (in ACUÑA, Carlos et al., *Juicio, castigo y memorias. Derechos humanos y justicia en la política argentina.* Buenos Aires: Nueva Visión); LÓPEZ, Ernesto (1994): *Ni la ceniza ni la gloria: actores, sistema político y cuestión militar en los años de Alfonsín* (Bernal: UNQ); MIGNONE, Emilio (1991): *Derechos humanos y sociedad: el caso argentino* (Buenos Aires: CELS-Ediciones de Pensamiento Nacional); PUCCIARELLI, Alfredo (2006) (comp.): *Los años de Alfonsín. ¿El poder de la democracia o la democracia del poder?* (Buenos Aires: Siglo XXI); SANCINETTI, Marcelo (1988): *Derechos humanos en la Argentina postdictatorial* (Buenos Aires: Lerner); VERBITSKY, Horacio (2003): *Civiles y militares: memoria secreta de la transición* (Buenos Aires: Contrapunto). It is of course a very rich bibliography, which postulates extremely diverse conclusions in many aspects, but which in essence share the marks we identify as those of the "conventional vision".

Arguments

We begin by outlining the principles which form the common denominator of what in our opinion is the current standard or conventional critical view of the subject at hand. These principles can be summarized in the following eight arguments, logically and chronologically connected to each other:

1. Alfonsín devised his policy so as to contain the pressures of human rights movement and their impact on a public opinion increasingly sensitized to the question of human rights.
2. The determination of the levels of responsibility and the number of defendants obeyed, from the outset, this need to delimit a process of institutional mobilization and activation which had already been spontaneously launched towards investigation of the violations.
3. In these terms the dispute arose between creating a *Comisión Bicameral* (Bicameral Committee) or a commission of experts (which was ultimately what was chosen, with the name of *Comisión Nacional sobre la Desaparición de Personas*: CONADEP: National Commission on Disappeared Persons). This opposed a political alternative which was participatory and in agreement with the public consensus on the one hand, to one which was limited, technical and practical, and inspired by a depoliticized vision of the problem in question and of the conflicts it generated on the other.
4. In these same terms we can explain the dispute over the role the Executive sought to attribute to the *Consejo Supremo de las Fuerzas Armadas* (the Supreme Council of the Armed Forces: the highest military court, composed of retired officers, with jurisdiction over crimes committed by soldiers in the exercise of their duties), with a second level centralized in the *Cámaras Federales* (Federal Courts), versus the option of leaving everything to ordinary criminal judges. This was equivalent to a choice between a decentralized and unrestricted justice on the one hand and a restricted and centralized justice on the other.

5. Both CONADEP and the *Cámara Federal* (Federal Court) of the Capital escaped the control of the national government, expanding the scope the latter had wanted to give to their interventions. Alfonsín had hoped for a limited number of trials, but when CONADEP made a more comprehensive report than expected, and the Cámera included Point 30 in its decision, the process broke the banks. His own creatures betrayed him.
6. The failure of moderation on the part of the human rights movement (and its best expression, APDH) is the result of the transactional or "moderate" nature of government policy in an area where demands are necessarily expressed in terms of principles and the moderate way is doomed to leave most of those involved unsatisfied.
7. Alfonsín's inability to address the social demands which express the consensus achieved by the movement is what leads to the decline of the social support which the government had initially attained in this field.
8. The quest for reconciliation through a middle way is the goal which contaminates the whole politics of Alfonsín and which signals its end, preventing it from imposing itself on the military resistances. These could have been contained either by a more comprehensive and consistent politics of trials or by a politics which did without them from the beginning. The former course was the one demanded by the human rights agencies and the latter is the course the Partido Justicialista would have followed had it won in 1983 and the one which would animate the corrections made by Menem from 1989.

Each of these statements must be analysed critically and in light of a thorough review of what we know of the facts involved. Looking ahead to the presentation of this analysis, we can group the conclusions we have arrived at into three types of objections which the judgments contained in these eight arguments deserve. In several of them (1 to 6) some facts are favoured over others, and the latter are ignored or dismissed as explanatory factors without further justification. In others (particularly, 1, 2, 3 and 5) the actions in question are judged by their later effects, not by what the actors could have known was going to happen if they took one course or another. (Thus they fall into temporal fallacies such as the attribution of efficacy to certain factors in periods prior to those in which they actually made themselves present.) Finally, several of the arguments (mainly 6, 7 and 8) are resorted to so as to point to a moral and practical failure, the "unwillingness" of the government of the day, without sufficient evidence in that respect. The available alternatives, the general course of governance and the preferences of other actors are not sufficiently considered, thereby losing sight of the context in which policy was developed. In what follows, we will first carefully analyse each of the claims mentioned, contrasting them with facts not taken into account and with alternative, more comprehensive and consistent explanations, and then formulate a number of conclusions which can be drawn from them so as to offer an assessment of achievements, failures and errors of the Alfonsínist administration in this sphere.

1. Alfonsín's policy created a demand, first by enabling access to an unlimited truth (which also was "made official" through the CONADEP report, *Nunca Más*, a detailed study of the crimes committed during the dictatorship, and in particular of the thousands of cases of abduction and forced disappearance), and second, by creating a channel for judicial intervention on which strict time limits were imposed (the first request in the *Consejo Supremo* [Supreme Council] could not take up more than a few months). It was through these decisions and the effects they produced that the demand for justice would be legitimized and would expand in public opinion such that, what was the "best which could be imagined" in 1983 (the prosecution and conviction of a few senior officers and some members of the military juntas for the crimes), would become a "minimum acceptable" between 1985 and 1986. Therefore, the demands cannot be considered as an external and autonomous determinant of government policy. It is the initiative of Alfonsín which opens the social consensus to a debate over the issue of human rights and offers a way of solving it. Thus Alfonsín becomes the channel through which the demand of an impassioned minority, the human rights organizations, is linked to public opinion. It is he who thus gives form to an ever more consensual and ambitious social demand between 1983 and 1986.

This explains the fact that when this channel weakens and finally disappears there are no alternative routes for the movement; it has no way of converting its denunciations of the violations and the judicial roadblocks on the one hand, and its demands for access to justice on the other, into a minimally effective social and political force. Supplementary evidence of this is provided by a number of facts. These include the positions of the *Partido Justicialista*, both that adopted by the presidential candidate, Italo Lúder, during the campaign of 1983 and that which Vicente Saadi (head of the Peronist bloc of senators) argued throughout the first years of democratic government. Lúder, for his part, announced the irreversibility of the amnesty dictated by the last military junta just before the elections; Saadi, on the other hand, combined the charge that the CONADEP and the intervention of the Supreme Council were expressions of a "covert amnesty" with a direct demand for a general and open amnesty. To these considerations we must add the few votes received by maximalist and diffuse groupings, such as the *Partido Intransigente* (Intransigent Party) and the Christian democratic sector known as *Humanismo y Liberación* (Humanism and Liberation) and the limited ability of the agencies to mobilize against Alfonsín's proposals.

The only mass demonstrations of the period from 1984 to 1986 were, symptomatically, those which accompanied the delivery of the CONADEP report in September 1984 (in which the *Madres de Plaza de Mayo* refused to participate, arguing that the report was intended to "close the matter" and show the invalidity of the demand of "appearance with life"), and those which repudiated attacks on the premises of the Commission and the UCR. The reluctance or ambiguity of other institutional actors to act as channels for the movement, and in particular the unwillingness of Peronism to support the official policies, thus removing institutional support for the trials, are frequently ignored in conventional critical analysis. The same goes for the simultaneous demands of the Partido Justicialista both for more trials and none.

2. Alfonsín's unwillingness to narrow the scope of trials is more significant, above all for being more effective, than the specific initiatives to the contrary. The latter existed, but failed conspicuously to obtain results until 1987. This was attributable to at least three factors which conventional

analysis often overlooks. First, his strategy of "move and see", faced with many different, even contradictory, actors, whom he sought to make converge towards the centre in its support. Second, the criteria that the procedures and not just the result of the policy should be consistent with respect for the separation of powers and the law. Third, what was, perhaps, more important, the growing reliance of the government on its achievements in this arena *vis-à-vis* problems in others. Alfonsín's acceptance of the amplification of the potential number of "accused" on the basis of the weakening of the criteria of *Obediencia Debida* (Due Obedience), reveals his early disagreement with limiting the trials. This was introduced into the Senate during the treatment of the reform law of the *Code of Military Justice* (CJM) by a party with very little influence (the *Popular Movement Neuquino*, MPN), who managed to exclude "heinous and abhorrent" acts from the "excuse" of obedience.

And not only that: a provision was soon added to keep expanding the initial objectives. This resulted from the need of Alfonsín's government to achieve objectives, given the limited results which it had yet attained in the fields of the economy, the trade unions, etc., and his own reluctance to impose discretionary brakes from the standpoint of the Executive on an institutional process which he himself had opened.

This combination of republican self-restraint and political necessities will become visible on three occasions. The first is when he refuses to pressurize the deputies to correct the extensions to the reform of the CJM introduced in the *Senado* (Senate), thus partially vetoing the law. The second happens when he allows independent action on the part of the judges of first instance, the courts and the *Corte Suprema* (Supreme Court), which contradicts his initial objectives. And the final occasion happens around 1986 when he refuses to endorse and support the "instructions to prosecutors" with which the *Secretaría de Justicia* (Ministry of Justice) sought to re-establish *Obediencia Debida*. The tension between his initial perspective and the role he assigned to the division of powers in the management of the politics of trials is, in large measure, behind all of these conflicts, which are dragged out over time without finding a solution. Beyond the general criteria introduced with his bill to reform the CJM, his assumption was that, to the extent that they were an example of the republican functioning of the institutions, the trials had to be legitimated by Congress and implemented autonomously by the courts. The priority granted to judicial impartiality was from the outset in tension with the necessarily centralized, uniform and rapid political character which the process had to take.

An episode which illustrates this point nicely is the previously referred to reform of the CJM. Here are the details. When the *Cámara Baja* (Lower House) had to review the changes made to the executive's project in the *Senado* (Senate), the president had the opportunity to put pressure on the Deputies, even threatening to veto such changes if they did not return to the original plan. Several officials raised with Alfonsín the need to continue on this road so as to avoid greater evils in the future, even if it meant paying costs, and clashing with their own legislators and those of other parties. The response they received from the president is supremely eloquent: "we'll let things pass and then we'll see" (according to the testimony given by the then presidential adviser Carlos Nino in his book *Juicio al mal absoluto*, and confirmed by Alfonsín himself in the Oral History Archive, 2007, and also by Jaime Malamud Goti, AHO, 2005). But there is another no less interesting episode, in particular because it takes place more than two years later. In April 1986, contrary to which has tended to be argued in the literature, Alfonsín overruled the instructions to prosecutors improvised by his Secretary of Justice, even before the human rights organizations had mobilized to repudiate them. He did so under pressure from the Radicals themselves and the Federal Court.

3. What is expressed in the debates about the best way to address the review of the past is a competition between different versions of the politicization of the problem and its solution, and not one of the opposition between "political participation" and "depoliticisation and technique". Included in these different versions of politicization is the one in which is at issue here: whether it is better to create a Bicameral Commission or the CONADEP. The ruling party sought to politicize the responsibilities of the military leadership in order to establish a general criterion for a trial, and the production of a truth at once formal and consensual about what happened plays a decisive role in this regard. It permitted the deactivation of the pre-existing polarizations in terms of "versions of history", shed light on the repressive plan as a whole within a limited time, and opened the door to distinguishing the direct commission of crimes from the capacity of taking decisions in this respect.

At the same time, attributing a leading role to the intellectuals and leading professionals in the CONADEP would have permitted provision of an explanation of what happened, including the issue of multiple responsibilities in the origins of the political violence, transcending the dispute between political parties. This objective is fulfilled quite satisfactorily. In this respect, although it is true that the argument of the *dos demonios* ("the two demons": the military and the guerrillas) "depoliticized" specific crimes on both sides (those who were "driven to act"), the fact remains that it offers a key which acknowledges the political nature of the decision to resort to illegal violence, as opposed to moral arguments about the objectives pursued which, ironically, intended to depoliticize victims or victimizers. In the end, the problem behind the objections to the CONADEP (not just those directed at it by the human rights movement, but also by the military), is not the conflict between a political and a depoliticized view, but rather dissent concealed behind the apparent consensus as to what the observance of human rights involves and demands. Neither the revolutionaries nor the counterrevolutionaries were willing, at that point, to renounce their moral justification for the violence they had practiced, nor to attempt to take advantage of the struggle between political parties so as to denounce the crimes of the enemy.

Of note is another symptomatic fact, which the literature, again symptomatically, also often overlooks. At the beginning of the democratic government a large part of the human rights movement, as well as the political leadership, was suspicious of any possibility of progress in the courts, whether military or civilian, and of achieving any conviction, and imagined the intervention of Parliament as a way of conducting an investigation and a "political" trial which would have the role of condemning the repression in a generic way, even if specific responsibilities could not identified. The Bicameral Committee would play a decisive role in this plan, for it could allow the committed minority of the parliamentary parties to take an active role, putting pressure on the executive and the courts. Thus the CONADEP offered the Executive a way forward without multiplying the number of institutional actors involved, or granting more influence to Congress.

On the other hand, however, it should not be overlooked that this strategy helped give voice to a social actor which would help to establish the so-called "official truth", but which in doing so would gain increasing autonomy, as a result of which the government would lose its ability to be the only actor to investigate, report, and postulate responsibilities and therefore accuse. The autonomy of that "voice of society" is an additional difficulty when it comes to reconciling unlimited truth with limited justice. Although the role of the CONADEP in the validation of levels of responsibility and the theory two demons has been highlighted, this is specified within the framework of a highly extensive and accurate identification of illegal and immoral behaviour in the commission of specific crimes, which will help to modify the social consensus about what is punishable and what is unforgivable. This allows us to specify in what sense the CONADEP "burst the banks" of Alfonsín's plans.

4. The intervention of the *Consejo Supremo* was not in the end the greatest obstacle to the progress of trials. What was much more problematic, rather, was the heterogeneity of criteria and speeds with which the civil courts acted in this respect. This is true of both the courts of the first instance and those in different parts of the country. The alternatives on hand to deal with the trials were not ordered simply according to the number of potential defendants, nor in terms of the options of civil versus military jurisdictions. The basic problem to be solved was the degree of centralization and political coordination *vis-à-vis* the legitimacy and impartiality of the process. In these terms, not just two, but three alternatives can be identified. First, a centralized political trial which determined once and for all the political responsibilities. Second, decentralized civil and / or military litigation, preventing the political power from intervening in the actions of the judges who presided over the trials. Third, an intermediate formula which combined to some extent the division of powers and the regulations of the law with a political criteria of judgment. As is known, Alfonsín chose the third alternative. He wanted to take advantage of the trials both as, on the one hand, an example of the rule of law and of the republican form of conflict resolution, thus respecting the separation of powers, and, on the other, as a moral victory for democracy, an expression of the definitive rearrangement of the civil-military relations and the effectiveness of the moral principles of the new regime, thus establishing respect for individual rights.

In this context, the error which can be attributed to the implementation of the policy was, if anything, that there was not enough centralization, that its full reconciliation with the division of powers was not achieved, and therefore that it was impossible to quickly determine the number and condition of the defendants. With respect to these objectives, the role played by the *Consejo Supremo* may even vindicate it. Its intervention was a necessary instance of the transition between a corporate and authoritarian regime and one subject to impartial and republican rules, enabling the strengthening of the Law as an independent constitutional power. This was so because it permitted respect for "due process" (given that "natural justice" was respected and retroactive application *in toto* of civil justice avoided), while at the same time bringing about a centralization of the cases. These came to it from courts in different parts of the country, in the most diverse terms in which they had been raised by the plaintiffs and dealt with by the judges. Achieving these goals through a single double instance trial would turn out, however, to be at the same time both narrowly useful to legitimize the process in terms of impartial and unquestionable procedures, and very costly both in terms of the time spent and the wear and tear on the moderate consensus. In this respect it becomes clear for the first time that to make the trials a case of division of powers runs counter to the goal of achieving quick, centralized and definitive results, over those which force the different actors to cooperate. This is because, while the formula does centralize, it still leaves to the discretion of too many actors the times and criteria to apply. These include not only the *Consejo*, but above all the different Federal Courts, including the judges of first instance, who may have resisted or delayed the elevation of cases to the military courts and the *Corte Suprema*, which ought to have ensured the consistency of the decisions of individual judges and cameras. Centralization through a second hearing, in short, would take years; and the unification of criteria would not succeed at all. From the above we conclude that it was the sum total of the objectives pursued, not mutually compatible, in an ambitious strategy, which needlessly complicated matters for government, not its "moderation".

In the conventional criticism, however, the significance of the intervention of the *Consejo* is often ignored or underestimated. It intervention did not only mean self-judgment, but the centralization of cases and the criteria which the federal courts and trial judges of the first instance had to apply. If that was the decisive question, giving a homogeneous composition and criteria to these courts was essential. And to have allowed its composition to be settled with the decentralized criteria of federalism and by the division of positions in the *Senado* (Senate) into lots amongst the parties, was a serious mistake. An even greater centralization by case through the single intervention of the *Cámara de la Capital* (Chamber of the Capital), would have allowed it to turn the whole process into a single initiative: it is known that that option was considered, but never seriously.

5. During 1986 Alfonsín's government was more dependent than ever on its achievements in the field of human rights, which explains the loss of another whole year in delimiting its policies, i.e., in returning to its initial objectives and criteria. The above-mentioned reluctance on the part of the party and the president himself, in April of that year, to maintain the instructions to prosecutors, prove it. The very logic of *Punto Final* (Full Stop) also illustrates the point. According to the criteria of conventional criticism, Alfonsín bet on carrying out a few trials, but the process had escaped his control, first with the reform of the CJM, then when CONADEP made a more comprehensive report than expected, and finally when the House included Point 30 in its ruling on the former commanders (enabling new trials of the cases which had been taken as proven). His own creatures had betrayed him.

A more accurate description of the process would be that Alfonsín's goals in this field gradually expanded to the extent that steps were taken towards the objectives initially pursued, and not only as a result of sectoral pressures, but because his government was pursuing a strategy of "move and see". This left much room for independent initiatives arising both from their own factions and from other actors and, above all, because the government became more and more dependent on achievements in this field, in the light of the disappointing results achieved in others. We have already mentioned two facts which show evidence in this respect: the tolerance with which Alfonsín received notice of the changes to his proposed reform of the CJM and his attitude towards the instructions to prosecutors. To these can now be added the logic which animated the law of *Punto Final*, which was adopted in December 1986. This law largely insists on the premises which had guided previous decisions, and even takes them for granted, because the scope of his trial policy could not be retrospective, but at most limited in time. Hence the essential part of the project is the unification of criteria and the coordination and acceleration of the courts and trials, rather than the imposition of limitations on the number of cases. Seen from this perspective, the immediate effect it had, the processing of hundreds of officers, both those on active duty and retired, should not really have surprised the executive, except perhaps in terms of the number achieved.

6. The APDH entered into crisis before the politics of Alfonsinism did, and this crisis was due rather to a process internal to the human rights movement than to external factors. The growing pre-eminence acquired by the rights of blood of the relatives of the victims over a public and liberal notion of rights is the fundamental fact in this regard. The responsibility of other organisms for this happening, and therefore for the collapse of the APDH, is at the same time impossible to ignore. The disagreements underlying the "mock consensus" on human rights must have come to a head for this to have happened. We have already referred to this and it is something which directly affected the possibility of reaching a consensus about initiatives aimed at creating political and institutional conditions which would make possible the enforcement of these rights. Liberal republican ideas which place emphasis on the impartiality of justice and its "condition of exercise" were from the outset much weaker in the *ethos* of the agencies than the universalist discourse of rights and, in particular, than the legitimation of demands by virtue of the "rights of blood" of the relatives of the victims. These turned out, at the same time, to be very useful instruments for legitimizing populist, anti-liberal and revolutionary perspectives about the objectives which the movement should assume (e.g., the rehabilitation of the "ideals of the disappeared" and the denunciation of "all forms of domination"), and tended to prevail over the aim of strengthening judicial and representative public institutions, capable of guaranteeing rights. This was a tendency, we should add, which would be facilitated by the role of the "authorized voice" which Alfonsín's own policy (through the CONADEP) had bestowed on morally motivated actors of civil society. The voice of "interested" or affected parties, the victims and their families, and the rights of blood, in combination with a universalist

and humanist discourse predominated at the expense of a possible link between the human rights agencies and a much richer and more complex political and social system (composed of parties, interest groups, a multitude of public institutions, intellectual domains and other social actors), with which they would be obliged to coexist according to shared rules. It would determine their progressive isolation.

The consequence of this tendency would be the reabsorption of the demands relating to violations committed during the dictatorship in terms of the revolutionary struggle, and the politicization of the movement's agenda in a populist and leftist key, on the basis of the decline of the Alfonsinist consensus. To this corresponded, therefore, at the same time their progressive loss of influence on the institutional processes and public opinion and the strengthening of a self-enclosed, encapsulated, identity. Eloquent evidence of the above is that offered by the adoption of the "appearance with life" of the disappeared as irrenounceable objective, first by the *Madres* and later by the whole movement. At the same time, several episodes have been recorded in its midst between 1984 and 1987 which shed light on the reluctance of the mothers in particular, and the relatives and those who assume the position of victims in general, to submit their claims to scrutiny and public legitimation, which would have involved respect for rules of law and the strengthening of the institutions as a fundamental condition for channelling such claims. The campaign to delegitimize the action of the CONADEP and the subsequent appropriation of its report is perhaps one of the most significant. A number of other things should also be noted. These include efforts to avoid any discussion of the problem of political violence, the denunciations of the actions of the Federal Court as part of a "Alfonsinist circus", and the process of electing new leaders of the *Madres* in 1986, which leads to the rise of Hebe de Bonafini and the break-up of that organization.

But undoubtedly the most telling issue in this regard was the dispute this movement and other institutions promoted in the heart of the APDH. This, we shall clarify, was practically the only agency which promoted the integration of political actors and institutional representatives within its framework, and had advanced from the time of dictatorship in the direction of providing itself with a committee with a pluralistic composition of political forces, interest groups, and religious denominations. This condition, however, soon began to put it into opposition to the rest of the movement. When it faced the need to establish positions on government policies, which it did by attempting to reconcile the positions of its moderate members with those of the more militant (as a rule generally members of other agencies), the latter began to question it and even to exclude it from their activities and meetings. Hence, after the high point of the involvement of many of its leaders and activists in the CONADEP, its activity declined rapidly. The final straw came in 1987, after the passing of the law of *Obediencia Debida*. The *Madres*, together with other institutions, promoted the removal Alfonsín from among its members and encouraged the exclusion of moderates from its committee. Since then the institution has lost virtually all of its influence.

7. The results of the September 1987 elections, held after the vote on the law of *Obediencia Debida* in April of that year, were bad for the Radical government, but not "so" bad. They show that it retained much of its electorate and, therefore, to some extent that important sectors of the latter supported its accommodation to the need to halt the trials and negotiate with the military. Had it failed to do so, that is to say, had it not been able to show a firm agreement with the military, would in the end have been more damaging to its consensus than pushing through the laws of *Punto Final* and *Obediencia Debida*. The unresolved tension between using the trials to keep the military on the defensive, and stopping the trials so as to appease them, had led to the mutiny of the *carapintadas* during Easter 1987. This was something which the government interpreted at the time as an opportunity to demonstrate to one and all the need to agree. And to some extent it succeeded, convincing its own party of the need to vote for *Obediencia Debida*, but not sufficiently with respect to the *carapintadas*, who would mutiny again. And this damage would make itself obvious again with the subsequent rebellions in late 1987 and during 1988. However, the most significant fact is that once the Alfonsinist consensus weakens and its orientation changes, every political channel for the incorporation of the demands of the human rights movement into the public agenda disappears. This reveals to what extent Alfonsín's human rights policy was the only possible option

We must be clear that this does not mean the extinction of the consensus about the illegal repression, but merely a change in the priority accorded to the prosecution of those responsible. The ambiguity which had characterized that consensus from the outset is now revealed in all its complexity. Behind a general rejection of the disappearances and torture, there had existed from the beginning very different views about why they had happened, whether they were in some measure justified by the circumstances, whether or not to condemn the persons responsible, whom to condemn and how. This helps us to understand that the "Alfonsinist solutions", including the law of *Obediencia Debida*, continued to have some degree of consensus. Of this law it can at least be said that it was not enough to generate a massive shift in political and electoral preferences.

Moving on, it is quite risky to argue that the UCR lost the 1987 elections because of that law. It must be remembered that on that occasion this force lost only 6 per cent of the votes it had received two years earlier, and that between these two elections, as well as the trial of the former commanders and the Law of *Obediencia Debida*, the monthly rate of inflation had increased from 2 per cent to about 20 per cent. Even if the electorate generously assigned equal value to both circumstances, we cannot say that for more than 3 per cent of the voters this law had been a motive for changing their vote.

8. Moderation was not an option doomed to failure from the beginning but, rather the opposite, was the most reasonable and profitable choice in a complex context such as that faced the by Alfonsín government. The problems of the design and implementation of its human rights policy can be attributed, not to the fact that it was moderate, but to its not being sufficiently so, that is to say, not being firmly enough defined as such. It was not necessarily a question of carrying out more or fewer trials, but of carrying out a definite number of trials which had been established from the beginning. Nor was it one of preventing the use of civil courts or that of military ones, but of ensuring a centralized process as rapidly as possible at different levels, which would grant less autonomy to the actors in each step involved. Therefore, it was not necessarily the case that more intervention should be granted to the Parliament, to the parties, experts or other social actors, but of making more extensive and fuller use of presidential powers.

There is also no objection in principle to the search for a certain equilibrium with the military power, but rather of the way in which it was conceived.

The notion of reconciliation with which Alfonsín was effectively working from the start corresponds to an idea of the rule of law as a constitutional and normative covenant between players. It is motivated primarily by a regenerative expectation, namely that these actors can agree and coordinate themselves according to some consensus and shared goals. It is this idea of a regenerative covenant or agreement, rather than that of reconciliation itself, which is the origin of some of the problems we have identified in the human rights policy of the period. We can illustrate this point by means of a comparative exercise: it should be pointed out that if the policy of reconciliation which Carlos Menem would face up to was more effective than that of his predecessor, this was not due solely or primarily to the amnesties he dictated in 1989 and 1990. Just as important is the fact that he did not implement them with a view to compromise, but with a view rather to the use (and abuse) of presidential powers in a context which is defined as an emergency, without granting the least autonomy or authority to the intervention of other actors.

The conventional argument of some critics that Menem's amnesties continue and deepen the policy of the last years of Alfonsín (and even that during the transition the latter would have negotiated signing them jointly), has no empirical basis whatsoever and is, in analytical terms, inconsistent. For neither the goals pursued by two leaders, nor the tools with which they work can be compared. The truth is that Menem will bring with him a completely different vision of the problem, which leads not only to amnesties, but to the defence of repression. This vision can be summarized by the postulation of a "political liberalism" which is no longer that of the rights and guarantees, but that of the most minimal rules of the game which ensure legitimacy in the exercise of power. In sum, it is a governmental liberalism more than a liberalism of procedures and limits to power.

Peronism in power from 1989 will eventually resort to the discourse of rights, but for other purposes. It will do so primarily to legitimize privatization and the withdrawal of the state, while expressly excluding the issue of violations during the dictatorship, and more generally, that of access to justice. In these terms, a completely new account of the process of democratization will seek to impose itself, by displacing the Alfonsinist consensus and putting aside the landmarks which it had left behind, the *Nunca Más* and the Trial of the Juntas. However, to the extent that this emerging consensus will offer neither long lasting nor sufficiently consensual solutions, the result will be more of a chronic lack of definition of the dispute between competing narratives and foundational of the set of events which define the terrain of the dispute. Thus it will be a self-justifying and partisan use of the two registers of liberal discourse (in doctrinal terms not necessarily mutually incompatible), which, with the conclusion of the cycle of the Alfonsinist consensus, will hinder their progress towards the strengthening liberal and republican traditions. Although not entirely lost, they might find only a tenuous continuity in actors and institutions. Contributing to this, of course, not least of all, is the fact, already noted, that the liberal culture of rights will find otherwise ambiguous promoters in the bodies acting on its behalf, and that if they recognize the trials and *Nunca Más* they will do so from the point of view of traditions and principles of legitimacy which take us back to the cycle of Argentinean politics in which the partisan use of material and symbolic resources wrecked collective coexistence.

The New Approach to the Issue with Menem

With Menem we effectively encounter a strong will to resolve the issue once and for all, but with a radically different approach to that taken by Alfonsín, even at the end of his term. For the governing vertex, it was now a question of incorporating the military as subordinate participants in the two fundamental strategies of the government: structural reforms and the redefinition of foreign policy. Only in this context did it make sense to consider the issue of human rights. Menem, therefore, devised a strategy of pacification which entailed closing down definitively the review of past trials, as a step to ensuring the firm obedience of the military in view of the objectives which really mattered: integration into the unipolar world which resulted from the fall of the Berlin Wall and the collapse of the Soviet bloc, and the adaptation of the state apparatus to a new phase of capitalist expansion. In order to do so, he based himself on an assumption which was shared by a significant sector of the PJ (and also, we would say, of the UCR) from the period of the transition. This maintained that the crimes committed by the state were not enough to delegitimize what the Armed Forces had felt forced to do for good of the state and the country, namely, suppress the guerrilla organizations.

In this spirit, Menem would proclaim the end of the long cycle of instability and would declare himself the architect of the final pacification of the country, a work in progress since the time of Videla. This would mean embracing the cause of reconciliation and forgetting, and its most enthusiastic supporters in the Church, politics and the military. At the same time, following the same logic applied in the reform strategy, he promoted various types of compensation for the victims of repression and their families. With this he did not aim so much to moderate criticism from human rights organizations, as serve the sectors of Peronism linked to them. Yet, his strategy was not as successful and as free of obstacles as many analysts have wanted to believe. The truth is that he paid high costs in terms of legitimacy for the decisions he took. And he also largely failed to establish a new narrative about the past, one which, if it could not erase the moral gravity of the crimes of state terrorism, would at least play them down. In the final analysis, this will result in a reopening of the debate about repression, and, gradually, of the trials.

The most serious difficulty for the strategy of forgetting emerged from the courts. There we will find, even among judges and prosecutors close to the government, sustained commitment to the task of continuing or initiating trials. These include both the loopholes left open in the laws of *Obediencia Debida* and *Punto Final*, that is to say, the reference to "aberrant acts" (theft of babies and property, etc. ...) and the so-called "truth trials", trials which would not have penal consequences for the repressors but which would keep open the debate about the illegal repression. Sometimes this commitment on the part of judicial officers, particularly in the case of those affiliated to the government, was related to the search for a source of legitimacy which would offset or dilute the criticism they and the judiciary in general deserved for their conduct in cases of corruption involving government officials. It contributed, on the other hand, to the recognition of international conventions against so-called crimes against humanity, which would be a milestone in the reform of the Constitution in 1994. It also led to compensatory initiatives (such as the payment of compensation to relatives of disappeared persons and former prisoners who had not enjoyed a fair trial or who had been detained by executive order), which deserved extensive support from the executive and the parliamentary groups of both the government and opposition.

This process of the reopening of the trials would be of great importance for the revival of the human rights movement in the second half of the 1990s. But this revival, however, did not mean a recovery of the public influence which it had achieved in the previous decade. On the contrary, the human rights organizations, particularly those representing the victims and their families, evolved in a particular direction, which generally led to their divorce from the main body of the currents of opinion which animated the society during the 1990s.

BRUNO NAPOLI

Memory, Truth and Justice: Ideas of an Institutional Justice

Argentina is passing through an unprecedented political moment. Almost 600 repressors from the last civil-military regime, which lasted from 1976 to 1983, have been arrested (accused of the kidnapping, torture, murder and forced disappearances of citizens). Of this number, sentence has been passed on about 170 and the rest are in prison awaiting trial. Another 800 participants in the dictatorship's extermination plan are found at liberty, but charged in different cases in more than half the national territory.[1] This unusual situation contrasts dramatically with ways of reading recent history which have tried, from the perspective of distinct government administrations, to close in different ways a question impossible to close: that of state terrorism in Argentina.

The changes brought about in recent years in the politics of human rights in the country contrast not only with the situation three decades ago, but also with that of five years ago. To undertake a revision from a political point of view, contrasting previous state administrations, and especially those of the same political tendency (Peronism), with the current situation, is just one attempt to understand a turning point in the field. Another is to attempt to understand the political meaning which first the "military question", and later the consequences of the genocide,

1 According to the calculations of CELS (December 2010), adding the figure of thirty-seven deserters and 257 deaths before being sentenced (Página/12. 26/12/10). This data differs from that of the UFC, which adds up to about thirty persons sentenced (196) but only 41 with unappealable sentences of *incapable of being annulled*. It details, moreover, 498 detained on trial and 820 accused in total (data of the Unidad Fiscal for control and monitoring of cases of violations of human rights 29/12/2010).

have had when it comes to assuming the leadership of the country at any moment. The decisions taken about the crimes against humanity have been fundamental to the frameworks of legitimacy of the later political actions, establishing limits of the law and its interpretation.

The current measures, enshrined in an absolute respect for the judicial system (and its timings) have helped to negotiate the scope of the legitimation necessary in order to take decisions in other fields. And alongside these changes, the political actors involved in the story (within the system of democratic representation), have established diametrically opposed political positions in less than a decade.

The tensions generated by the conjunctural political conflicts interacted in such a way that these same actors took the meaning of institutional justice as a political positioning of democratic strengthening for the future. *Memory, Truth and Justice* acts as a new location in the notion of a universal institutional path, and has been recorded in the declaration of the *Cámara de Diputados de la Nación* (Chamber of Deputies of the Nation) as an objective to be pursued. It sheds light on the unprecedented direction in which we have been travelling in terms of the criminalization of the recent past in the country.

The Attempts at Closure and the Construction of Responses

At the start of the 1980s there resounded like the shots of an intense gunfight which had only victims but no perpetrators, the announcements of the end of the "war against subversion", the "pacification of the country",[2] or "in Argentina there are no disappeared, they are all dead". Declarations

2 The concept of "pacification" has been maintained even under democracy by different political sectors as a justification of the policies of impunity enacted with tools of the state, but has also been a narrative which has gained little acceptance as a way of reading this politics.

of this kind bore the imprint of the political position of the dictatorship on the question of "detainees-disappeared".[3] It was the first attempt to close the subject, without giving further explanations of the fate of thousands of citizens kidnapped alive from their homes, their workplaces or their places of study. It imprinted the logic of an unfinished story which did not answer fundamental questions: Who kidnapped them? Why? What happened to them? Where are they? Without these answers, a foundational political slogan of the human rights movement emerged in opposition: "Aparición con Vida" ("Appearance with life").[4]

Meanwhile the civil-military regime assiduously invited journalists from the mainstream media to meetings, press briefings or conferences, in order to explain the political changes taking place in the country, without going into details on the subject of the disappeared (and without even being challenged by the "guests" of the event).[5]

3 The dictatorship, which held that the disappeared were "a pipe dream, are neither living nor dead" (in the words of former dictator Jorge Videla), changes its position in 1979 and starts to take them for dead. On Army Day (29/05/79) the former dictator General Viola spoke of the "absent forever". That year laws 22,062 (the "right to a pension") and 22,068 ("presumption of death") are enacted so that the relatives of the disappeared who had reported the crime between 6/11/74 and 9/12/79 (the date the Law was passed), would accept them as having died and have the right to the benefit of a state pension. On 28/10/79 the Pope speaks of "the lost or disappeared in Chile and Argentina" in front of 70,000 people in Rome and asks them to pray for those who "have no hope now to embrace their loved ones". "In Argentina there are no disappeared, they are all dead," and "everybody knows they are dead" are statements made by Ricardo Balbín (UCR) to the magazine *Cambio 16* (Spain) and the TV show *La Clave* (Spain) during his trip to the Iberian Peninsula (April 1980). B. Neustadt vindicated Balbín's "favour to the nation" in *La Opinión* (23/04/1980) in the note entitled "El favor de Balbín" ("Balbín's favour").

4 The slogan was accepted by the Asociación Madres de Plaza de Mayo 5/12/1980 as a political response to what we call the discourses of "death".

5 The journalists were invited to witness the achievements of the "Process" or simply to be told what they had to write. An example is the meeting which one of the greatest perpetrators of genocide in Argentina's history, General Albano Harguindeguy, then Minister of Interior of the dictatorship, organized for "18 women journalists" in order to "fill them with information so that afterwards they make use of it" – such

Once in the democratic stage (1983), the reading of *a superseded war*, the debtor of the "*theory of the two demons*", would be the way of making the years of the dictatorship intelligible. The state would adopt it as its own in order to offer an account of what had happened with state terrorism. It would at the same time have an acceptable functionality for the implementation of a legal structure of gradual impunity which Alfonsín's government would apply haphazardly but effectively, although paying a high political price in dong so. In this context the *Juicio a los Comandantes de las tres primeras juntas militares* (Trial of the Commanders of the First Three Military Juntas),[6] will be the space from which to untether a previously contained thirst for justice, to be enforced as a reading of a "possible" but not complete punishment. But it is also conceivable that there was not much more space within the reasons of state, living yet with prosecutors, judges, politicians and journalists, who only a short time before had coexisted in turn without conflicts with the dictatorship. However, the Trial will be a political gesture of institutional strength which will endure over time as a possible reading of the resolution of the theme. Later, through the so-called "laws of impunity",[7] the liberty of more than 1,000 repressors will be engineered in another attempt to close the question. It is an attempt which will be undermined by the series of three military uprisings[8] undertaken by

---

were his words to those present. Attending this meeting of 04/07/1980, were, among others, Magdalena R. Guiñazú, Mónica Gutierrez, Mónica Cahen D'Anvers, Nelly Casas, Reneé Sallas, Clara Mariño, Emiliana Lópéz Saavedra (*Siete Días*, No 882, 9 to 15/07/80, text photographs of the meeting: Luisa Delfino/Jorge Grupali).

6 This trial cannot be thought of as the "Argentinean Nüremberg" (the title of a film by R. Arias from 2004) for it was not the product of the victory of a foreign army that put those military commanders on trial; here an existing penal code was applied, with the participation of many of the judges and prosecutors of the previous period. This does not make it more (or less) simple, but rather signals its enormous distance from that event. General R Bignone (commander of the 4th Military Junta) handed over the presidential flag to Alfonsín and retired to write his memoirs ("*El último de facto*" published by Planeta).

7 *Ley de Punto Final* ("Full Stop": 23/12/1986) and *Ley de Obediencia Debida* ("Due Obedience": 05/06/1987), in that chronological order.

8 April 1987–; January 1988; December 1988.

the middle ranks of the army, uprisings which were more closely related to the internal problems of the armed forces than to the achievement of an "amnesty" (such a thing was accepted) and which restored the sensation of an unfinished chapter. Meanwhile, as part of the dual stance of the state on state terrorism, the government still held in prison political prisoners[9] inherited from the dictatorship, and subjected the organizations of the human rights movement to pressure in order to put an end to their demand for the "justice and punishment of all those culpable". This applied in particular to the Madres of the Plaza de Mayo and their successive marches and the questions they raised, who were treated as terrorists.[10]

"Another Contingent of Mothers"

In 1989, in the context of a politico-economic crisis, with the looting of shops, a rate of inflation which liquidated salaries on a daily basis, and the early renunciation of the constitutional president, Raúl Alfonsín, Carlos Menem assumes the presidency. Immediately, one of his ministers speaks frankly about the policy with respect state terrorism and declares that "the Argentinean government will pardon the military rebels and those accused of violating human rights as part of its strategy of increasing the credibility of the country and attracting foreign investment [...] the investor

9 In 1988 there are still 5 political prisoners: A. Carrizo, R. Emperador and J. Paz are liberated in December; F. Nuñez and T. Cormack in July 1989. Amongst them, Graciela Daleo, ex-detainee-disappeared in the ESMA, is imprisoned again by a lawsuit on the part of the dictatorship in 1988. Liberated a few months later, and benefited by the amnesty of 1989, she is the only one to reject it and reopen in the case in 1990.

10 On 21/12/1984 Alfonsín declares at a press conference that "the political objectives" of the Mothers "do not coincide with the national interest" (while the March of Resistance is undertaken); 6/07/1985, he declares on German television that the Mothers" defence of "those who occasioned this whole tragic spilling of blood in the country, with an elitist conception leading to subversive terrorism" is "negative for democracy". In Bayer, Osvaldo, *Ventana a la Plaza de Mayo*. Periódico MPM, 1985.

is no philanthropist, he takes a risk; if there are no clear rules of the game which allow him to calculate profitability, he will go to another country: (he needs) legal safeguards; clear rules in the economic field and the military conflict resolution amongst other things" (*El Cronista Comercial* 25/08/1989, Italo Lúder,[11] Minister of Defence and later Ambassador to France in the government of Carlos Menem). A month later it is the president himself who announces, in the context of an historical revisionism which his campaign had affirmed, that "there still remain some wounds to be closed and I, as president of the Argentineans, pledge before God and before my people to heal these wounds, so that on the basis of national unity we march towards the Great Fatherland which Rosas, Urquiza, Sarmiento, Quiroga, Peñaloza, Guemes and all the great men and caudillos who were born in this land dreamed of" (*Dársena Norte*, 30/09/89 receiving the repatriated remains of the federal caudillo Juan Manuel de Rosas). A week later (07/10/89) he will sign the first amnesties setting at liberty more than 250 repressors. The following year (30/12/90) he signs the last ones, liberating the rest (amongst them those condemned in the Trial of the Commanders).

With this beginning of Menem's administration, the 1990s find our country with every person guilty of acts of genocide at liberty as a result of the accumulation of spaces of impunity by means of constitutional mechanisms. They enjoyed liberty and speculated on the possibility of a vindication of the actions they had taken on the basis of a reaccommodation with their own ranks: "They agreed almost unanimously that the military leadership will converge on Jorge Rafael Videla because of the almost mystical way in which he survived his five years in prison without moments of spiritual weakness [...] the behaviour of Videla was in every way unobjectionable" (Editorial, *Ámbito Financiero* 22/08/1989).

11 In October 1975, I. Lúder, provisionally in charge of the presidency in the absence of Isabel Martínez de Perón for reasons of health, signed the decrees N° 2.770/71/72. In its Article No. 1, the latter establishes that "The Armed Forces under the Supreme Command of the President of the Nation, which will be exercised through the Consejo de Defensa (Defence Council), will proceed to undertake military and security operations such as are necessary to the end of annihilating the action of the subversive elements throughout he country". The ministers C. Ruckauf, A. Cafiero, A. Robleto, T. Vottero, C. Emery and M. Arauz Castex signed the decree.

The amnesties mark a space for a very different balance of forces with Peronism back in power. The decision to liberate those with greatest responsibility for the terrorism of the state (and the loftiest symbols of the regime) fell to a one-man action without need for consensus. In contrast to this, Alfonsín needed two Congressional laws and his personal intervention during the vote in order to achieve the impunity of the middle-ranking officers of the terror, its less visible faces.

If, during his electoral campaign Menem, tired of repeating the phrase "only an idiot could confuse pacification with amnesty", these initial gestures (the amnesties) signal the beginning of a profound change for Argentina (in terms of political economic structure) and the concepts of "national reconciliation" or "pacification" are soon replaced (without confusion) with the most brutal sincerity. In February 1991 a bomb explodes in the offices of the newspaper *Página 12*. In April the ex-detainee / disappeared Graciela Daleo is detained again. In March the *Madres de Plaza de Mayo* are accused by Menem of betraying the country and in June suffer their fourth attack (robbery and the destruction of the house of the *Madres*). The following month the president links the newspaper *Página 12* with the events of La Tablada[12] and with drug trafficking. In November Menem begs that "they cease to bear their dead and forget, that they let the dead weep for the dead".

This crazy situation is accompanied by a state posture which lays bare the political framework of the of this new "*pacification*". The President of the nation warns the population which participates in the marches in repudiation of his political economy, and above all the young people who repudiate his plans for education, that "it is not going to be the case that we will have again another contingent of Madres de Plaza de Mayo calling for their children" (Página/12. 09/07/1992).[13]

12 In January 1989 a group of left wing militants of the MTP tried to seize a military regiment in the locality of La Tablada, resulting in more than thirty deaths, some of them shot after surrendering, and others "disappeared", in the re-taking of the barracks by the armed forces.

13 He also added that "the resurgence of subversion [...] is a latent danger throughout Latin America. And that is why, he said, they had to be very careful, show themselves, making use of liberty, but not overdoing things, because here these criminals meddle and try to take advantage of this type of situation". This reversal of the terms of the

The Myth of the Absent State

The paradoxical thing about this situation is that the readings which the political leaders eventually make a decade later (and which still endure) is that the state was absent during those years of "neoliberalism". This is paradoxical because neither the policy of impunity nor the realization of a plan of spoliation of the national resources which were passed into private hands would have been possible without the involvement and approval of representatives of the state as a whole, whether the *Congreso de la Nación*, the *Corte Suprema* or the Executive. This is true also of all the symbols of the 1990s: amnesties, labour flexibility, the regulation of the right to strike, the support given by Isaac Rojas and Martínez de Hoz to the economic policy, the sale of state enterprises, massive layoffs, sending troops to the Persian Gulf, the policy of submission to the USA. It was a strong state, legitimated symbolically, which was present at the signing of those agreements and which managed to give a legal framework to the policy of impunity in all its terms; it was also the guarantor of the fulfilment of those "pacts". The sensation of "necessary" impunity (as Lúder put it) was what functioned as a demiurge of a political class which assumed responsibility for the imposition of dramatic changes regardless of the consequences, at a point when the country had got out of hand. As a corollary, it is worth mentioning that the trade union leaders of a CGT[14] were divided in two internal camps (both Peronist at root), which made pronouncements on

---

responsibility for what happened during the dictatorship, blaming the activists and their neglect by their mothers, is linked to the worst tradition of the dictatorships in Argentina. Alberto Bonnet (2007) reminds us of a similar campaign was launched by the federal police in the days of another dictator, Onganía in 1966, with the phrase "know where your child is now". A few days after the president's remarks, the *Madres de Plaza de Mayo* (Mothers of the Plaza de Mayo) initiated the campaign "know where the murderer of your child is, know what office he holds or what activity he carries out, know where he lives".

14 The Confederación General del Trabajo, which undertook fourteen general strikes against the government of Alfonsín.

the amnesties. Güerino Andreoni (*Sindicato de Comercio CGT-San Martín*, liaison committee) declared: "it is a highly contentious subject. Society has suffered much and in this sense no one can deny what happened in Argentina. But on the basis of disagreement and incomprehension, we cannot rebuild a country. I appreciate that the President (Menem) has taken a decision of this nature". Saúl Ubaldini (*CGT-Azopardo*) will say: "it is a power which the Constitution grants to the Comrade President, and I am no one to criticise him".[15]

The Changes of the Narrative and their Limits

It being inevitable that closure was impossible, the country's successive administrations had to take responsibility for the question of state terrorism in Argentina. The contrast will be given, on the one hand, in the "terminality" attempted by Raúl Alfonsín" (with an "exemplary" trial), Carlos Menem (with the amnesties of "pacification") and Fernando De la Rúa (with the rejection of extraditions and of international penal cooperation); and on the other, in the "progressive" politics of Néstor Kirchner, who prompted the replacement of the idea of impunity by that of a *justicia universal* (universal justice) and the reopening of cases.

Every attempt at closure had implications for the future, but also marked limits to the construction of the past they were trying to close off. The downside was the unwanted debates with various "storm fronts" which drove the matter still further forwards (generating in part the conditions for the current situation). In addition, at each moment, "political militancy", the relation to (and between) the organizations of the human rights movement, the "evidence", or the judicial system in other domains, took different routes.

15 Three years before, Menem had declared that "the *Punto Final* for the murderers is prison" (*La Razón*, 09/12/1986).

The first attempt at closure referred to above (the laws of 1979 and the "incomplete narrative"), generated a debate amongst the human rights organizations which affected the unity of action of the movement, and led to the slogan "*aparición con vida*" (appearance with life), as forceful as it was resisted (and still is) by the same protagonists. But at the same time, this attempt aimed to put precise dates to the criminal action to be judged in the future: 1974–1979.

The second attempt (by Raúl Alfonsín), by means of the *Trial of the commanders*, tried to close the subject in order to advance a gradual amnesty mediated by levels of responsibility.[16] The government completed this scheme with Law 23.062 (in agreement with Peronism), known as the *Ley de Reparación Histórica* (Law of Historical Reparation).[17] This regulation established the impossibility of judging any crime committed by the state before the coup of 24 March 1976. Thus, with these two tools (the trial and the laws of historical reparation), it managed to cancel history backwards and its limit a reading forward, covering the period of state terrorism. This double movement is politically interesting (in its effects) because it supposes that the crimes of the state began on the day of the military coup, thus hiding the images of terror before this date with their roots in the attempt at Trelew in 1972 and put into practice from 1973 with the massacre at Ezeiza and the "Triple A" organization organized by Perón's secretary. It is nonetheless also true that with this scheme Alfonsín avoided a new confrontation with (and within) the ranks of Peronism, which would

16 This manoeuvre has two judicial setbacks: the confirmation of the sentence given by the *Corte Suprema de Justicia* in 1986 (amplifying the "levels of responsibility" to the chagrin of Alfonsín who wanted them limited to only a few military leaders) and paradoxically the law of *Punto Final*, which instead of putting a stop to the trials, acted as an wake up call for the criminal processing of more that double the number of accused before that date.

17 Thanks to this law (passed in May 1984), Isabel Perón avoided being extradited from Spain in April 2008, when an attempt was made to investigate the crimes of the state in the period 1973–1976, perpetrated by the "Triple A" organisation (which in turn counted on provincial organisations, such as the "liberator commandoes of America of Córdoba), whose aim was to eliminate political opponents of the government.

bleed again with accusations intersected by a history which still allows us to listen to its most profound cries.

The third attempt (the amnesties) generated a series of unwanted debates which called into question, socially and through the mass media, the theme of the terrorism of the state and its consequences in collective memory. On the one hand, the "testimonies" have seen light in works of investigation, historical reconstruction, or academic essays on the subject, which dispute their validity, but also in the television studios, where impunity and morbidity meet in a dramatic way for the victims. On the other hand, these testimonies have given rise to a new discussion with some organizations of the human rights movement through the dispute of being the "authorised voice of those who are not". If the 1980s were marked by a victimization of the disappeared (cancelling the political militancy of each individual, and presenting them as victims of "an absolute and perverse evil"), the 1990s will be a fertile ground for a change which comes from the "heroism" of the disappeared but also from the "doubt" of the word of the survivors (who came to be treated as traitors for having managed to save their own lives).[18]

But it also opens up the opposite phase of "reparations", the legal road of the financial compensation of the victims of state terrorism. It recognizes legally the figure of the detainee-disappeared,[19] the financial compensations increase, and the numbers are surprising for the beneficiaries number in the thousands in each case, revealing a reality which had been hidden in the previous decade. At the same time, the closure of the local judicial road opens the road of trials abroad, and towards the middle of this decade (with testimonies which multiplied, both of victims and of perpetrators, with the cancelling of the possibility of being sent to prison), trials take place *in absentia* in Spain, France, Italy, Sweden, Switzerland and Germany. In the face of these facts, demands for international penal collaboration arise, and Menem resolves the question with a decree[20] which establishes "the refusal

18 The object of a lucid analysis in the work of A. Longoni, *Traiciones*, Norma. Bs. As. 2007.

19 By means of Law 24.321 (10/06/1994), opening the possibility of assuming the death of a relative; and economic indemnity by means of Law 24.411 (07/12/1994).

20 Decree N° 111 of 09/02/1998.

of international judicial cooperation" for cases of crimes against humanity. Half way through the year of the decree (1998), echoing a demand which acquired new force, some deputies in the *Congreso de la Nación* (National Congress) tried to repeal the "Laws of Impunity". It was a failed session. The *Madres de Plaza de Mayo* were not permitted to enter the premises, symbolically awaiting outside (in a rain which accompanied them like a persistent lament the entire day) the negative decision about the proposed repeal. That is to say that the government itself, through its obligatory closure of the issue, opened a flood of alternative routes which found cracks.

The following administration endured the pressure of a year which contained glimmerings of a possible opening. In 2001 the judges Cavallo and Bonadío declare the nullity of the laws of impunity and the *Cámara Nacional de Apelaciones* (National Appeal Court) ratifies their decisions. Fernando De la Rúa, however, will close his ephemeral administration by impeding the demands for the extradition of those accused of genocide through another decree,[21] one which establishes *rejection in limine* of any move in this direction.

The Moment of Legitimation

Having reached this point, the collapse of representation in 2001[22] required new perspectives on the part of the political class, but also a demand which from the symbolic point of view might change the course of a reading which could touch the heart of this leadership. This pragmatism constructed a new possible understanding of the recent pasts (which included the

21 Decree N° 1581 of 05/12/2001, scarcely a few days before his escape in helicopter from the roof of the "Casa Rosada".

22 A new political economic crisis which resulted in the renunciation of President De la Rúa on 20/12/2001, and the election of the senator Eduardo Duhalde as head of the executive power until 2003.

state violence of the 1970s and of the 1990s); and the political expressions of that present articulated in turn battles already fought, crossing a field where pragmatism and political necessity united, marching together. In the reconstruction of these pasts, the symbolic played a dominant role. And with the return to power of Peronism (that deeply-rooted narrative of political practice which marks the times of our current history), a new attempt was possible. If the reading of the neglected sectors united two forms of impunity (of the dictatorship of Menemism) and in 2001 they questioned everything from an impossible "*que se vayan todos*" ("they must all go"), the pragmatic leadership understood that it could combine these two themes by presenting a new model of understanding. The dictatorship killed thousands of citizens (now recognized as political activists) in order to implement an economic plan which was concretized during the 1990s. So to punish the impunity of the 1970s implied at the same time punishing the impunity of the 1990s, while preserving at the same time the figure of the state ("absent" in the act) in a precise way, so as to monopolize new (and urgent) decisions with authority. This new notion approached sectors of the centre-left and progressives (in the broadest sense) so as to be able to advance a legitimate need to consolidate all the demands under another politics of memory, truth and justice.

Thus things stood, and with a practical need, in May 2003 when Néstor Kirchner assumed power with an extremely meagre 22 per cent of the votes and a divided Peronism which had to reconstruct legitimacy on the basis of this percentage (and the limited party apparatus which went with it). The cascade of gestures is overwhelming. Within a week he decapitates the leadership of the army and receives the *Madres de Plaza de Mayo* (08/06/2003). Within a month he repeals De la Rúa's decree and re-establishes international cooperation in criminal matters.[23] That same year the *Congreso de la Nación* (National Congress) declares null and void the laws of impunity and on the International Day of Human Rights in December Kirchner convokes another meeting with the Madres in the Casa Rosada, while a crowd marches for 24 hours in front of the

23 Decree 420/03 of 25/07/2003.

government house, in a new edition of the *Marcha de la Resistencia por los Derechos Humanos* (Resistance March for Human Rights). The new anniversary of the military coup (24/03/2004) finds him giving a speech in the ESMA and turning the place into the *Museo de la Memoria*, while he takes down from the walls the portrait paintings of the generals of the dictatorship. In December 2007 the first sentence since the re-opening of the trials is handed down. In 2008 the country subscribes to the Convention on the Forced Disappearance of Persons (only two nations do so at this point: Argentina and France) and in only three years there are almost 200 convictions.

2001–2008: The Collapse of Legitimacy and Corporate Delegitimation

The brief (but intense) period mentioned in the previous section invites a review of the comings and goings which in so few years resulted in new demands. The demands for reparations which a society in crisis expresses do not always coincide with the results obtained in their partial resolution. But they can serve as an apprenticeship for pragmatic political leaders who are capable of confronting and overcoming those crises, according to a necessary and desirable equilibrium. In many cases these demands are expressions of the political paradox which they contain. Constituent demands of the political system such as "*que se vayan todos*" may conflict with demands such as "todos somos el campo" ("we are all the country").[24]

24 The first was expressed in 2001, in the face of the political economic disintegration of the fiscal adjustment applied by the government Fernando De la Rúa (an alliance of radicals, socialists and dissident Peronists) which had replaced that of Carlos Menem in 1999. The second slogan was unfurled in 2008 by rural producers in the face of the increase of the withholding tax on the sale of their crops during a year in which the price of soya broke records internationally.

The first assumes a craving for renewal which could wield the desires shared by vast sectors (although their interests be different), embarking on a road with no clear destination, which achieves a partial renovation of the spaces of discussion and consensus (which could be an enduring state assembly, which carried alternative democratic forms within the same system of representation). The second emerges from the vice of corporate radicalization which seeks to unite in one symbolic space ("el campo": "the country", that unbridled metaphor of the Argentinean "wide boy" or "spiv") sectors of society who could never even set foot freely in the vast national territory which has been plagued with "enclosed" lands for the last two centuries.

The paradox is interesting because an objective of getting rid of some resulted in attempts to take on a different task collectively when it came to deciding the political destinies. This other, which simulated adding to the lands of few owners the dreams of the many (to such a precious good) led to the polarization of political and corporative stinginesses which were finally swept away by their own grief over titles to property. In the heat of these two slogans, separated by less than a decade, the changes which the country had added together as a hope for renewal were gradual but concrete. The desperation generated by the crisis of political legitimacy of the first slogan (2001) was reordered by the candid legitimacy which the neglected sectors of political activism pushed for on the basis of causes considered to be already closed (sectors which in turn achieved a space which they do not intend to give up without a fight). And many of those who "went away" encountered in the second slogan (2008) the possibility of a return, although this time the space was not the space of the executive leadership, but rather the virtual regrouping which on the basis of certain hegemonic mass media acts as the "media party". It is an enclosure of new ways of conducting politics (from a newspaper or a television set), without spreading out into the street or in elections, but as generators of new forms of dismissal which take up ideas which are outmoded but by no means less potent for that. In the seven years which separate one slogan from the other, the status of legitimacy, the forms of representation and the sensation of a justice which put brakes on the illegal acts of the state, have changed dramatically. It is a change "in two stages" which accounts for successive landmarks as unforgettable watchwords of our times.

Epilogue

A number of contrasts in this recent history of Argentina which we have narrated deserve a remark. Alfonsín received the *Madres de Plaza de Mayo*, along with Adolfo P. Ezquivel and the APDH in November 1983, being then president elect but not yet in office. Once in charge of the executive power he receives (6/08/85) a succession of military personnel accused of the crimes of the dictatorship and listens to their complaints. He does not appear at the final meeting with the *Madres* (24/06/86), but goes instead to a gala in Teatro Colón (and the *Madres* occupy the government house for 20 hours waiting for him). After this, he never receives them again, operating passively in his internal division of 1986. Menem, who undoes the weak but essential notion of justice which Alfonsín had established, not only does not receive them but attacks them ruthlessly in every forum in which he can. De la Rúa does the same. And Kirchner, who receives them early, vindicates them, and calls them regularly, transforming them into a symbolic and material part of his administration.

In this context, the notion of the "political activism" of the victims of state terrorism suffers similar limitations. If during the 1980s, faced with the danger of being imprisoned (in accordance with Alfonsín's decrees for judging military personnel and "terrorists" equally), there is a liquidation of political activism, in the 1990s this danger disappears and from the victimization of the disappeared he or she passes to a heroism (brought about by the organisms of the human rights movement) which seems to find an equilibrium in the following decade. In the speech at ESMA in 2004 (and also before the United Nations Organisation), the recognition of the struggle of the families of the disappeared results in President Kirchner's request of to take up again as an example the social activism of the disappeared. In fact, in the last sentences, the political activism of the victims has been considered as aggravating the crime, something unthinkable in the *Trial of the Commanders*.

This new situation, now of recognition, traces a narrative which takes up its protagonists and returns them to their political place. But it is recognition not of the "revolutionary" component of the activists of the 1970s, but of their political and social activism in a "national popular project" which does not specify very precisely the nature of this project. And it also informs an interesting debate, an irresolvable tension, between the political orientation of the majority of the disappeared (members of different strands of Peronism) and that "account of politics" which Peronism in power itself made at every historical stage. It is a movement which presented violence from below as a form of resistance to proscription and which once in government rid itself of its own activists (during the 1970s); and which on its return to government thirteen years after these events pardoned "right and left" openly.[25] And again at the helm of the nation it reopens history from a new direction profoundly respectful of the law, but without being able to pass the limits of this contradictory history and in conflict with its origins.[26] Thus, perhaps, the distance between the good that it does now and how it is presented, impose for moments an abysm where unhidden but rather "veiled" realities play with tensions without settling debts. But, in addition, perhaps it is because of that delicate care for wounds which have still not been healed, that we can maintain that the situation is unprecedented not only in our recent history, but in the century and a half which separates us from the formation of a state which has decided its class conflicts with an unprecedented violence and never since revised the notion of institutional justice in the direction of the victims.

25 And he establishes a wounding identification: "Only a little time ago, we knew that it was very difficult to go out into the street [...] we had to fight hard, yourselves, your families, and those who we understand, because of a stupid and absurd ideology which bled humanity to death" (Menem, July 1992, during a ceremony in the Liberator Building).

26 Alfonsín's Law of "historical reparation" still remains in force and the crimes of state of the period 1973–1976 are not reviewed.

PART II

Memory and Truth

CHIARA FORNERIS

The Narrative as a Formative Influence on the Norm: The Experimental Aspect of the Critical Interpretation of the Argentinean Past

The processes of democratization which follow dictatorial, authoritarian or totalitarian regimes are never simple. Once democratic mechanisms are re-established it is necessary to address the complex problem of how to situate and develop them in the socio-political fabric of the country. The obstacles to the assertion of a genuine rule of law are numerous and insidious. Among these it is possible to identify a convergence point in the plurality of narratives, which are anchored to a single past.

From the twentieth century onwards, during the experiences of transition to democracy, the presence of memory and the weight of the past have been augmented by a number of factors. These include, first, the centralization of the issue of justice and the confirmation of individual and collective responsibilities in relation to major rights violations committed under dictatorial, authoritarian or totalitarian regimes. Second, the need to rebuild and reorganize a collective national identity based on democratic values and the principles of cohesion and social harmony. Finally, the need to enter fully into an international order based on the principles of freedom and justice, in which the recognition of historical truth is accompanied by the freedom of expression and of the debate necessary so as to try to achieve it.

In the stages and modalities through which the politics of memory has developed in the course of the last twenty years, common characters and different nationalities, histories and cultures can be traced, in which they have played a crucial role not only because of the historical context, but also because of the role of judicial battles and of the cultural confrontation relating to collective identity.

The question of transitional justice is a phenomenon around which some of the more complex issues relating both to the transition to democracy and to national identity have often been found, not only in the recent past but even up to several decades ago. These issues will be placed in the centre of the theoretical and methodological reflection on memory, which has frequently developed in a way which cuts across different disciplines.

In the reconstruction of the rule of law the process of assimilation of grief assumes different forms. On the one hand, one part of civil society (the human rights movements, victims, survivors and relatives), demands that the still fragile and incomplete newborn institutions unequivocally distance themselves from the previous regime. On the other, the institutional actors, tendentially closer to closing the painful chapter of the past in the name of a totalizing future, concentrate efforts on the consolidation and strengthening of institutions and propose policies of forgetting and of "reconciliation". Finally, there are those who applaud and exalt the splendour of the regime. From this brief overview the different social, institutional and political factors can be deduced which may influence the public horizon in relation to the debate about memory and justice. Whether you look at the issue of memory from a deductive point of view, or whether you look at it from an inductive perspective, it is clear that the analytical course can not be a consistent and unambiguous linear path, but rather must be addressed by multiple approaches.

Memory is a multifaceted concept which brings together different levels of investigation, ranging from the intimate and sentimental proper to personal memories, to the dialectical, even contraposed, about the meaning which the different actors attribute to the past. Collective memory is different. Whether it is the repetition of memories or mere speculative abstraction about the past, it is the result of a complex and difficult work of recovery through which we carry out the process of the constructive reintegration of evil, or of the reprocessing of the past. To be precise, it is to use a key which can locate the source of intellectual need and not to attribute society's change of direction to a certain dimension of historicity.

In this introductory phase a premise becomes necessary which must be made explicit as a tool which can guide and direct the reflections which will continue to address the binomial of *memory* and *right*, which, based on the common denominator of the narratives, develop between themselves a two-way relationship.

The underlying idea which is presented as the subject of our reflections here is that the narrative is the literary genre which permits the objectification of value. While the conviction of understanding law as a literary genre may seem suggestive, it is actually very precise. If the law is stripped of its – wrongly attributed – cloak of self-referentiality, and due regard is given to the complexity of the juridical phenomenon, it seems quite evident that the latter manifests itself as the effective action of human relations.

Although the narrative of history and of the tribunals, law and memory of the past are manifestly different, the convergence between them and their tendency to overlap have become ever more frequent. For there to be the narrative, and consequently to have not only history but also law, there must be the will not to forget. The narrative, therefore, can not withhold, any more than the documents can, the memories which, nevertheless, are emotive and ethically partisan, and therefore influence notably the formation of the historical narrative.

The collective memory is built on the basis of the most varied stories. It endorses, in a way which is not always recognizable, the impressions of the personal accounts and the lessons of history, the insinuations of journalism and the findings of the courtroom, in addition to the evidence of archival documents. But the memory as an active faculty of the present time responds especially to the requirements of the era and to the psychological and cultural climate which characterizes society. It is characteristic that the law is inspired by the narrative as the objectification of the rule, whether in its training or in its evolution. In fact, the work of the interpretation of the rules undertaken by the courts is nothing else than the reduction *ad unum* of a plurality of legal meanings, which are precisely based on the stories, in the attempt to reconcile the evolution of society (understood as a text in slow and constant movement), with the polyhedral articulations of culture which begin to be delineated.

The law, therefore, should not be attributed an identity separate from the context; that would be to prefer the form to its meaning in an unwarrantable separation of the "before" and the "after" understood as absolute moments. On the contrary, law is integral to the project of life, whether individual or collective, and realizes itself precisely through experience as a collective mediation in which the today stands as an inclusive synthesis of the whole story. In light of this, if the law contributes to the construction of collective memory, which includes (but is not limited to) legal "truth", memory for its part, sustains the science of law so as to develop a decisive role in consolidating support for fundamental principles and commitment to a shared life project to be carried out through the law. Over time, this adherence and commitment are learned, reinterpreted and accepted by the society. Memory, here, should be understood not as an exact restitution of the facts but rather as the reconstruction of the past in terms of the present.

The analysis of the role of criminal law in the construction of collective memory demands confrontation with a series of remarkable complexities which a society, such as that of Argentina, creates when it initiates a journey of democratic development and of the reconstruction of justice in the face of crimes against humanity. These include crimes no less brutal than disappearance, the method used scientifically with the idea not only of eliminating the opposition, but also its vision. Significant in this respect are the words with which Simon Wiesenthal ends *Los asesinos están entre nosotros*: "Maybe there will be suspicions, discussions, and investigations undertaken by historians but there will be no certainty, because we will destroy the evidence along with you. And even when some evidence remains, and some of you survive, people will say that the facts you relate are too monstrous to be believed: they will say that they are the exaggerations of Allied propaganda and will believe us, who will deny everything, and not you. It will be us who write and impose the history of the concentration camps".[1]

The demand for the public management of memory, as a requirement for recognizing solemnly and publicly the wrongs done, emerged after the

1 S. Wiesenthal, cited by P. Levi in the opening of his essay about memory, *I sommersi e i salvati*, Turin, Einaudi, 1986, p. 3.

Second World War and was augmented progressively. Its emergence coincided with the simultaneous appearance of the need for a redefinition of collective identities and renewed attention to the issues of international justice, the new and different forms with which to confront the problem of the punishment of crimes committed in the most tragic phases of the history of different countries and of reconciliation within the society in which these events took place.

Memory is recognized as a fundamental right of peoples. It is the sum and fundamental element, not only of the social group, but also of the rule of law, as it contains within itself three time periods: past, present and future: "[...] the present is the moment in which we remember and relive a past from which we come (but which we do not we want), the intentionality of the future and, generally, their association with what is happening at this point in time".[2]

There are three key concepts to which Argentinean society – and not only Argentinean society – refers. These are in fact Truth, Justice and Memory, and they highlight a principle which has universal value. It is not only a question of not forgetting a past of oppression and repression, but also of not forgetting the ideals of justice and freedom, emancipation and equality: for these very principles people resisted and fought against dictatorships and totalitarian regimes. It is not accidental that these principles are among the key elements of the rule of law. The socio-historical and cultural identity of a society is based precisely on the "reciprocity" between the struggle for memory and the struggle for the recognition of and respect for fundamental rights. Fundamental rights evolve precisely from the dialectic between memory and forgetting. If to this consideration is added the fact that memory cannot be a guarantee of *nunca más* ("never again"), but only a hope, it is clear that a positive exercise of democratic action is demanded of a state and imposed through the assumption of a politics of memory.

2 E. Jelin, *La construcción de la memoria a veces da para debatir, otras no*, a work cited in P.A. Brodsky, *Discurso y decurso. Reflexiones sobre la memoria histórica y la identidad en el judaismo post-Shoá*, in *Nuestra Memoria*, Year XI, Number 25, Buenos Aires, 2005, p. 103. The italics are mine.

The relation between the private and the public administration of memory imposes, therefore, the need to address and resolve impediments to the different forms of the institutionalization of the binomial of law. To the threat of forgetting and the development of a politics of anti-memory, a state can respond only by granting legal protection to memory.

The aim now is try to look at the most significant stages in which the law (particularly the criminal law) has, so to speak, discovered in the narrative (trials, inspections, debates, laws) a complex and sometimes contradictory relationship with both the history and the memory (or rather, memories) to which to those facts belong.

The action of the legal protection of memory on the part of a State can be articulated in three ways. First, through the legislative *sanctioning* of a rule of memory, by emphasizing the need to remember and to contribute to the building of a collective memory through a so-called "politics of memory". Second, by *prescribing*, from a normative point of view, a collective memory, i.e. the need to remember in a certain way. Third, *by guaranteeing* the exercise of penal action by overcoming impunity through the annulment of laws of amnesty, understood as an instrument of forgetting, and by means of an affirmation of justice which becomes memory.

The first level of institutional intervention is that of the construction of collective memory – the acquisition of the responsibility of the duty to remember through the development of the politics of memory.[3]

3 Examples of policies of memory include the support given to the creation of places of memory, such as. in Argentina, the proposed conversion of the School of Naval Mechanics (ESMA) into a museum of memory and an institution containing the National Archives from 2003; or even the use of the legislative instrument, with which the affirmations and celebrations of shared memory are sanctioned. The so-called laws of memory, based on the need of every society come to terms with its past, and of every rule of law to recognize itself in a nucleus of values, acknowledge that if they are to admit the historical reality, the people must first of all know it. Therefore, it must be taught in school and publicly commemorated, with, for example, the introduction of Day of the Memory: in Italy this was done by means of law 211/2000 (27 January), in France law 644/2000, or United Nations resolution 60/7, 2005. The Spanish law of historical memory (Law 52/2007) makes history in itself, in as far as this has had the ability to synthesize the two levels of state intervention,

We will not stop at this level because it represents the convergence of the plurality of stories linked by a common past. The so-called laws of memory are based on the need of every society to settle accounts with its past and every state based on the rule of law to identify itself in a nucleus of values. These laws recognize that in order to admit the historical reality, people must first know it and ratify the affirmation and celebration of shared memory.

In this investigation it is not the reconstruction of individual and collective identity following the serious human rights violations which deserves particular attention. This will be given to the process of the transformation of symbolic meanings with which the ambiguity of the institutional actors is realized.

Faced with the demand to define the value of the memory there is a very strong risk of reducing memory to a mere legend which chains contemporary societies to an obsessive form of learning from the past, but does not have the power to reveal. The same mechanism is at work in the emergence in many European (and not only European) legal systems of the use of the criminal law to prescribe an obligation to remember in a certain way in opposition to the despicable phenomenon of Holocaust denial.

The transformation of memory into a legal right worthy of protection – which has as its constituent element the public character of denial – generates the complex problem of the identification of interests which may be offended by the behaviour in question, of an uncertain and abstract nature, of the legal right which it aims to protect. This stretches from the disturbance of public order, public peace, national security, and terminates with the protection of the reputation or the right to honour, under the laws of one country or another.

---

i.e. the legislative and that part which relates to guaranteeing the implementation of the prosecution. For a broader view of the great intellectual debate about the political use of memory, see E. Traverso, *Il passato: Istruzioni per l'usage. Storia, memory politics*, Verona, Ombre court, 2006.

In recent years there has been a steadily growing tendency, both at the international and national levels, to repress denialist behaviours by means of the criminal law.[4] Thereby the limitation of a fundamental, but not abso-

4 In most contemporary countries, the use of history by public authorities is a reality which is in constant growth and diffusion. Not being able to restore an exhaustive "map" of denial, we will limit ourselves to indicating the legislation of some European countries. France, in 1990, recognized as an offence the public denial of the Holocaust and other Nazi crimes against humanity as defined by Article 6 of the Charter of the Nüremberg Tribunal (L. No. 90–602 which modifies the 1881 Act in relation to freedom of the press, introducing Article 24 a: Denial of crimes against humanity: "Article 24a. They shall be subject to the penalties provided by the sixth paragraph of Article 24 those who have challenged, by the means listed in Article 23, the existence of one or more crimes against humanity as defined by Article 6 of the Statute of the International Military Tribunal appended to the London Agreement of 8 August 1945 and which have been committed either by members of an organization declared criminal under Article 9 of that statute, or by a individual convicted of such crimes by a French or international court".). It only penalizes the denial of crimes against humanity committed during the Second World War, with the exclusion of denial against other genocides. Likewise, on 23 March 1995, Belgium adopted the law "On the repression of the denial, trivilialization, justification or approval of the genocide committed by the German Nazi regime during the Second World War". The Spanish penal code Article 607 bis C.P. 1995 suppresses the spread of ideas, acts of genocide denial or the attempt to vindicate regimes to or institutions which adopt practices causing such crimes, setting up perhaps a debt of apology. According to this Article: "Those who, with intent to destroy in whole or in part, a national, ethnical, racial or religious group, perpetrate any of the following acts shall be punished: 1. By imprisonment for fifteen to twenty years, if they have killed any of the members of such a group. If two or more aggravating circumstances come together in the act, the penalty which will be imposed is of a higher level. [...] 2. Dissemination by any means of ideas or doctrines which deny or justify the crimes under the preceding paragraph of this article, or intend the rehabilitation of regimes or institutions which generate such practices, shall be punished with imprisonment of one to two years". In contrast to other countries, the Swiss penal code (art. 261 bis as codified in the law of June 18, 1995) provides for the punishment by means of a fine or the arrest of "[...] any person who publicly, by words, writings, images, gestures, violence or, in any other way injurious to human dignity, disparages or discriminates against a person or group of persons because of race, ethnicity or religion or, for the same reasons unknown to us, grossly minimizes or seeks to justify genocide or other crimes

lute, right is accepted: that of the freedom of thought. The introduction of the norm in relation to the need to remember in a certain way is none other than the identification in the criminal codes of the crime of denial as an instrument of punishment for abuses of freedom of expression.[5] In the face of the historic importance of crimes such as serious violations of human rights, for the international the national community the reworking of grief implies both the claim of memory and the need for punishment, and, often, the commitment to the defence of the memory of the past against the phenomena of deniers and / or revisionism.[6] This past is thus

---

against humanity". Article 130 of the German Criminal Code, written in 1994, disciplines the crime of *Volkesverhetzung*, that is, of assaults on human dignity of part of the population, outlining a crime of abstract or perceived danger. It comes from the fact of omitting either any reference to the conduct, or the author's subjective identification with Nazi ideology, so that the legally protected right matches only the tutelage of the public peace. Belgium, on 23 March 1995, approved the "Act to suppress the denial, minimization, justification or condoning of genocide committed during the German Nazi regime during the Second World War". Turkey punishes anyone who affirms the Armenian genocide (Attack on Turkish national identity, Article 301 of the Penal Code). At the level of regional legislation it will be recalled that on 15 July 1996 the Joint Action of the Council of Europe was adopted, on the basis of Article K3 TEU (July 24, 1996, Vol L 185, GUUE, p. 5), according to which Member States are called on to suppress the public denial of crimes of which Article 6 of the Charter of the Nuremberg Tribunal exactly when such denial includes a contemptuous or degrading treatment in relation to a group of individual persons based on skin colour, race, religion, national origin or ethnicity.

5 Highlighted in this respect is the opinion of Article 19 of the International Covenant on Civil and Political Rights, adopted on 16 December 1996, that after having passed the right to freedom of speech and press, the last paragraph states that "The exercise of the freedom provided by paragraph 2 [...] implies duties and responsibilities. This may therefore be subject to certain restrictions which must be expressly established by law and are necessary: a) respect for the rights or reputations of others; b) the defence of national security, public order, health or public morals".

6 It is necessary to establish precisely the lexical scope of the term "revisionism" which in the text is used in its negative sense acquired from the beginning of the twentieth century, i.e. indicating the intellectual behaviour of those who obstruct the evidence of (historical) fact, who do not demand testing by a historiographic review, and push things to the point of outright denial. According to the broadest sense, the

crystallized in an absolute moment.[7] It is at this moment that, through the attempt to bequeath memory to a stable and "objective" picture within a legal framework, a dramatic shift of relations between form and meaning is completed. Legislative interventions of "one and only one" particular memory are intended as a tool, transforming the collective memory into a legal right to be protected, bending the law, in particular the criminal

---

term "revisionism" indicates the tendency of the historian to change its own judgment, his historiographical discourse, on a given fact, when a series of facts, so far unknown and overestimated, are rearranged in the judgment so as to lend a different perspective on the past. It follows that all historians are revisionists, still prevalent in their own way of acting to continually review previously acquired knowledge, and that history is an open reflection on the mechanisms which contribute to the resolution a conduct in relation to others, and with reference to the modes and times in which they were ordered. For an overview of denial, see, among others: V. Pisanty, *L'questione delle camere irritating gas. Logica's negazionismo*, Milan, Bompiani, 1998, P. Vidal Naquet, *Gli Assassini della memoria*, Rome, Editori Riuniti, 1993; C. Saletta, *Per il contro revisionism storico Vidal-Naquet*, Genoa, Graphos, 1993, P.P. Poggio, *Perstorica un'analisi critical revisionism, revisionism in Lezioni sul storico*, AA.VV., Milan, Fondazione Luigi Micheletti, 1999, pp. 21–51, P.P. Poggio, *Nazism and revisionism storico*, Rome, Manifestolibri, 1997; C. Mattogno, *Il mito dello sterminio ebraico. Introduzione storico – bibliografica alla storiografia revisionista*, Monfalcone, 1985.

7 On the issue of transformation of the "defence of the memory in a claim of memory against history," see, among others, P. Ricoeur, *Memory, storia, l'Oblio*, Milan, Raffaello Cortina, 2003; T. Todorov, *Gli abusive della memoria*, Naples, Ipermedium Libri, 1996. For a more general overview of the subject of the relationship between history and memory its and possible political uses, see among others: P. Ricoeur, *La memoria, la storia, l'oblio*, Italian edition under the direction of D. Iannotta, R. Cortina, Milan, 2003 and *Ricordare, dimenticare, perdonare*, Bologna, Il Mulino, 2004; M. Halbwachs, *La memoria collettiva*, Italian edition under the direction of Paolo Jedlowski, Milan, UNICOPLI, 1987, and *I quadri sociali della memoria*, Naples, Ipermedium, 1997; P. Connerton, *Come le società ricordano*, Rome, Armando Editore, 1999; A. Pugiotto, *Quando (e perché) la memoria si fa legge*, in *Quaderni costituzionali*, 1, 2009, pp. 7–36; D. Bidussa, *Dopo l'ultimo testimone*, Turin, Einaudi, 2009; G. Braga, *La libertà di manifestazione del pensiero tra revisionismo, negazionismo e verità storica*, in M. Ainis (directed by), *Informazione, potere, libertà*, Turin, Giappichelli, 2005; M. Manetti, *Libertà di pensiero e negazionismo*, in M. Ainis (ed.), *Informazione, potere, libertà*, op. cit.; G.E. Rusconi (ed.), *Il passato che non passa*, Turin, Einaudi 1988.

law, and making it an instrument of the recomposition of the events of the past through the renewal of the same legal fact which distinguishes the crime of denial.

Furthermore, linking criminal law and the process of reconstruction of collective memory incurs the danger of transforming the judge into an arbiter of history. This creates two problems. On the one hand, to submit memory to judicial logic with its continuous appeal to ethics, perpetuates the ruling characteristic of dictatorial, authoritarian and totalitarian regimes, under which the distinction between law and morality is imperceptible. It has, on the other hand, robbed the law of its sovereignty and its value, with a relative disregard for the criminal proceedings which have as their precise purpose that of accepting and determining individual responsibility in relation to the events delimited and not that of reconstructing and telling the story. The crime of denial, by superimposing the two methods, legal and historical, can generate dangerous distortions. In fact, among the criteria for establishing whether the statements can be punished, is that of the correct method used by the historian who consents to curb abuses of the freedom of expression. The legislative[8] and judicial[9] guidelines for the

8 See note 4. For a comparison between Europe and the United States, see also F. Schauer, "Freedom of Expression Adjudication in Europe and the US", in G. Nolte (ed.), *European and US-Constitutionalism*, Cambridge, Cambridge University Press, 2005, 49ff. In relation to this subject, see also E. Fronza, "Profili penalistici of negazionismo" in *Riv. Dir It. Proc. Pen.*, 1999, p. 1034 et seq.

9 For an overview of case law regarding denial, see the judgment of the Supreme Court of Canada: 27 August 1992, *R v. Zundel* [1992] 2 SCR 731. For continuation, see: Tribunal canadien des droits de la personne, 18 January 2002, *Citron v. Zündel*. At the European level, see among others: *Glimmerveen and J. Hagenbeek v. the Netherlands*, nos 8348/78 and 8406/78, Commission decision of 11 October 1979, Decisions and Reports (DR) 18, p. 187; *Kühnen v. Germany*, no. 12194/86, Commission decision of 12 May 1988, DR 56, p. 205; *BH, MW, HP and GK v. Austria*, no. 12774/87, Commission decision of 12 October 1989, DR 62, p. 216; *Ochsenberger v. Austria*, no. 21318/93, Commission decision of 2 September 1994; *Walendy v. Germany*, no. 21128/92, Commission decision of 11 January 1995, DR 80, p. 94; *Remer v. Germany*, no. 25096/94, Commission decision of 6 September 1995, DR 82, p. 117; *Honsik v. Austria*, no. 25062/94, Commission decision of 18 October 1995, DR 83-A, p. 77; *Nationaldemokratische Partei Deutschlands, Munich-Upper*

punishment of denialist behaviours tends to identify the role of the judge not only as one called upon to protect historical truth, but also as that which the method of the historian defines, emphasizing the assessment of the context, aims and the method, in addition to content.

However, I think that although it is insufficient by itself, penal action constitutes, in any case, in conjunction with other mechanisms of recall, a key instrument. The act of judgment is a symbolic act of reparation. Contrary to what may occur with the inclusion of the crime of denial, this is not to identify justice with memory, but means rather doing justice to memory. It is necessary to be clear that we are talking about crimes against humanity, which the legal system recognizes and in relation to which imposes, moreover, a duty to remember, from the moment it converts them into imprescriptible crimes.

From everything which has emerged, it can be said that the approach to the great debate on the relationship between memory and law, so to speak, of the already consolidated (e.g. European) democracies, is characterized by the propensity to give memory a legally protected "official" value. This approach, fortunately, does not exhaust the different modes of presence of memory and justice within the historical judgments. The experience of South America, and particularly of Argentina, delineates a semantic binomial between law and memory in relation to the objectives of creating a new collective identity and a new platform of shared values within society, developing, in a completely reconsidered way, new theoretical approaches on the basis of the idea of law as literature.

Bavaria v Bezirksverband. Germany, no. 25992/94, Commission decision of 29 November 1995, DR 84, p. 149; *Rebhandel v. Austria*, no. 24398/94, Commission decision of 16 January 1996, *Nachtmann v. Austria*, no. 36773/97, Commission decision of 9 September 1998; *Witzsch v. Germany (dec.)*, no. 41448/98, 20 April 1999; *Schimanek v. Austria* (dec.), no. 32307/96, 1 February 2000, *Garaudy v. France* (dec.), no. 65831/01, ECHR 2003: *IX v Norwood. United Kingdom* (dec.), 23131/03, 16 November 2004. For some examples of American jurisprudence see: *NY v. Times.* Sullivan 376 US 264 (1964), *Brandenburg v. Ohio* 395 US 444 (1969) and *National Socialist Party of America v. Village of Skokie*, 432 US 43 (1978).

Subsequent to an administration of political power which culminated in the ignoring of the past in a mere matter of amnesty and pardon, Argentina, today, has chosen to decipher the meaning of the social disruption within the courts through the condemnation of the soldiers indicted for serious violations of human rights. Argentina's experience in the collection and preservation of individual and collective memories takes place at a veritable crossroads of disciplinary approaches from which new legal perspectives may be formulated.

For a better understanding it is necessary to follow – synthetically – the stages of evolution of the binomial of law and memory in Argentina. This can be summarized in the demand for the satisfaction of the right to truth with regard to the crimes of state terrorism. Until 1983, there was complete disregard for this, with the relative simplification of some excesses justified by the context of fighting a just war, and therefore with the democratic election of President Raul Alfonsín, a special commission of inquiry (*Comisión Nacional sobre la Desaparición de Personas* – CONADEP) was established. The Commission was conceived of as a study group with the aim of searching for the truth and with a persecutory possibility limited to those responsible for state crimes who belonged to the upper reaches of the hierarchy.

The outcome of the activity of the CONADEP is a rich report – *Nunca Más* – of 50,000 pages in which "the reconstruction of the *modus operandi* of state terrorism and a survey of its infrastructure were carried out. 8,960 cases of missing persons were accounted for and about 380 clandestine detention centres were identified".[10] *Nunca Más* is followed by a series of exemplary trials of members of the junta,[11] including, as will

10 As recognized by President Alfonsín, in Alfonsín, Raúl, *Carlos Nino, jurista y filósofo de los derechos humanos y la república democrática*, Prologue by C. Nino, *Juicio al mal absoluto*, Buenos Aires, Ariel, 2006, p. 17.

11 The choice in favor of "selective justice" in relation solely to the military hierarchy and not against all those who had plotted serious crimes against humanity, was issued for reasons of political stability, or rather so as not put "[…] in serious jeopardy all the processes of transition themselves […] our objective could not be the judgment and condemnation of everyone who, in one way or another, had violated human

be recalled, the trial of General Jorge Rafael Videla and Admiral Emilio Massera. In 1986 the trial for the reconstruction of the truth is interrupted by the adoption of the Law of *Punto Final* (Full Stop) which places a time limit of sixty days on filing complaints about violations of human rights, after which no appeal can be taken into consideration. This provision is followed by another law – that of *Obediencia Debida* (Due Obedience) – which grants an amnesty to those responsible for carrying out crimes against humanity, except for the acts held to be unpardonable (crimes against minors and against property).

The path to impunity is perfected by the Menem government, with the pardon which covers every trial still in progress and erases previous convictions passed on all members of the military junta regardless of distinctions between levels of command. The only crime excluded from the amnesty measure continues to be that of the misappropriation of children. It will be the judiciary, in 2001, which reverses the trend of impunity,[12] and this will be cemented in 2003 with congressional repeal of the laws of *Punto Final* and *Obediencia Debida*, initiated by President Néstor Kirchner and confirmed by the Corte Suprema in 2005.[13] Since then old trials have been reopened and new ones have been initiated.

In that sense Argentinean judges have devoted themselves to taking up the social narrative instead of persisting as the guarantors of what had been solemnly ordained by state power, responding to the responsibility for assuming some constitutional visions and not others. The courts, even in the face of political power, became guarantors of democratic renewal, waiving formal logic in favour of the legal meaning contained in national

---

rights, because this is impracticable without achieving an exemplary punishment which would prevent the recurrence of similar acts in the future". See: Alfonsín, *Carlos Nino, jurista y filósofo de los derechos humanos y la república democrática*, op. cit., p. 21.

12 To this end, observe Sentence n° 4 of 6/3/2001 of Juzgado Nacional in the Criminal y Correcional Federal, with which the laws of *Punto final* and *Obediencia debida* are deprived of certain legal effects.

13 Cf. CSJN, expedient S. 1767. XXXVIII *Simón, Julio Héctor y otros s/ privación ilegítima de la libertad, etc.* causa n° 17.768, resolution of 14/6/2005.

and international law. To the question of how to ensure continuity between this "reconstructed" present and current history, Argentinean legal action responded by concretizing the descriptive image of the law as a bridge linking the present to the future, where the story forms "the material which integrates what the legal world is, what it should be and what it is capable of being".[14]

The complex relationship between justice, history and memory is born of the relationship these have with the notion of truth. Or it might be more correct to say, with the notion of cognition in which *non veritas auctoritas facit legem*. In accordance with this principle, for their part, the *Comisión* and the *Corte Interamericana de Derechos Humanos* recognized a duty on the part of the states to make available to individuals and societies all necessary facilities and information in their power, in order to reveal "the full, complete and public truth about the events, their specific circumstances and who participated in them"[15] and thus to develop their own mechanisms of disapproval and prevention so as not to reiterate the violations in the future.

The *Comisión Interamericana de Derechos Humanos* (CIDH) recognizes in the right to truth not only a "private" dimension of the families of the victims "allowing a form of reparation" but also a "collective dimension, which enables society to have access to information essential to the development of democratic systems",[16] although it does not clarify whether the judicial investigations are necessarily punitive or merely epistemological. It will be the *Corte Interamericana de Derechos Humanos* which brings back within the criminal law the right to know what happened. In other words, the Court charges the state with the duty of guaranteeing the victims an investigation with the aim of "identifying those responsible, [...] imposing appropriate sanctions [...] [and] ensuring that the victim receives adequate compensation".[17] The fact that a state must make available all the means

14 Cf. R. Cover, *Nomos e narrazione. Una concezione ebraica del diritto*, al cuidado de M. Goldoni, Turin, Giappichelli, 2008, p. 24.

15 Cf. Report N° 25/98, par. 95 of CIDH.

16 Cf. Report n° 25/98 of the CIDH, para. 88.

17 See the judgment *Velásquez Rodríguez* of 29/7/1988, para. 174.

necessary for the realization of a group's right to the truth is an obligation of means and not of ends. It does not necessarily imply the involvement of the judiciary and the aim of punishment, just as, conversely, this function is not ignored *a priori.*

I think the objection that the use of penal logic in the field of memory is risky[18] can be overcome by always making its limits explicit in advance,[19] but at the same time highlighting that these are linked to an idea of "formal" law, a forgotten aspect of "socialization" as a public space around which the community expresses itself, such as *jurisgenesis*.[20]

The dialectic as process is extinguishing, if not eliminating, the sublimation of the past (understood as a salvational remedy for the hostile antagonisms), with its boundaries and fragmented vision imposed by the limits of the adversarial structure. It makes its contribution through the renewal of dialogue. By perpetuating the story, moreover, it obliges the parties to the criminal process (both victim and accused), and indeed the whole of society, to confront the historicity and absoluteness, and the indelible and incommensurable nature of this event.

18 See in particular C. Ginzburg, *Il giudice e lo storico. Considerazioni in margine al processo Sofri*, Turin, Einaudi, 1991.

19 The most frequent problems which become evident through debate on the theme are subject to the fact that the judge acts out of respect for and within the formal limits of the verification of the truth imposed as a guarantee in favour of the accused, developing a verification action among the various accusatory hypotheses. The fact on which the judge must rule is a fragment and he investigates only the facts restricted to the accusation. He can carry out the investigations for a limited period, in line with the reasonable duration of the trial whose epilogue is a ruling, which tends to a definitive finding and is characterized by its trenchant nature of judgment (one of a single version of events, or *res judicata*). He narrates in order to resolve clearly between guilt and innocence and fulfils his function even if he does not reach an absolute conviction (acquittal *in dubio pro reo*). He cannot relive the fact and modify the analysis of already established interpretations or add new ones, the case of appeal being an exception.

20 The concept of *jurisgenesis* was coined by Robert Cover so as to describe the process of creation of juridical meaning in R. Cover, *Nomos e narrazione*, op. cit.

When determining the truth about what occurred, the judge includes in his decision, among other things, first and foremost, recognition of the existence of the victim. This is an essential and fundamental action wherever crimes against humanity have been committed on a massive scale and, even more so, at the end of a dictatorship which is characterized precisely by serious crimes against humanity. With the recognition of the victim the existence of a *culprit* is made apparent. Therefore, the second function of judicial action is the identification, without the possibility of denial, of all those responsible. In conclusion, it is the recognition, in itself a form of reparation for the damage suffered by the victim, which imposes the obligation, not only of individual redress on the part of accused, who is admonished with the corresponding penalty, but collective restitution, on part the of the whole society.

It is therefore clear how the court decision affects the lives of social and political relations. It does so by warning a society which, through actions or omissions, allows the violation of rights; it reaffirms or alters key aspects of the story we tell and the way we tell it.

It could be objected that reopening a judicial episode after almost thirty years is an anachronism and an overemphasis of "ideological" sectarianism in relation to Argentinean society. Against this position I would like to cite Nietzsche's concept of "irruption of timeliness" as anomalous temporality where the instant and the present take precedence over the regular narrative process of a collectivity. It advances on the construction of a "text" in a slow and perpetual process of formation, especially when referring to the process of adhesion to fundamental principles which, with the passage of time, are first understood, then reinterpreted and eventually accepted by the community.

So far we have examined the different forms assumed by the process of assimilation of the past. At this point in our reflections, however, it seems appropriate to investigate the use of legal logical itself in the Argentine model of reconstruction. The question is whether the decision to such logic as an interpretive scheme of memory has represented the theoretical ground for the objectification in norms those social narratives born of the prolongation of contradictions both within and outside the courtrooms. An example comes to us precisely from the legal reasoning contained in the ruling of the Corte Suprema in the confirmation of the repeal of the amnesty laws.[21] This represents, in my view, a high point in the recognition of the promotion and protection of human rights. The reasoning of the Supreme Court justices, which describes the legitimacy of the decision itself with reference to the Constitution, finds its own basis in the ability to grasp the legal significance proposed by the international community.[22] It is a meaning which goes beyond mere legal recognition, since it is addressed to the "can be" of the law as an alternative to the established rules but anchored to the text of the Constitution.

I believe that being aware of the difficulties and contradictions arising from the use of criminal law in the construction of memory is not to deny its role, but rather to further clarify our relationship, as individuals and as a society, with the field of law; for this is the fundamental nucleus of communal life around which a society founded on respect for basic rights is constructed. Therefore, we must not forget that the judge is one of the

21 See *Simón, Julio Héctor y otros s/ privación ilegítima de la libertad, etc.* – Case number 17.768, opinion of the Señor Procurador General, 29 August 2002. The judgment of the *Corte Suprema* was adopted due to the referral to the constitutional judge of the facts of a criminal case brought by the President of the *Centro de Estudios Legales y Sociales*, Horacio Verbitsky, in relation to Héctor Simón, a member of the Argentinean Police Force, who kidnapped Jose Poblete Rosa, his wife, Gertrude Hlaczik Martha, and daughter, Claudia Victoria Poblete in Buenos Aires on 27 November 1978. These latter were transferred one after the other to the clandestine detention centre known as "El Olimpo", where they were tortured for approximately two months, in such a way that subsequently no more news was to be had of them.

22 The *Corte Suprema* affirmed the unconstitutionality of the amnesty laws in the light of some arguments of international law, such as the incompatibility of these laws with international obligations under the *Convención Interamericana de los Derechos del Hombre* (American Convention on Human Rights) of 1969 and the International Covenant on the meaning of Article 75, paragraph 22 of the *Constitución Argentina* (Constitution of Argentina), which confers internal constitutional status on such international agreements. The Court goes on to assert the primacy in the hierarchy of sources of international standards over national, as this appears to imply that international law, especially American regional law, imposes on States the duty of repealing such criminal law principles, with the end of ensuring the effective implementation of obligations international field of human rights.

central pillars of the rule of law and that his task of protecting and ensuring respect for fundamental rights is essential to the existence and survival of a democracy. The fact that there are moments in which the judicial role is overemphasized is a logical consequence of the development of the process of democratization of a country like Argentina which is emerging from its own dark age. If we start then with the consideration that a just society thus needs to include in its DNA a collective memory as the "history of injury", as the history of the victims, it is clear that the criminal trial is a fundamental mechanism enabling such a requirement to be absolved.

At the root of my concluding considerations is the concept of the interconnectedness and interdependence of fundamental rights and of the different disciplines of the humanities. Instead of using a sense of identity which distinguishes and separates, this conception places the emphasis on the inclusive and multifaceted aspect of identity. It is sufficient to think of the witness, who, as a survivor, has the dual role of denouncing and recounting, both in court and to society, thus protecting memory.

As a guarantee of the right to know what happened, the criminal law is the right to truth. It is the right to know the facts and those responsible, to ensure their non-recurrence and the possibility for a society to meet, rethink and redefine itself. This obviously requires the contributions of other actors, such as the historian, but also of the movements of opinion which track the economic, social, political and cultural structural causes which favoured the establishment of a dictatorship. Methodologically the criminal process concluded with the verification of the accusatory hypothesis – isolated from the normative circumstances with difficulty – where the search for truth is not the goal but only one of the instruments. Precisely because of this, the procedural debate is a long dialogue in which different truths (accusatory and defensive), which must never be taken as the official truth, confront each other.

This reflection on memory as an historical-theoretical aspect of new legal meanings is by definition temporary and incomplete, having chosen to reject any form of rationalization and thus of condemnation of memory.

It is clear that the law has the duty not only to "build the boundaries" but above all to "... establish instruments of communication between people whose life together is continually endangered by new men who are born.

[...] The laws circumscribe each new beginning of barriers and at the same time these ensure their freedom of movement, the potential of something entirely new and unpredictable. The boundaries of positive law are for the political existence of man what memory is for his historical existence: they guarantee the pre-existence of a shared world whose continuity transcends each one of the beginnings, and therefore of a reality which contains in itself all the new sources and is nourished".[23] And this is because a story is readable and codifiable if the survival of the communication based on the existence of internal coding systems is guaranteed.

Memory, history and law are three different, but not contradictory, instruments, which converge together in the pursuit of truth and the pursuit of a justice which institutional actors have a duty to protect with morality. Therefore, the legal result can never be one and only one, the *nomos* being by nature plural and therefore subject to the will, based on the interpretation of the guarantee of pluralism and the valorization of cultural differences.

The Argentinean courts are sites in which many things happen and which do not assume a purely symbolic role, in which the individual is guaranteed legal personality, the denial of which is the first step towards totalitarianism.[24]

23 H. Arendt, *Le origini del totalitarismo*, Milan, Edizioni di Comunità, 1996, p. 637.

24 On this theme, see Arendt, *Le origini del totalitarismo*, op. cit.

CARLOS SLEPOY

Impunity and *Justicia Universal* (Universal Justice) in Relation to Crimes Against Humanity

Seneca reflected: "There are things we do not do because they seem impossible, but they are impossible because we do not dare to do them". Until a few decades ago, it seemed unrealistic to think that norms would be established to sentence those responsible for the most serious crimes against humanity. What was normal, and what had been naturalized during the whole of history, was absolute impunity. The Holocaust had to occur in order that, for the first time, a tribunal was established so as to judge them. The Nüremberg Military Trial was severely criticized for different reasons: for having been set up by the victorious powers, establishing itself subsequent to the events, creating a special statute in order to judge those responsible. It offered, however, a response, albeit partial and limited, to the aspiration for justice, opened a fruitful road and initiated a new stage in the development of International Criminal Law. On this basis, international and regional treaties, resolutions and recommendations whose objective was the prevention and punishment of these crimes began to multiply, and councils and commissions were established to watch out for and report violations of fundamental human rights. That this happened was due fundamentally to the determination and demands of the victims themselves. Ad hoc tribunals were created which have handed down many important sentences. Permanent tribunals have been established on different continents, and more recently, the International Criminal Court.

Following Gastón Bachelard or Jacques Derrida we could say that an epistemological obstacle has been overcome, namely one which hampers or prevents thought from imagining a reality different from the one which already exists. In spite of their importance, the previously referred to instruments suffer a number of profound limitations and conditioning factors.

I do not propose to analyse these here. I would only reply that, in spite of the enormous advances which have happened in less than half a century, impunity remains essentially in force. There are two fundamental related reasons which make this possible from the standpoint of the juridical field: first, the lack of punishment of those who promote it and consent to it and, second, the ineffectual international prosecution of those responsible for crimes against humanity.

Impunity

The nature of criminal punishment has been and will continue to be the object of discussion. That over which there is no debate whatsoever is that it is needed for at least two powerful reasons:

a) Its deterrent effect: the so-called common crimes continue to happen despite the fact that all the laws in the world provide a penalty for those who commit them. Such crimes would multiply if this was not applied effectively. Those who perpetrate this type of crime know that the transgression of the laws which sanction them will be followed ineluctably by punishment. A good of the person who commits the crime is thus harmed: they lose their liberty, their inheritance, their right to exercise public functions or administer their goods, as a response to the infringement of other juridical goods which they have previously harmed. Only exceptionally does the penalty fail to be imposed, when the criminal is left without punishment as a result of the ineffectiveness of the administration of justice or of other circumstances outside the scope of the institutions of the state.

Something entirely different, and inverse, occurs in relation to the great crimes against humanity. Their authors know that it is highly likely that they will not be punished. This is not because they manage to avoid the action of justice but because in the majority of cases, through distinct and deliberate mechanisms, they are protected by impunity. The sentencing of common crimes is a fundamental task which the whole state assumes. The failure to penalize the more atrocious crimes, on the contrary, is the rule. If with their effective punishment the proliferation of ordinary crimes is avoided, the absence of punishment for crimes against humanity favours their development. They would happen to a much lesser extent if, as happens in the cases of common crimes, they were punished. The corollary is that, the greater the impunity of those responsible for crimes against humanity the more crimes of this kind there are.

b) The defence and production of a social value: when a criminal law establishes a penalty for unlawful conduct, it supports a good which is understood to be estimable. Whoever goes against such a law goes against a right that is protected by social consensus. If the law does not reproach the conduct of whoever harms this good, this conduct would not be unlawful but, moreover, the good which is harmed would not be, or would cease to be, socially valued. The intention of the penalty is, in this respect, to defend and promote the social value of given goods or rights: to life, liberty, bodily integrity, property. If their violation is repressed, this is because they are understood to be worthy of being defended. If they were not the object of protection, this would mean that they were unimportant. This is exactly what happens when the criminal law exists but is not applied.

This latter is what happens in a generalized way with respect to the great crimes against humanity. Laws exist in every country, and also internationally, to punish those responsible, but they are either not applied, or only in a limited way, or in some cases only exceptionally. A profound social disvalue is thus established: the message is that the rights of victims of these crimes and those of the societies which suffer them do not deserve to be safeguarded. These elementary findings produce indignation and unease. The more serious the crime, the greater the impunity of its authors; the greater the social value to be enhanced, the more it is scorned. We know the powerful interests which conspire to make it so. We know that the problem lies here and that it is necessary to search for a solution, and that from the point of view of the law, it can and must be found. This has been done laboriously with respect to the punishment of crimes which were not previously considered such (slavery or torture) and the promotion of rights previously non-existent (votes for women or divorce).

Concealment and prevarication

The Spanish *Código Penal* (Penal Code) (Article 451) punishes the crime of concealment, as do the criminal laws of different countries. Concealment is what is committed by those who have knowledge of the commission of a crime but, without having participated in it as authors or accomplices, do any of the following: take part subsequently to its completion, assisting the perpetrators in order to benefit from the proceeds thereof; conceal, alter or render useless the body, effects or instruments with which the crime was carried out so as to prevent its discovery; or help the alleged perpetrators to evade investigation by the authorities or their agents or to circumvent their search and arrest.

Interestingly the cited Article of the Spanish law – very badly drafted, by the way – for no apparent reason does not include the concealment of every type of crime. By contrast it criminalizes those which, given their precise nomination, should be understood to be considered the most serous: murder, treason, rebellion, terrorism, genocide, crimes against humanity and those committed against persons and property in times of armed conflict. It provides that if the accomplice, as they are rightly described, had acted to abuse a public office – in this case regardless of the crime in question – they would be subject to punishment. These punishments include imprisonment from six months to three years and specific disqualification for any employment or public office for a period of up to two to four years if the offence was less serous, or covert disqualification of six to twelve years if serious. In summary, it prescribes that whoever participates in abusing public functions to help those who have committed a crime to evade the action of justice, take advantage of its results or hide its proofs, has also committed a crime: that of concealment.

The question is particularly relevant in relation to the crimes of genocide, crimes against humanity and war crimes. This is so because, fortunately, there exists a vast international body of jurisprudential regulations which establishes that penal action is imprescriptible with respect to such crimes and that those responsible may not benefit from any regulation or practice which leaves them without punishment. That is to say, no state may claim the right of leaving its officers without punishment, as if they could possibly do so with respect to any other type of crime. What has been pointed out implies that the authorities of any country – be these governors, parliamentarians or any other kind of public functionary – who have abused their competences in order to promote the concealment of those crimes, themselves commit a crime. In consequence, they must be tried and, if found guilty, sentenced with the penalties which these very laws provide.

It is well known that, when enacting laws or decrees in order to exonerate of responsibility the authors of these crimes, those who do so argue that they had the purpose of avoiding greater evils or acted for reasons of *force majeure* or out of need. These circumstances, as is well known, can attenuate or excuse criminal responsibility. But whoever commits a crime must demonstrate that the crime was in fact committed in such circumstances. And they must do so in a criminal trial, not before the judgment of History. And the attorneys and judges who, ignoring their obligation to pursue these crimes, provide opinions and resolutions which support norms and practices of impunity and, in consequence, cover up for their authors, must also submit themselves to trial.

As with concealment, the laws of different countries of the world punish prevarication. In the Spanish Criminal Code (Article 446) this crime is committed by judges who knowingly give unjust judgments or resolutions. Their author can be punished with specific disqualification from any employment or public office for a period of ten to twenty years. Any judge ought to know that any resolution or ruling handed down with the object of eluding the investigation of crimes against humanity is not only unjust but unlawful and, therefore, commits the crime of prevarication. To sum up, the failure to put on trial those who commit these crimes, the generalized lack of punishment, favours, as has already been said, the continued committing of the crimes which conceal or with respect to which they prevaricate. There is no harm to those who damage the goods which should be the most valued and those who so decide do not suffer any injury either. Not only do those who have injured humanity emerge unharmed, but those who promote and consent to it do so too. Impunity is unharmed. Crimes are committed with impunity unscathed.

Concealment and prevarication in Spain

In Spain we have recently seen a comprehensive example of the commission of such crimes, and their consequences, on the occasion of the judicial inquiry initiated by Judge Baltasar Garzón into the crimes against humanity committed by the Franco regime, an investigation which has now been finally sunk by the *Corta Suprema* (Supreme Court). Because they reveal the full awareness which they had of having committed them, it is illuminating to take into account the following antecedents. On 15 October 1977 the *ley de amnistía* (amnesty law) was passed which covered anyone who had committed crimes with political intent (Article 1). This law answered in its day to the demand of the Spanish democratic forces that those who were in prison during the dictatorship should be liberated and that thousands of persons should return from exile. From the text of this law it could not be inferred that it was intended to shelter those who had committed crimes detrimental to humanity. But even if this had been intended or it had been desired that it be interpreted in this way, this would not be admissible: those crimes cannot rely legally on political motivations or intentions. Unless, of course, it was understood that the genocidal Nazis, for example, could have been or could be exempted from responsibility for similar reasons.

In those days there already existed international treaties and resolutions such as the Convention on the Punishment and Prevention of the Crime of Genocide of 9 December 1948, the International Covenant on Civil and Political Rights of 16 December 1966, the Convention on the Imprescriptibility of War Crimes and Crimes against Humanity of 26 November 1968, or the Resolution of the United Nations of 3 December 1973. With respect to such crimes, the latter declared that wherever and whatever the date on which they had been committed, they will be the object of investigation, and that the persons against whom there existed proofs of culpability in the commission of such crimes would be sought out, arrested, judged and, if found guilty, punished.

These and other provisions of a similar nature have become mandatory rules of international law, that is to say, they require compulsory observance by every state and against which there can be no agreement or provision to the contrary. To grant them this character, different resolutions and decisions of national and international tribunals were gradually added during the second half of the twentieth century. From the final years of the twentieth century the Spanish courts were particularly active in this process. Successive resolutions made by courts of the first instance and orders and judgments by the *Salas de lo Penal* of the *Audiencia Nacional* (Criminal Chambers of the National High Court) and of *Tribunal Supremo* (Supreme Court) and the *Tribunal Constitucional* (Constitutional Court) passed resolutions in relation to crimes in several countries of the same nature as those committed in Spain. They established an invaluable national and international jurisprudence and consolidated a doctrine which, in essence, determines that those responsible should be prosecuted in any place, the principle of *justicia universal* (universal justice) being applicable at all times, because of its imprescriptibility and without there being a law or practice which may prevent their investigation or prescribe their impunity.

However, when the above mentioned judge decided to apply these principals to those responsible for the planned and systematic repression which millions of Spaniards suffered, those same judicial organs resolved that the same laws did not govern Spain. That is to say, they resolved that the *Audiencia Nacional* (National High Court) does have competence to instruct proceedings against criminals in any other country, but not against those of its own. The same Criminal Division of this court which had once, by unanimous vote, declared is competence to judge such crimes, now resolved by majority vote that they could not be investigated. In consequence they passed a resolution which includes those two crimes to which we have alluded: concealment, on the one hand, by protecting those responsible and helping them to preserve the outcome of the crime; and prevarication, on the other, by dictating a manifestly unjust resolution, in full knowledge of the fact that it was the same Chamber which had founded the previously cited doctrine. The names of the three judges who voted *against* this resolution deserve to be highlighted: José Ricardo de Prada Solaesa, Clara Bayarri García and Ramón Sáez Valcárcel.

As is known, this judicial rebuff, which certainly does not have an equal in comparative jurisprudence nor indeed in Spanish, does not stop there. In its day the Criminal Chamber of the *Corte Suprema* (Supreme Court) condemned Adolfo Scilingo for murders and illegal detentions of persons committed in Argentina. The action brought by the plaintiffs against the decision of the Criminal Chamber of the *Audiencia Nacional* (National High Court) had not yet been resolved, however, when it decided to prosecute the judge Garzón, accusing him of prevarication. To this crime it is necessary to add that of calumny – which is committed when someone is charged with a crime in full knowledge of the falsity of the charge or with reckless disregard for the truth – both of which crimes have been committed by the judges of the *Tribunal Supremo*.

The consequences of these authentic judicial abuses is disturbing and saddening. In the short term these include the suspension of Garzón's functions as judge, the absolute abandonment of the victims, the paralysing of every criminal investigation into one of the oldest genocides committed during the last century and the implicit warning to every Spanish judge who agrees with the suspended judge. In the longer term, it gives notice that when material interests are involved, there are ideological or political crimes which will not be investigated and criminals who will not be judged. The reproduction of the one and the other is thus assured. In spite of the evidence that it is the impunity which favours and perpetuates the crime, it is a settled and universal practice which seems to be part of the natural order of things. This is so much the case that those who authorize it even seem unaware that they are committing crimes. It is necessary to make them know.

As has been outlined above, existing legal rules have solutions for combating these crimes. It is only necessary to apply them, and to this end the first step is awareness that it can be done and should be done. As has always been the case, together with judicial initiatives in different locations in pursuit of fulfilment of these laws, a broad social movement is what is necessary so as to guarantee it. In this sense, just as only the undaunted efforts of thousands of persons and hundreds of human rights organizations around the world made possible the birth of treaties and resolutions which condemn crimes against humanity, it is necessary now to create international instruments which explicitly declare that impunity is a crime and that those responsible for promoting it or consenting to it must be judged. Thus a huge step would be taken in combating the mass violations of human rights.

Justicia universal

Theoretically formulated a long time ago, *justicia universal* (universal justice) has been effectively applied for a little more than a decade in which time the principal of *justicia universal* or *jurisdicción universal* (universal justice or universal jurisdiction) has revealed itself to be a formidable instrument in the international struggle against impunity for the serious crimes against humanity. *Jurisdicción universal* (universal jurisdiction) is defined by the nature of the crimes to which it applies: international crimes. Among them and in particular these include: genocides, crimes against humanity and war crimes. The principle of *jurisdicción universal* is fundamentally different from the classical *principle of territoriality* or the *principle of nationality* or of *active or passive personality*. According to the *principle of territoriality*, jurisdiction is attributed to the courts of a country when the crime is committed in its territory; according to the *principle of nationality or of active or passive personality*, action is taken with respect to crimes which took place abroad when the author or the victim of the crime are, respectively, nationals of the state in which jurisdiction or *protection* is exercised, extra-territorial intervention being possible because the illegal act affects the interest of the person's state. The principle of *jurisdicción universal* (universal jurisdiction), by contrast, is alien to the notion of territory, nationality or interests. The territory is the world, the nationality is universal and the interests are those of humanity. It has therefore been pointed out repeatedly that, in applying it, the court which acts does so in the name and in representation of the international community.

Thus the Spanish *Tribunal Constitucional* declared with utmost clarity in its sentence of 26 September 2005 with regard to the genocide committed in Guatemala: "The international and cross border prosecution which the principle of *justicia universal* (universal justice) seeks to establish is based exclusively on the particular characteristics of the crimes submitted to it, whose harmfulness (paradigmatically in the case of genocide) transcends that of the specific victims and affects the International Community as a whole. Consequently their prosecution and punishment constitute, not only a commitment, but also an interest shared by every state (as we had occasion to affirm in *STC 87/2000, of 27 March, FJ 4*), whose legitimacy, therefore, does not depend on ulterior interests particular to each one of them. Likewise the conception of *jurisdicción universal* (universal jurisdiction) currently in force in International Law is not configured around connecting links based on particular state interests, as shown in our own Article 23.4 Ley Orgánica Poder Judicial (organic law), the previously cited German Law of 2002, or, to dwell on examples, the Resolution adopted by the International Law Institute in Krakow on 26 August 2005, which, after highlighting the aforementioned commitment of every state, defines *jurisdicción universal* in criminal matters as "the competence of a state to prosecute and, if they are found guilty, punish suspects, regardless of the place of commission of the crime and without consideration of any active or passive connection of nationality, or any other criteria of jurisdiction recognised by International Law". If the declared objective of the application of the principle of *justicia universal* is to enforce the international prosecution of those who have been classified as enemies of humanity, the cooperation which puts an end to impunity in the country where the crimes are committed it is no less important.

Application of the principle of *Justicia Universal* by the Spanish courts

This was what happened in the highest example which has existed until now of the implementation of the principle and of which I will therefore make special mention: the judicial proceedings staged by the administration of Spanish justice system in relation to the mass violations of human rights in Argentina and Chile. The victims, deprived of the possibility of bringing their demands before the judicial organs of those countries as a consequence of the existence of the laws and practices of impunity, had had recourse to the jurisdictions of European countries which had acted in some cases with notable efficiency. However their performance was governed by the principle of nationality or passive personality, which limited them substantially: only the nationals of those countries found protection in these courts; the rest were not protected.

On 28 March 1996, however, the Spanish attorney Carlos Castresana brought before the Spanish *Audiencia Nacional* an accusation in relation to the crimes mentioned, committed in Argentina, which fell under the responsibility of Judge Baltasar Garzón in the Central Court of Instruction Number 5. On 28 June, that is to say, three months after the accusation was made, Garzón declared Spanish law, and specifically his court, competent to instruct in this case. A few days later he would intervene in a dispute about the crimes committed by the Chilean dictatorship which fell to Central Court of Instruction Number 6 under the responsibility of the magistrate Manuel García Castellón who, equally, would admit his competence. A year and a half later, in November 1998, he would decline it in favour of focusing first on the connection between the crimes committed in both countries under the so-called Plan Condor, as it was designated by the leaders of he coordinated repression in the southern cone of Latin America.

Although for a long time the idea was put about that, as had been the case in the courts of other countries, the judicial processes initiated in Spain were directed at the investigation of crimes whose victims had been Spanish citizens, this was never the case. From the beginning they were dedicated to the knowledge of the totality of the crimes independently of the nationality of the perpetrators and the victims. It seemed unusual then, scarcely fourteen years ago, that the courts of one country could act with respect to crimes committed abroad if these did not affect it directly. In the course of this short period of time, not only has the idea been accepted, but its necessity and legitimacy is today universally admitted. The legal framework in which the judicial processes developed is established in Article 23.4 of *Ley Orgánica del Poder Judicial*, which lays down the principle of *justicia universal*, differentiating it from the other attributive principles of jurisdiction to which we have alluded.

The only limit which this statutory provision established for the exercise of jurisdiction by the Spanish court was that one of the accused had already been tried elsewhere. Because of this, the judge could not take further action with respect to this person, but this did not prevent him from continuing to do so with regard to the others. He therefore sanctioned, along with the principle of *justicia universal*, that of the *concurrencia de jurisdicciones* (concurrence of jurisdictions). This is a principle of great importance. Some of the results of these judicial cases are well-known: the detention of Pinochet in London for 503 days; the trial the Argentinean Adolfo Scilingo and his sentencing to 1,084 years in prison by the *Tribunal Supremo*; the detention in Mexico of the other naval officer Ricardo Miguel Cavallo, his extradition to Spain and his later handing over to Germany to stand trial there.

But other events, which permitted them to harvest these fruits, are generally ignored. The scope of the investigation enabled the instruction of the trial to be free of any limiting restrictions. For years the courts acting in the case received the testimony of hundreds of victims, together with multiple documents and reports; they attested to the method used, the intention pursued and the identification of a large number of repressors. Before long more evidence had been concentrated in a single trial than had accumulated during more than twenty years in any office or court. The injured parties produced their accusations, brought their grievances, presented themselves as witnesses, and sent their testimonies to the trials through the Spanish consulates abroad. A huge social mobilization moved public opinion and gave life to the trials. This would not have been possible if they had been constrained to investigate only those crimes committed against Spaniards. The application of the principle of *justicia universal* permitted the participation of all the victims, who became the main protagonists, and, with them, wide sectors of Argentinean, Chilean and Spanish society, who also felt themselves to be part of what became a genuine epic.

A new and unforeseen road had been opened. The explicit objective which informs the principle of *jurisdicción universal* had been focused: The enforcement of the prosecution of criminals under international law. The Argentinean and Chilean victimizers could no longer pass at liberty through the world. The issuing of hundreds of international warrants for their search and capture warned them that they could be detained in any part of the world, although, paradoxically, the only one in which they had protection was the one in which the crime had taken place. There, in the heart of the societies they had destroyed, they found refuge. The Chilean authorities made huge efforts to prevent the extradition of Pinochet to Spain. The Argentineans refused to service the requests for detention placed by Judge Garzón. They could not, however, prevent the acceleration of the process of the delegitimation of impunity. At first timidly and only a little later at breakneck speed, some judges in those two countries began to declare the unconstitutionality and lack of conformity with international law of the laws which consecrated it. Later the superior courts endorsed these criteria and then the executive and legislative powers arranged rules which would allow the prosecution of those responsible. Today in Chile and Argentina hundreds of repressors have been tried and dozens sentenced. There is still along way to go, but the bone of impunity had been broken. Thus a second, implicit, objective of the application of the principle of *justicia universal* (universal justice) is fulfilled: working to put an end to impunity in the country in which the crime is committed.

Subsidiariedad or *concurrencia*?

No one seriously contends, as so many did until only yesterday, that sovereignties are encroached upon when the perpetrators of genocide are pursued internationally by courts other than those of the country where the crimes were committed. Given the excellent results obtained, this argument is no longer presentable. Another more subtle argument is now sought in order to perpetuate impunity. Its promoters, recognizing and even extolling the importance of *jurisdicción universal*, immediately use the adjective: *subsidiaria* (subsidiary). That is to say: accessory or secondary. It is claimed, in short, that courts outside the country where the crimes were committed should only intervene when those inside the country in question do not do so. At first glance this seems reasonable. It would not make much sense for judges in other states to act when those of the country itself are doing so. However, the so-called rule of *subsidiariedad* (subsidiarity) is theoretically incompatible with the goal of laying siege to impunity and in practice is a shortcut for its perpetuation.

The very concept of *subsidiariedad* is untenable in relation to the principle of *justicia universal.* On the one hand, *jurisdicción universal* seeks to facilitate the prosecution of the perpetrators of crimes prejudicial to mankind. The number of perpetrators of mass killings is so high, they have so many accomplices and accessories, so many resources they can count on, that the greater the number of courts which act, the more effective the search will be. Moreover, the victims would not resort to foreign courts if they knew themselves to protected by their own. They inevitably turn to another country because they are not supported, or not sufficiently so, by their own. In any case if these courts are acting they will feel comforted rather than offended by international aid and support. Of course, there are several reasons for this: better reparations for those affected and the societies assaulted, the immediacy of the events, the ease of producing proofs, etc. It is desirable and preferable that all involved be tried in the country laid waste, but until all the barriers of impunity have fallen in it, the performance of *coincidente* and *sincrónica* (coincidental and synchronic) jurisdictions in different countries around the world in pursuit of *justicia universal* is necessary, and invaluable. Not secondary but primary. Not accessory but principal. Not alternative but simultaneous. Not *subsidiaria* but *concurrente* (concurrent).

With respect to this the *Tribunal Constitucional* said in the aforementioned statement: "the ultimate basis of this attributive rule lies in the *jurisdicción universal* of states and their organs for the knowledge of certain facts in the prosecution and adjudication of which all States have an interest, so that its logical consequence is the *concurrencia* of powers, or in other words, the *concurrencia* of competent States". And then, challenging the decision of the *Audiencia Nacional* which it would ultimately nullify: "This consideration regarding the basis of *jurisdicción universal* permits us to enter directly in weighing up the constitutional significance, from the perspective of the right to effective judicial protection, of the resolution of the Order of the *Audiencia Nacional*, inasmuch as the theoretical assumption from which it departs in order to establish the absence of jurisdiction, the principle of *subsidiariedad*, does not appear *prima facie* to be coincident with the principle of competence, which this Court has considered preferential". This principle, on the other hand already forms part of the international legal imperative and, in this sense, is enshrined in Article 9 of the Statute of the International Criminal Court ad hoc for the Former Yugoslavia, created by Resolution No. 827 of the Security Council of the United Nations dated 25 May 1993, laying down *concurrente* competences: "The International Tribunal and national jurisdictions are simultaneously responsible for Prosecution of Persons responsible for serious violations of international humanitarian law committed in the territory of the Former Yugoslavia since 1 January 1991". In an identical manner this rule is laid down in Article 8 of the ad hoc International Criminal Tribunal for Rwanda. In virtue of this simultaneity in the exercise of jurisdiction, the courts of various states, especially European ones, have been judging and sentencing persons responsible for genocide and crimes against humanity committed in these countries. The fact that there are investigations in one of them does not prevent action being taken in others. This is exactly what has happened – and is still happening despite the fact that many criminals are being tried in their own countries – with the multiple and overlapping legal proceedings which, under different rules conferring jurisdiction, are held in various European courts with respect to the "punishable acts" which occurred in Argentina and Chile.

In the event that the courts of different countries seek the prosecution of the same suspect responsible for different actions, which one of them takes precedence would be elucidated by means of the same rules laid down every treaty of extradition: the severity of the crime, the nationality of the perpetrators or victims, the place of commission of the crimes, which court acted first. Once judged by this court, he or she would be handed over on a temporary basis to the next in priority and so on. If the prosecution was for the same offence the sentence pronounced by the court which was preferred would produce the effect of *double jeopardy* in the others. The theoretical fallacy of the concept of *subsidiariedad*, however, pales before the real purpose with its promotion pursued. Is intended that, at the news that there is a trial in progress, be its criminal content real or not, or whether it covers one or a few of those responsible among thousands, the courts of other countries will refrain from taking it up.

Current contents of Article 23.4 of the Organic Law of the Judicial Power of Spain

It has already been noted that Spanish law has upheld the principle of the *concurrencia* of jurisdictions. Under pressure from Israel, China and USA to paralyse the trials which are being carried out in various courts of the *Audiencia Nacional* (National High Court) in relation to crimes committed in Gaza, Tibet and Guantanamo, the parliamentarians of the major parties decided to distort the principle of *justicia universal* established in Article 23.4 of the Organic Law which had made so many transcendent lawsuits possible. A reform was needed to improve it which explicitly included international crimes but which did not contemplate, but, instead, eliminated from the model the principle of *concurrencia* of competent States. Pursuant to this, in the words of the *Tribunal Constitucional* (Constitutional Court), the activities of the Spanish courts must cease only when a sentence in another country should fall with respect to those who, among others, had been accused in Spain and only in respect of them. Instead it provides that: "Without prejudicing what international treaties and conventions signed by Spain could provide, in order that the Spanish courts may know of the foregoing offences, it should be established whether its suspects can be found in Spain or that there are victims of Spanish nationality, or that some relevant connection with Spain can be found and, in any case, that a trial which involves investigation and successful prosecution, where appropriate, of such offences has not been initiated in another competent country or within an international court. Criminal proceedings initiated before the Spanish courts will be dismissed temporarily when a record of the beginning of another trial relating to the events reported in the country or by the Court to which the previous paragraph refers".

The principle of *jurisdicción universal* (universal jurisdiction) is thus subject to any of the following circumstances:

1) "That the alleged offender is present in Spain". This rule does not apply to any serious criminal offence. The judicial process is direct and if there is evidence of the commission of a wrongful act and the person or

persons who allegedly committed them is or are identified and he or they are not in the country, a warrant for search and capture is issued in the context of a request for extradition. The more so when the law refers to international crimes. To quote again the decision of the *Tribunal Constitucional* previously invoked: "Undoubtedly the presence of the alleged perpetrator in Spanish territory is an unavoidable requirement for prosecution and conviction, given the lack of trials *in absentia* in our laws (excluding non-relevant assumptions in the case). Because of this, legal institutions such as extradition are effective building blocks for achieving the purpose of *jurisdicción universal*, the prosecution and punishment of crimes which, by their nature, affect the entire international community. But such a conclusion cannot lead to the erection of this circumstance as a *sine qua non* for the exercise of jurisdiction and the opening of the trial, especially when to proceed thus would be to subject access to *jurisdicción universal* to a profound restriction not contemplated in the law, a restriction, moreover, which would be inconsistent with the rationale and objectives inherent to the institution".

2) "Or that there are victims of Spanish nationality". The principle of passive personality or nationality which is introduced has nothing to do with *jurisdicción universal*. This, as we have seen, is based solely on the nature of the crimes and seeks equal protection for all victims.

3) "Or that some important connecting link with Spain can be seen". Besides the fact that this requirement contradicts the essence of *jurisdicción universal*, it is not clear what the criteria for determining the existence of this link is. Its accuracy is left to the interpreter, which will generate multiple remedies and hence the prolongation of the trials, or their closure, when, given the gravity of these crimes and the support which their perpetrators usually enjoy, it is essential to exercise maximum speed and efficiency.

4) "In any case, that a trial which involves investigation and successful prosecution, if any, of such offences has not been initiated in another country or within an international tribunal". Furthermore: "The criminal proceedings before the Spanish courts will be dismissed temporarily when record is made of the beginning of another trial of the events reported in the country or by the Court to which reference is made in the previous paragraph". This means that although the alleged offender is present in

Spanish territory, their victims were of Spanish nationality or are found to have a bond of relevant connection with Spain, the Spanish courts should refrain from considering whether a trial has been opened in another competent country – as if Spain were not such a country – or in an international court. This not only violates the already mentioned constitutional doctrine of the *concurrencia de jurisdicciones* and *jurisdicción universal*, which does not require a greater point of connection than that which arises from the nature of the crime, but that the law now refers to "facts punishable" or "allegations". The difference from the previous wording is abysmal; previously the law alluded to suspects and the inhibition of the Spanish court was struck down if any of them had already been judged, continuing its actions with respect to the others. Now the mere news there is an investigation of the facts is enough for the court to decline its competence, even though no record of who is being investigated or in what state are the cases are to be found.

It is argued that the rule of *subsidiariedad* reflects the fact that it is unreasonable for the courts of one country be transformed into an international tribunal. This, again, at first seems reasonable. But such an explanation is superficial and conceals, again, the purpose, that of avoiding international commitment. As we have seen there are statutes of *ad hoc* international tribunals, which, far from discouraging, call on States to exercise jurisdiction jointly. The Statute of the permanent International Criminal Court, for its part, expressly declares that its action is complementary to the relevant national courts exercising *jurisdicción universal* without differentiating between the territory in which the crime is committed (Article 1). The creation of this court therefore does not have the effect of supplanting *jurisdicción universal*, as with an undeniable sense of relief the promoters of impunity wanted to see.

Constraints on the International Criminal Court

The existence of the International Criminal Court is the result of a long-standing aspiration of the international community. It answers the need for a supranational tribunal for the prosecution of those responsible for crimes enshrined in dozens of international conventions and resolutions. However, until the Statute is fundamentally reformed it can not fulfil its function for several reasons:

1. the five permanent members of the Security Council of the United Nations – including the four biggest arms exporters in the world – the United States (30 per cent), Russia (24 per cent), France (8 per cent), United Kingdom (4 per cent) – can agree unanimously not to start proceedings or to halt proceedings before the Court for a period of twelve months, extendable indefinitely (Article 16);
2. the reporting of a crime before the Court can only be made by a State, the Security Council or the Prosecutor (Article 13);
3. the charge is exclusively in hands of the Prosecutor (Articles 15, 42 and 52);
4. even when the commission of crimes under the Statute is proven, the prosecutor may decline to investigate if he considers that an investigation is not in the interests of justice (Article 53.1.c);
5. the Court can only test crimes committed after the entry into force of the Statute (Article 11.1), i.e. 1 July 2002;
6. the statute consents to covenants of immunity, that is to say, impunity, which the United States has already made repeated use of, agreeing with different countries that their citizens will not be delivered to the Court for crimes committed in those countries (Article 98);
7. various states have not signed the Statute and the Court can not act in relation to crimes committed in them (Article 12), including the United States, China and Russia, permanent members of the Security Council.

Moreover the influence which the major powers and their allies have on this organism is notorious. In its present condition the Court is intended to prosecute violators of human rights committed in countries which do not have their approval.

In opposition to this reality, the rules proper to the principle of *jurisdicción universal* are:

1. Only the courts, without any political interference, decide the opening and continuity of the proceedings;
2. the complaint may come from different sources without restriction;
3. the prosecution may be brought by the victims, their organizations, social agencies and human rights organizations, as well as from fiscal and even against his opposition;
4. in the interests of justice the courts act when the commission of crimes against humanity is verified;
5. its application is retroactive without limitation, in accordance with the applicability of the crimes for which it applies;
6. it does not consent to pacts of immunity;
7. it applies to any person in any country in the world.

In short it allows the victims and the societies to be the fundamental actors in the judicial process which is directed against the perpetrators, whoever they may be. It is an instrument in the hands of the weak and underprivileged.

Even if we leave aside for a moment the relations of power to which the International Criminal Court is subjected, and we stand on the assumption that it did not suffer them, the exercise of *jurisdicción universal* would remain the only effective way to combat crimes against humanity. Even with huge financial resources and a vast number of officials, a single court is unable to confront the many crimes of this type which occur in the world. The only effective way to pursue those responsible is through the national courts of different countries with settled judicial structures. There is nothing to impede it and everything suggests that, to this end, courts specialized in this field ought to be enabled in each State, before which the victims can channel their complaints. An International Criminal Court whose aim was the realization of justice could act as a supervisory body for their actions and claim for itself, in any case, knowledge of specific cases. This would mean a veritable structure of international justice. This is therefore to generalize the principle of *jurisdicción universal*, not restrict it. It is not to pass limiting laws under the pretext that lower courts of a country can not undertake this great task, but rather that each one promulgate rules which will enable full and unrestricted exercise.

I conclude by affirming that only through the undaunted efforts of thousands of people and hundreds of human rights organizations around the world was the birth of treaties and resolutions condemning the crimes against humanity possible. It is therefore necessary to create the international instruments obliging States to establish, and their courts to exercise, concurrently with other countries, *jurisdicción universal*. The fight against impunity must face new challenges, because others have been overcome. The conditions are created so that, soon, other fruitful experiments will definitely enshrine the sole principle which corresponds to *justicia universal*: *concurrencia de jurisdicciones*. A giant step would have thus been taken in combating widespread violations of human rights. There is a growing universal awareness of the need to end these crimes. The punishment of those who leave them unpunished and the prosecution of those who commit them in all times and places by the courts of different countries, is the only way to deal with them. A new epistemological break, the bearer of a new paradigm of justice is in the making. We must help at its birth.

GIANCARLO MANIGA

The Trials in Italy

Premise

The last military dictatorship in Argentina carried out the planned repression of all kinds of dissent, through the elimination of all opposition, including peaceful opposition. It did so by means of kidnappings, clandestine detentions, torture and murder, all of which were hidden or disguised in various ways. Approximately 30,000 people were made to disappear, identified by that horrible neologism, established since then and made sadly famous internationally, *desaparecidos* ("the disappeared"). Among them – disproportionately so even in the context of the substantial representation already present for decades in the Argentine population – were many Italians.

In the course of the difficult path of recovery of a long inactive and brutally suppressed democracy, the termination of the bloody dictatorship should have been followed by the identification and prosecution of numerous officials, from the leadership of the Juntas and commanders of zones or of regions to the many perpetrators, often in the military hierarchy, as well as intermediate and subordinate cadres, including the most abject footsoldiers. As is well known, this did not happen.

The few trials of the commanders of the Juntas, which resulted in merely virtual convictions, the amnesties granted to the highest military ranks, and above all, the shameful laws of the cover-up – together these have ensured and guaranteed until very recently, the most incomprehensible and indescribable impunity for almost all the criminal perpetrators of what, not surprisingly, has been called a veritable genocide.

It is, moreover, natural that remedies have been repeatedly searched for as surrogates for this denial of justice, which constitutes an outrageous neglect of the victims and their families. In this spirit, in addition to the specific need for the persecution of the crimes of which their fellow citizens turned out to be the victims, it is necessary to attempt to recreate justice in other countries, at the very least partially, where Argentina was and would have been absent for decades, and to repeal the declaration of unconstitutionality, "the laws of impunity": *Punto Final* (Full Stop) and *Obediencia Debida* (Due Obedience).

In this spirit, in fact, the criminal proceedings could be carried out in Italy.

The basis of the prosecutability of these crimes in Italy: Articles 8–11 of the Italian Criminal Code

When determining the sphere of efficacy of the framework of criminal law, Italian law has adopted the principle which is often defined as *territoralità temperata*. That is, like most modern states, it has adopted the principle of territoriality. (Article 3 of the Penal Code: The sphere of efficacy of criminal law is defined by the State's territory, obliging all those who are found in it, both citizens and foreigners; Article 6 of the Penal Code: the crimes committed in the territory of the state are punished according to Italian law.) But this has been mitigated through the introduction of the criteria of the criminal protection of the state authority and of the Italian citizen abroad. Therefore, as provided for by Article 7 of the Penal Code, the prosecutability in Italy and under Italian law of particular crimes committed abroad by citizens or foreigners, as prejudicial to the administrative and monetary sovereignty of the state, has also scheduled, under Article 8 of the Penal Code the prosecutability in Italy of "political crimes" committed abroad, including those committed by foreigners, to the detriment of Italian citizens. The final paragraph of Article 8 of the Penal Code says: "For the purposes of criminal law a political offence is any offence which harms a political interest of the State, i.e. a political right of the citizen (Constitution, 48–54)". Such a prosecution is prepared at the request of the Minister of Justice. Article 11 of the Penal Code also says that – in those cases specified in Article 8 of the Penal Code – the foreign citizen who has already been tried abroad, may be tried again in the Italian state if the Minister of Justice requests it. The extremely serious events with which we are dealing, are configured, in the greater part of the cases, as crimes of aggravated murder and aggravated kidnapping. The political connotations of these crimes is evident.

The presence among the victims of numerous Italian citizens resident in Argentina permits application of the previously mentioned criminal regulations. This makes it possible for Italy to pursue these actions and proceed against those Argentineans responsible for the crimes, with the important distinction between the few cases already judged in Argentina (for which prosecution in Italy would be subject to the request of the Minister, in accordance with Article 11 of the Penal Code) and the overwhelming majority of cases in which people have walked free from the trials owing to the laws of amnesty. In Italy they may – indeed should – be judged, as it now appears inconceivable that those shamelessly unconstitutional laws would find recognition and enforcement outside of Argentina. They can be tried in Italy and in other civilized countries, as has been done in France, and as is being done in Spain. In Italy, as we will remember, justice has moved in this direction, initially with faltering steps. For example, the Minister of Justice could have – I would almost say, ought to have – applied for renewal of judgment, under the above-mentioned Article 11 of the Penal Code, for those cases already tried, ineffectively, in Argentina; the expiry of the deadline for the application did not allow it. Only more recently, with the introduction and favourable conclusion of the trials, were the misgivings overcome, consolidating jurisprudential principles which can be described as definitive. This is also a useful way forward for other similar initiatives involving crimes against humanity perpetrated in other countries but definable as political crimes against Italian citizens, in accordance with the rulings of our courts, particularly the *Corte di Cassazione* (Supreme Court of Appeal) with the judgment which closed the first trial, which we will discuss below.

The progress of the first trial in Italy in the *Foro di Roma*

Summary to 1989

A variety of actions were undertaken by the relatives of the disappeared during the repression and immediately after the end of the dictatorship, although these actions which often became bogged down in the face of the silence of the authorities, including both the executive and the judiciary. Among these was a series of denunciations before the consular authorities, all of which were received by the Consulate General of Italy in the City of Buenos Aires, the capital of the Argentine Republic. Following complaints made to the Court of that city, the investigation arrived at the Court of Rome, under the above cited Article 8 of the Italian Penal Code. Although attempts to bog down the process were observed, the case was filed in the Public Prosecutor's Office before the Court of Rome. The court started to gather the first witness statements and documentary evidence; it also began to locate some of those responsible in the cases which had been brought to trial, above all, the commanders of the military juntas who in the meantime had been tried in their entirety and through the most important oral and public trial which has been carried out in Argentina. If, pursuant to Article 11 of the Penal Code, the Minister of Justice at that time had not requested the renewal of the trial against of these latter, the renewal itself – as has been pointed out previously – would have been prevented. Moreover, the attempt by the examining magistrate to formally notify the Argentinean suspects of the court proceedings had to confront, then, the strong opposition of the local judicial authorities; with this the trial suffered a sharp bureaucratic setback. The political stonewalling did everything else: the investigation was stopped.

Preliminary investigations subsequent to 1989

With the entry into effect of the new Criminal Procedures Code and the intervention of the advocates of the affected parties, among whom this writer was included, the case gained renewed vigour. The office of the investigating judge having been abolished by the new procedural code, the case resumed with the preliminary investigations in the hands of the public prosecutor. The Public Prosecutor welcomed the new testimonial depositions, expert reports and extensive documentary evidence and he did everything he could to boost and care for the defence of the injured parties. It should be pointed out that in Italy in that period there was a change in the attitudes of the political parties and the executive. This was due, in particular, to the presence in the direction of criminal affairs of the Ministry of Justice of Giovanni Falcone, an attentive and passionate judge, whose premature death at the hands of the mafia did not allow him to dedicate himself to these events with the meticulous care which he had personally announced.

The application for letters rogatory for the hearing of witnesses in Argentina

The facts of a series of cases having been outlined, the opportunity was presented for hearing from numerous witnesses (relatives, survivors, individuals aware of the facts and other persons), all residing in Argentina. The usual long lead times and concern about wasting a good opportunity suggested to the defence of the private parties the idea of proposing their hearing through the taking of evidence introduced by the new Criminal Procedures Code (Articles 392 CPP and following). This would enable them to support the witnesses with full guarantees of due process and render the depositions capable of being acquired, without their repetition in future hearings. The suggestion was accepted by the Prosecutor and welcomed by the Judge for Preliminary Investigations, who ordered the trial of letters rogatory to be carried out in Argentina. Although the efficiency of the ministerial and diplomatic authorities was not entirely obvious, the request was accepted – apparently as an exceptional case – by the Argentinean authorities.

A judge from Buenos Aires scheduled a series of hearings for the examination of the witnesses; the two Italian magistrates, the Judge for Preliminary Investigations and the Fiscal, made their way to Argentina in February 1994 to carry out the request. Unexpectedly, the very day scheduled for the first hearing, the stonewalling which seemed to have been overcome, was revived: by the action of one Attorney, the warrant was blocked. The Federal Court of Buenos Aires, revoking the previous ruling of the judge, declared its exclusive competence to decide in order of the warrant, thus divesting the judge in question of authority. A few days later, the same Federal Chamber, judging on the basis of its self-proclaimed competence, rejected the request for letters rogatory: it thereby prevented the scheduled hearing of the witnesses and hindered the Italian magistrates from performing their legitimate work. The lawyers for the affected parties quickly took appropriate measures: already present in Argentina, we rushed to collect the depositions, albeit in a different way. The witness statements were made in writing and signed before a notary or the consular authorities who certified their authenticity; once collected and appropriately set out they were then presented to the Italian Fiscal. This represented the final act of the private part, bearing a precise specification, for several cases, of the facts, circumstances and those responsible (who, in the end, were also identified with personal data). With such material, the prosecutor could close the investigation, formulate charges and direct the examining magistrate, in accordance with what the law stipulates, and the demands for the prosecution of the accused.

Request for dismissal by the Prosecutor and opposition to it

Contrary to expectations, the inactivity of Fiscal – which lasted for almost two years, in spite of our constant and persistent and even bitter requests – was interrupted in December 1995 by an absolutely unexpected request for a stay of proceedings. The unacceptable argumentations which the prosecutor used to found his application can be summarized as follows:

- The Federal Court of Buenos Aires, justifying the ruling with which it had rejected the request for of the warrant, had declared that all the cases mentioned in our cause had already been judged (double jeopardy).
- The presence of a previous judgment made necessary, in Italy, the application for renewal of judgment pursuant to the aforementioned Article 11 of the Penal Code. If the Minister had not previously requested the renewal, in the other cases, the request had to be considered still excluded;
- The Argentinean authorities, in any event, had already shown they would not provide any kind of collaboration, and this would have seriously hampered the prosecution of the case.
- We objected immediately to the request for dismissal, pursuant to Article 410 CPP, arguing, in short, against the arguments of the Prosecutor:
- That the statement of the Federal Chamber was absolutely generic, failing to cite the individual trials which, it said, were to be carried out in Argentina;
- That the statement was, in any case, false: almost all those cases had been blocked from the outset by the laws of impunity, *Punto Final* and *Obediencia Debida*, which, contrary to the assertions, had prevented any trial being held;
- That to anticipate the will of the minister – who, moreover, had not yet been put in a position to comment – was absolutely unacceptable and invasive of another constitutional power.

The *Giudice d'Indagine Preliminare* (the Judge for Preliminary Investigations, who is responsible for deciding on the requests for dismissal of the Prosecutor and of objections to them) scheduled a hearing for the month of May 1996. During this hearing, having listened to the parties, he demanded that the Prosecutor report back formally to the Minister so that he could decide whether or not to request the renewal of the trials, if it was revealed that there had been trials in Argentina. In the August of that year, the Minister declared that he had not been provided with data from the respective trials (which, as has already been said, did not exist) and invited the judges to evaluate the advisability of proceeding. On this basis, the duty passed to examining magistrate of deciding whether to archive or prosecute the case.

The closure of the previous investigations and the preliminary hearing

Having evaluated the actions and the copious documentation, the examining magistrate came to the conclusion that some of the cases on file, cases of confirmed homicide, were particularly rich in evidence. He arranged for the dismissal of others, because they had not been proven, and invited the prosecutor to formulate the charges for these cases and the requests to commit them for trial. The result was the request to commit for trial seven defendants, presumed guilty, respectively:

1. Guillermo Carlos Suárez Mason, Commander of the First Army Corps, responsible for Zone 1 in Buenos Aires, for the murder of the following Italian citizens:
   a) Laura Estela Carlotto
   b) Norberto Morresi
   c) Pedro Luis Mazzocchi
   d) Luis Alberto Fabbri
   e) Daniel Jesús Ciuffo
   and appropriation of the newborn:
   f) Guido Carlotto, son of Laura Estela Carlotto, who was killed after giving birth
2. Santiago Omar Riveros, commander of the Zone 4 Tigre – Campo de Mayo
3. Juan Carlos Girardi, commander of the Coast Guard in Tigre
4. Roberto Julio Rossin
5. Alejandro Puertas
6. Jose Luis Porchetto

7. Héctor Maldonado, all of them serving in the prefecture of Tigre, for the murder of
   g) Mario Bonarino Marras
   h) Mastinu Martino, two young Sardinian immigrants recently arrived in Argentina

The preliminary hearing is particularly controversial because, once there, the formal exceptions which the defence demanded were reiterated until the final stage of the hearings, ending with the committal for trial of the accused before the *Corte di Assise* (Assize Court) of Rome, in conjunction with the Decree of 20 May 1999. The first trial, identified as the Suárez Mason case after the main defendant, had, therefore, acquired public relevance, thus constituting a true novelty for Italy. Its importance was compounded by that fact that the Italian state constituted itself as a plaintiff.

The phase of the oral hearing

The trial commenced before the first *Corte di Assise* (Assize Court) in Rome on 21 October 1999. All the defendants duly summoned proved contumacious, with the exception of Suárez Mason, then in state custody; questioned by the Argentine judge about the possibility of his transfer to Italy for the trial, he rejected it. Thus, he was voluntarily absent. The oral hearings represented the living moment, emerging from the process, decisive, from that moment, of the significant dispute. Both for the public and accurate evocation of the historical context and the criminal offences which were derived from it, and for the treatment and the resolution of the main legal issues, they had of necessity, to deal, first and foremost, with to the question of Italian jurisdiction. The defence objected to this, questioning the application of Article 8 of the Penal Code. Numerous witnesses from Argentina gave statements about the historical context and events from which there emerged an exhaustive picture, usefully recalled not only because of the obvious legal reasons but also – widely reported in the Italian and foreign press, especially in Argentina – because of reasons of memory and truth. Memory: the truthful reconstruction of those events and the dutiful recollection of the victims.

It is not easy to summarize the painful experiences associated with each crime. Those victims represented, amongst other things, a few of the more numerous cases of murders of Italians perpetrated in those years. Of that larger number, they represented and still represent a cross-section, equally symbolic of those atrocities. We are permitted to recall, from among them, two representative cases. These include the case of Laura Carlotto, daughter of Estela Carlotto, current president of the association *Abuelas de Plaza de Mayo* (Grandmothers of Plaza de Mayo). A young student, pregnant at the time of her capture, she was made to gave birth and the newly born child was then taken away and allocated to one of the many horrific "adoptions" which took place in those circumstances. Subsequent to this, she was murdered in a fake shootout by shots fired at close range, carried out in the pubic area, almost as if to conceal the birth. And likewise, the cases of the brothers, Martino Mastinu and Bonarino Marras, young immigrants, recently arrived from Sardinia. The former was guilty of being a trade unionist who fought against the inhuman working conditions of the dockers. The latter was mortally wounded during a punitive expedition on a peaceful island in Tigre, while using his own body to shield his daughter who today, thus saved, has been able to exhume these tragic memories.

The legal arguments on which the defence of the accused was based are identified, in essence, as has already been noted, with challenging Italian jurisdiction. That is to say, they are concerned with challenging the power of the Italian judicial authority over those acts committed outside the territory of the Italian state and, therefore, outside of the ordinary jurisdiction of the latter.

In short, it was denied, with a variety instrumental arguments, that those events could be described as "political crimes" as envisaged in the aforementioned Article 8 of the Penal Code. From this connotation and from the circumstance that the victims are Italian, however, derives the exception to the principle of territoriality and, hence, the exceptional jurisdiction of this authority.

The exception raised immediately at the beginning of the oral proceedings was rejected by the *Corte d'Assise di primo grado* (Assize Court of the first instance); based on the evidence gathered, it convicted the accused with the sentence of 6 December 2000.

The sentence was later affirmed by the *Corte d'Assise d'Appello* (Assize Court of Appeals) and ultimately by the *Corte di Cassazione* (Supreme Court), with the repeated confirmation of Italian jurisdiction and, consequently, the legitimacy of the trial in Italy.

It is worth noting, in particular, judgment no. 541 of 28 April 2004, by which the *Corte di Cassazione* (Supreme Court) concluded this process. By providing a proper and comprehensive interpretation of Article 8 of the Penal Code, in the light of those events, this sentence determined a fixed and ineluctable point, which has not since then been eluded, with regard to the application of that rule. In addition it created the possibility that also, in the future, the fundamental rights of our fellow citizens will find protection under criminal law in Italy in all circumstances in which the injured are in foreign countries, under despotic authorities ignorant of the most elementary rules of democratic life.

In short, with that judgment, the *Sezione Prima della Corte di Cassazione* (First Chamber of the Supreme Court) has confirmed the application to the cases examined, of Article 8 of the Penal Code, considering those crimes, which are prejudicial to Italian citizens, to be political offences under objective and subjective aspects, as defined by the standard. These are understood as "political crimes objectively aimed at offending the political interest of the State or a political right the citizen" and "subjective political crimes, the common ones, determined wholly or partly by political reasons". The *Corte di Cassazione* (Supreme Court) explains:

> It cannot but share the conclusion reached by the lower courts concerning the political nature, both objective and subjective, of the crimes in question, especially if the definition of political offences given by Article 8 of the Penal Code be read in light of article 10 of the Constitution according to which "the Italian legal system conforms to the generally recognized norms of international law". Amongst those norms the Convention on the Protection of Human Rights and Fundamental Freedoms should be remembered, which obliges contracting States to respect certain fundamental rights of any person under their jurisdiction, including the right to life, the right to personal liberty, the right to a fair trial, the right not to be tortured, etc.

In uniformity with our findings, the Court concludes that the crimes under review had been committed "in the execution of a criminal plan aimed precisely at the physical elimination of opponents of the regime, without any respect for due process". It violated thus not only a political interest of the Italian State, which had the right to intervene to protect the rights of Italian citizens, but also the fundamental rights of the victims, including the right to life, the right to personal liberty, the right to freely express political ideas, etc. This decision of the Court of Appeal is a fixed point, a key reference for the other trials which were held later.

The development of the second trial in Italy in the *Foro di Roma*

This second trial was carried out with greater speed, thanks to the path already mapped out by the first, as a result of which the road was not so hard and bumpy.

Following the report made in 1999, the case was filed for the trial of the offence of aggravated homicide committed against three Italians, the father and daughter, Giovanni and Susanna Pegoraro, and Angela Maria Aieta, in 1977. It had been ascertained that the three victims, targeted for abduction, had, as was usual, been detained in the clandestine prison located in the School of Naval Mechanics (the ESMA), from which they were eliminated through the famous "flights of death". It should be remembered that this was one of the most important centres of detention and torture used by the members of the military dictatorship, in addition to being the principal focus of organization and action.

Following the investigations, the responsibility for the killings was attributed to the following officers, who exercised high level duties and functions in this criminal structure:

- Jorge Eduardo Acosta;
- Alfredo Ignacio Astiz;
- Jorge Raúl Vildoza;
- Antonio Vañek;
- Héctor Antonio Febres.

The commander in chief of the navy and, therefore of the School of Naval Mechanics, Admiral Emilio Eduardo Massera. Massera, as is well known, was a member of the first triumvirate (Videla, Massera and Agosti) of the Military Dictatorship.

Preliminary hearing

After the application for trial on the part of the Prosecutor, the accused were summoned before the judge of the preliminary hearing. All the accused – except for Massera and Vildoza – declared at the time of the notification of the relevant warning, conducted by letters rogatory, that they were not willing to be judged by the Italian judicial authority, thus denying and rejecting its jurisdiction. They were, therefore, declared voluntarily absent and the fugitive Vildoza, contumacious. Massera, however, sent an expert medical opinion issued by the Argentine military hospital, certifying his inability to attend the trial for reasons of health. An expert report carried out at that time by an Italian expert by order of the court, also came to the same conclusion. Massera having been declared temporarily unable to participate consciously in the trial, the proceedings against him were suspended, pursuant to Article 71 of our Criminal Procedure Code and his position was separated from that of the other defendants, pending further cyclical checks. The other defendants, with the order dated 5 April 2006, were sent for trial before the Second Chamber of the Corte d'Assise of Rome.

Oral Proceedings

The oral hearings of the first instance began on 8 July 2006. Having rejected the objection of the lack of jurisdiction, which had also been raised in this trial as well as in the preceding one, testimonial and documentary evidence were bought. The instruction of the oral proceedings echoed, in part, that of the previous trial, but many more testimonies regarding the reconstruction of events had been acquired. Particularly significant was the testimony of certain former detainees at the ESMA, who had fortunately survived, and were capable of evoking in an effective and often harrowing way, the places and the logistics of the arrests, the tortures they had suffered, the deliveries of pregnant detainees, almost always followed by the abduction of the newborn babies, and for many, the journey of no return, the "flights of death".

Following verification of the facts and of the fact of the crime of aggravated homicide committed by the accused, the latter were judged guilty and sentenced, with the ruling of 14 March 2007, to the penalty of life imprisonment. The sentence was upheld by the *Corte d'Assise d'Appello* (Supreme Court), with the ruling of 26 February 2009.

With that judgment this second chapter also closed, which had opened to examination, memory and justice, a particularly significant site and one which is symbolic of the criminal repression in Argentina. This is the ESMA, where side by side with the institutional functions of a council of the armed forces. based on noble traditions in Argentina and elsewhere, there were committed the most heinous and degrading crimes, with which and through which, havoc was wrought on those military traditions.

The position of Emilio Eduardo Massera

As has already been noted, the trial of Massena's responsibility was suspended and his position was separated from of the other defendants, pending checks: the law requires that the declared temporary judicial incapacity of a person must be verified cyclically, for the purposes of verifying its continued existence.

A subsequent expert report, dated 27 November 2008, gave a different result from the previous one, having established that many of the previously mentioned disorders were largely the result of simulations. This expert report declared him capable of standing trial and determined the revocation of the previous ordinance of suspension of judgment. With the decree dated 6 April the judge resumed the preliminary hearing and ordered the prosecution of Admiral Emilio Eduardo Massera at the Assize Court of Rome. With the defendant in contempt, the oral proceedings began with the hearing of 30 September 2009 and continued for a good number of hearings, all of them concerned with taking the statements of the witnesses for the prosecution. It is worth mentioning, among them, the deposition of Eduardo Luis Duhalde, later Secretary for Human Rights in the Ministry of Justice and Human Rights of Argentina, which accurately recalled the powers enjoyed by Admiral Massera and the chain of command, which was established in relation to the so called *Proceso de Reorganización Nacional* (National Reorganization Process), especially through the work of the structures of the navy, including the ESMA.

Incredibly discrepant was Adolfo Schilingo's deposition, provided by means of a video-conference link from the Spanish prison in which he has been interned as a result of the harsh penalty to which he has been sentenced in that country. During his deposition, he retracted everything he had previously declared, a position he has assumed recently in a desperate attempt to save himself from the life sentence, and has gone as far as to deny the peaceful circumstances, which he admitted to long ago.

A humble and personal consideration: Scilingo stained himself with serious crimes, just like hundreds, indeed thousands, of other Argentine military officers, all of whom have gone unpunished. He, however, has been the only one who has had the guts to confess and to describe the flights of death, which he did in the famous book *El Vuelo* (The Flight) authored by the journalist and president of CELS (Centre for Socio-Legal Studies), Horacio Verbitsky. But he is the only one who is now paying harshly – perhaps he had merited a fairer fate.

The instruction of the oral proceedings then envisaged the hearing of other witnesses. The death of the accused, which occurred on 8 November 2010, has transferred Admiral Massera to another judgment. History, on the other hand, has already condemned him.

Conclusions

The phase of these trials in Italy does not seem to have ended. Before the same *Corte d'Assise* (Assize Court) the oral proceedings against a Chilean military attorney, from Temuco, a city located in southern Chile, are currently in progress. He is accused of being one of those responsible for the death of an Italian professor, Omar Venturelli, during the dictatorship of Augusto Pinochet. The trial regarding the disappearance of Italian citizens as part the so called Plan Condor, would have to be held at short notice. This plan is imputed to military and civil personnel of several Latin American countries, among which Argentina is included.

However, after the repeal of the laws of impunity, Argentina seems to have discovered the road to justice and democracy. I truly consider that this is a journey undertaken seriously and that surrogate justice in other countries such as Italy is no longer needed. This would be the best result obtained with our breaking through of the veil of oblivion.

PART III

Justice

RODOLFO YANZON

The Trials from the End of the Dictatorship Until Today

The end of the dictatorship

On 10 December 1983 Raúl Alfonsín assumed the presidency of the nation after seven years of dictatorship. Thousands of people had been exiled, killed, disappeared and tortured and hundreds of children had been appropriated. There were about 400 clandestine detention centres where the kidnapped were systematically tortured in order to extract information which would allow the task forces to continue with the kidnappings. These were carried out in broad daylight, in workplaces and in homes, by the task forces of the different branches of the military, involving intelligence officers and with the collaboration of the police who would liberate an area, so that no state authority intervened, with the exception of these groups. No judge, prosecutor or lawyer could take action or have knowledge. No action of *habeas corpus* attempted on the part of families and human rights organizations had a positive outcome.

The media misrepresented the facts by calling the kidnappings "counterinsurgency operations" and the victims "terrorists" and even participated in mounting misinformation operations. They used the same vocabulary as the usurping forces. Thousands of people in secret detention centres were forced to endure inhuman living conditions. The vast majority of them are still missing today, as their final destination, decided by the intelligence agencies and the various commands, was the flights of death or some other form of extermination.

The survivors were subjected to a smear campaign. In keeping with the prevailing discourse propagated by the media and by the Armed Forces and supported by various political parties and leaders, they were branded as "terrorists", and some of them were put on trial by means of the very decrees the President had issued against members of the military junta. Thus the theory of the *dos demonios* ("two demons") was established, according to which Argentina had been the victim of two gangs of insane and violent outsiders which shared equal responsibility. Alfonsín's government inherited hundreds of political prisoners, many of them victims of torture and of trials fabricated by military courts. Only a handful were released, while most had to wait for solutions which appeared with the passage of time.

In order to investigate the human rights violations, Alfonsín created the CONADEP, in whose heart survivors and relatives gave evidence. Those proceedings served as the basis for criminal trials, although their validity as means of evidence was, and still is, questioned by the defence lawyers acting on behalf of the accused.

It was a scenario in which the survivors had to keep quiet about their political activism in order to avoid being prosecuted criminally by judges and prosecutors who had been inherited from the dictatorship and who claimed that the country had been under attack by international Marxism. As witnesses the survivors were obliged to explain why they had been abducted and subjected to torture. And, also, why they had survived.

The trial of members of the military juntas and human rights policy of President Raúl Alfonsín

The trial of the military juntas is considered a milestone in the fight against impunity. And it really was. However, it is necessary to address certain questions which are related to the practical and legal limits which existed.

The human rights policy of Alfonsín's government aimed to bring to justice only a few people: the most senior individuals in the chain of command. From the beginning, *Obediencia Debida* (Due Obedience) was thought of as a possibility. Law 23.049 was enacted, amending the *Código de Justicia Militar* (CJM: Code of Military Justice), which involved, on the one hand, separating the trials from the victims, who could not be plaintiffs, and, on the other, excluding the institutional responsibility of the Armed Forces. Thus, the Government introduced the idea of an individual origin of the crimes, ruling out the existence of an institutional plan and methodology. This brought it about that the *Consejo Supremo de las Fuerzas Armadas* (CONSUFFAA: Supreme Council of the Armed Forces), a military body, would start legal proceedings against military personnel. But the members of CONSUFFAA, like the rest of the Armed Forces, shared the methodology used in the massacre. The reform of the CJM anticipated that the Federal Chambers of civil justice would intervene only in face of delay and inaction on the part of CONSUFFAA; the inevitable of course happened.

Another negative decision made by the Government, which not only impacted on the progress of these trials but on the very functioning of the institutions, was to permit members of the judiciary who had served during the dictatorship to remain in their roles. These included, for example, members of the *Cámara de Apelaciones en lo Criminal y Correccional Federal de Buenos Aires* (CACCFBA: Buenos Aires Court of Appeals in Criminal and Correctional Federal) who eventually tried the former military commanders in Case 13. The limitation of liability according to rank was a measure which significantly reduced the chances of making progress in the trials. During the oral proceedings hundreds of testimonies were heard and a little over 700 cases were chosen in which to present charges. In December 1985 the decision was made public. It contained a number of troubling aspects. In the first place, it justified the military presence on the institutional plane as well as the actions of the armed forces; only their methods were subjected to criticism: according to the judgment, they were excessive. In the second place, the concepts used by the judges were similar to those used by the dictatorship and its mass media to describe its political opponents who it had planned to eliminate. Third, no soldiers were put on trial for the crime of rebellion. Fourth, they questioned the amnesty enacted 25 May 1973 in favour of political prisoners which the

Cámpora government had inherited from the dictatorship of Alexander A. Lanusse. As of that event, the judges said, everything which had happened in Argentina was the result of the actions of the guerrilla organizations. In doing so, they misrepresented history since, as we shall see, there had been secret military regulations from 1968 which anticipated the wide range of crimes which were carried out later. Finally, nothing was said about the nature of the armed forces during the previous 100 years or more and how they had had a negative influence on the institutional life of Argentina.

The convictions were open to criticism too. Admiral Armando Lambruschini, hierarchically responsible for one of the most important clandestine centres, ESMA, was sentenced to eight years in prison. Brigadier Héctor Agosti, was given just four years in prison. General Roberto Viola, was given seventeen years in prison but the *Corte Suprema de Justicia de la Nación* (CSJN: Supreme Court) reduced it to sixteen years and six months. Many cases resulted in acquittals.

The responsibilities were limited to what had been done by each force, and the coordination between forces was ignored. International law had little impact. The imprescriptibility of the crimes was not declared, their character of crimes against humanity was not established, and the notions of international law, including International Humanitarian Law, International Law and Human Rights, were not effectively applied.

Following the decision in Case 13 they began instructing the public prosecutors before the CONSUFFAA, through the Minister of Defence, and the instructions to the federal prosecutors, members of the *Procuración General de la Nación* (Attorney General's Office: at that time inferior hierarchies of the President of the Nation), so that they would paralyse or at least not promote criminal proceedings against the accused. The argument used was the need to harmonize the institutions with reconciliation within the Argentinean people. *The Corte Suprema* (Supreme Court) eventually upheld the policy of the Government and declared the laws valid. The trials were closed and only those already convicted in Case 13 and a few defendants, to whom the laws did not apply by virtue of their high rank, remained in prison.

The Laws of *Obediencia Debida* and *Punto Final* and the Amnesties

The law of *Punto Final* (Full Stop), which set a short deadline for making accusations, was passed. At the end of that period, they were removed from the investigations. This caused an avalanche of calls on the part of judges. As a response, regiments rose up in rebellion in opposition to the prosecution of their officers. In this climate, the *Congreso de la Nación* (National Congress) passed the law of *Obediencia Debida* (Due Obedience) which would permit exoneration of a large number of those responsible.

In July 1989 Carlos Saúl Menem assumed the presidency and announced amnesties for those convicted as well as for those few soldiers who had been tried. This was the case with General Guillermo Suárez Mason, the former Chief of the First Army Corps within whose orbit dozens of clandestine detention centres functioned, who had been extradited from the United States. Civilian members of the dictatorship were also amnestied. These included José Alfredo Martínez de Hoz, the defendant in a criminal case for the kidnapping of two businessmen, Michael and Federico Gutheim. Uruguayan military officers who had participated in crimes against Uruguayan citizens kidnapped in Argentina were also pardoned, particularly those involved in the clandestine detention centre known as Automotores Orletti. Members of political organizations who had been convicted or were on trial were also reprieved. Among them, Graciela Daleo, a survivor of clandestine detention centre in the ESMA, repudiated her inclusion on the list of amnesties next to her own torturers and was forced into exile in Uruguay.

Human rights organizations went before the *Comisión Interamericana de Derechos Humanos* of the *Organización de los Estados Americanos* (CIDH: Commission on Human Rights of the Organization of American States) to denounce the Argentinean State for impunity for crimes against humanity. The *Comisión* gave its decision in Report 28, in 1992, in which it stated that the laws were contrary to the *Convención Americana de Derechos Humanos* (American Convention on Human Rights), to which Argentina is a party, for violating the victims' right to justice.

The Trials abroad

One of the actions undertaken by family members and human rights organizations, with the support and collaboration of organizations in other countries, was to present denunciations in order to access the jurisdiction of other countries by invoking the principle of the nationality of the victim. In March 1996, however, twenty years after the coup, a complaint was filed with the *Audiencia Nacional* (Supreme Court) in Madrid, Spain. This was pushed by the *Unión Progresista de Fiscales* (Progressive Union of Prosecutors), using *jurisdicción universal* (universal jurisdiction) in virtue of the crimes committed. In view of the historical, cultural and linguistic affinity, it was a milestone. With the work of Judge Baltasar Garzón and the support of Spanish and Argentinean prosecutors and lawyers, survivors and family members gave their testimonies, the awareness of the Spanish community was raised, and a political, institutional and legal debate generated about the role of these trials and the need to explore other channels which might permit the prosecution of those responsible.

In France, Alfredo Astiz, a member of the Argentinean Navy, was sentenced *in absentia*, accused of infiltrating the human rights movement. Passing himself off as a brother of a disappeared person, he had infiltrated an organization in which two French nuns, Leonie Duquet and Alice Domon, cooperated in solidarity. This organization met in the Church of Santa Cruz to organize actions and complaints. France requested his extradition, which was rejected in 2009 as he was being tried in Argentina.

In Germany denunciations by relatives were made supported by the *Coalición contra la Impunidad en la Argentina* (Coalition Against Impunity in Argentina), an organization composed of German social, religious, professional and human rights organizations. They too used the principle of nationality of the victim. They advanced essentially two cases – those of Elizabeth Käsemann and Klaus Zieschank – who had been kidnapped, tortured and killed under the command of the First Army Corps. Their bodies had been found and identified, which permitted progress in the proceedings before the Nüremberg Tribunal. For both, the prosecution requested the extradition of Argentinean officers, among them Jorge Rafael

Videla and Emilio Eduardo Massera. The extraditions were rejected because, from 2003, the conditions for trial had existed in Argentina. The Embassy of the Federal Republic of Germany presented itself as plaintiff in the trial before the Oral Tribunal in the Federal Criminal Court (TOF) No 4 in Buenos Aires, carried out against several defendants in more than 100 cases of victims who were held captive and tortured in a clandestine detention centre known as El Vesubio. Between 2000 and 2001, in the face of the systematic refusal of cooperation on the part of the Argentinean Government, under the presidencies of Fernando De la Rúa and Eduardo Duhalde, the Embassy of the Federal Republic of Germany in Buenos Aires heard, through its Consul, Sven Krauspe, the testimony of more than sixty witnesses, most of them survivors of clandestine detention centres, which was then sent to the Office of Nüremberg. The importance of this testimony was highlighted above all by many survivors, who were thus listened to for the first time by a state authority.

Numerous testimonies were heard in Rome, using the principle of *nacionalidad pasiva* (passive nationality). An investigation was carried out over ten years into crimes against Italians in the context of what was called Plan Condor. This was the agreement between the dictatorships of South America (Chile, Uruguay, Argentina, Bolivia, Paraguay and Brazil), whose aim was to pursue and eliminate their political opponents wherever they were found. The principal scene of these crimes was in Argentina, because political activists escaping from the coups in Uruguay and Chile had gone to Argentina to ask the authorities of the United Nations High Commission for Refugees (UNHCR) for asylum on account of the political persecution they had suffered. Although they had obtained legal protection, many were later kidnapped, tortured and disappeared under the agreement. The *Fiscalía* (Public Prosecutor) has 150 defendants in its investigation, amongst them among senior and junior personnel. The accused will be formally charged and sentenced.

In Spain Adolfo Scilingo was tried. An officer of the Argentinean Navy, he confessed to having participated in the so-called "flights of death" in which the prisoners were drugged and afterwards taken onto planes so as to then be thrown overboard. Several bodies were located on the Argentinean coastline, which allowed their identification and the amplification of the charges for murder as happened in 2010 during the public trial carried out before the TOF 2 in Buenos Aires of 181 cases of victims who had been held captive in clandestine detention centres known as Atlético, Banco and Olimpo, or the case of the French nuns and mothers kidnapped in the church of Santa Cruz. Scilingo was put on public trial and is currently serving his sentence in Spain.

The sailor Ricardo Miguel Cavallo, alias "Marcelo" or "Serpico" was identified in 2000 in the Federal District of Mexico. His detention for extradition was solicited. While Cavallo was in custody awaiting public trial in Madrid, the Argentinean federal judge Sergio Torres, who investigates crimes committed in the ESMA, requested his extradition to Argentina and this was granted. Since late 2009 Cavallo has been one of the defendants tried in public trial by the TOF No 5 of Buenos Aires.

Towards September 2003 – the date on which, because of the annulment of the laws of *Obediencia Debida* and *Punto Final* on the part of the Congress of the Nation, the trials for crimes against humanity reopened – the *Audiencia Nacional* of Spain requested the extradition of dozens of members Armed Forces, the various Police forces, the *Gendarmería Nacional* (National Gendarmerie), the *Prefectura Naval Argentina* (Argentinean Coast Guard), and *Servicio Penitenciario Federal* (Federal Penitentiary Service). The successive administrations of the Presidents Carlos Menem, Fernando de la Rúa and Eduardo Duhalde had consistently refused all requests for judicial cooperation and extradition put forward by countries which had initiated criminal cases against Argentina for crimes against humanity. In the trial carried out by Judge Garzón, the arrest of the dictator César Augusto Pinochet, one of the main culprits of Plan Condor, was achieved in London in 1998.

Other extraditions were requested by Argentinean federal judges in order to prosecute crimes against humanity committed by the following: Julio Poch, who was in Holland working as an airline pilot, having participated in death flights of captives from the ESMA; Ricardo Taddei, a member of the task force of the clandestine centres Atlético, Banco and Olimpo; and Ricardo Almirón, a member of the far-right paramilitary group known as Triple A (*Alianza Anticommunista Argentina*: Argentinean Anticommunist Alliance).

Trials in Argentina before the annulment of the laws

The laws excluded all amnesty in the cases of rape and the wrongful appropriation of children. However, in practice only the trials for the search for appropriated children remained open, although their progress was delayed for many years for different reasons. On the one hand, many judges were not disposed to investigate; on the other, those who wanted to do so lacked the support of the different agencies necessary for investigating and establishing the whereabouts of the accused and of the children themselves.

In the so-called trials "for the truth" measures of proof were established for the sole purpose of determining the fate of the victims. The intervention of the CIDH was important. Carmen Aguiar de Lapacó, the mother of one of the disappeared, appeared before this tribunal, demanding to know what had happened to her daughter. The Argentinean State and Aguiar signed an agreement before the Commission by which the State became obliged to take all appropriate measures to seek the truth. After a period during which the judges resisted these trials, the trials for the truth began to open in the major cities of Argentina, having a special activity as the product of the human rights bodies and judges before the Federal Court of La Plata. Testimonies were received and documentary evidence was introduced, which resulted in criminal trials such as those formulated by the prosecutor Félix Crous, despite the impunity laws. That is, although the object of the truth trials was the discovery of the whereabouts of the victims, neither the families nor human rights organizations, supported by a small group of judges and prosecutors, ever neglected the criminal prosecution of those responsible.

In addition to these trials, and at the same time as trials were taking place in Europe, alternatives were sought in Argentina so as to overcome the impediments caused by the force of the laws of *Obediencia Debida* and *Punto Final* and the amnesty decrees. In 1998 there were denunciations against the Bolivian, Uruguayan, Paraguayan and Chilean military personnel who had participated in Plan Condor, as none of them had been favoured by those laws. This allowed the initiation of criminal proceedings which resulted in an investigation conducted by the *Fiscalía* (public prosecutor's office), in which numerous testimonies were received and documentary evidence introduced and which went as far as to seek extraditions. This investigation bore fruit in a trial which was conducted during 2001 to the TOF n° 1 in Buenos Aires.

The No. 5 TOF tried a Chilean citizen, Enrique Arancibia Clavel, a member of the *Dirección de Inteligencia Nacional* (DINA: National Intelligence Directorate) of Chile, whose head was General Manuel Contreras. Arancibia was accused of the murders of Chilean General Carlos Prats and his wife Sofía Cuthbert, which had taken place in Buenos Aires in 1974, and sentenced to life imprisonment for committing two crimes of aggravated murder and participating in a conspiracy to commit crimes against humanity. With the passing of time, this ruling became one of the milestones in this field because of its importance in terms of the legal criteria incorporated, such as the imprescriptibility of crimes against humanity. Different structures on which the task forces who carried out the kidnappings depended were denounced, because of the existence of a plan for the abduction of children. In 2011 the oral public hearing took place in Buenos Aires. This allowed the initiation of a criminal trial which resulted in an investigation instituted by the prosecutor of Tribunal No. 1 of Buenos Aires, which received numerous testimonies, incorporated documentary evidence and went as far as to seek extradition. This collection of such evidence comes as the result of a judicial investigation which began in 2001, but whose outcome still can not be predicted.

The military personnel who had benefited from the presidential amnesties were denounced for the crimes of the illegal deprivation of liberty committed against people who were still disappeared. The argument given in justification was that these amnesties only covered the period from the beginning of the crimes to the time when the amnesties were decreed, around 1990. From that year, the events, classified as continuing crimes, were not covered by the amnesties and therefore should be investigated and prosecuted.

As can be seen, numerous measures have been taken, both within Argentina, and abroad, to open up new avenues of investigation and prosecution, or to request the reopening of proceedings.

As part of the political and legal debate, we cannot overlook the many projects which have been presented to the *Congreso de la Nación* to discuss the repeal or annulment of the laws of *Obediencia Debida* and *Punto Final*. Finally, in 1998 the *Congreso de la Nación* sanctioned the repeal of both laws, which had an effect more declarative than real, since for Argentine law, this act did not change judgments which had been made previously. But the laws were no longer in force as of that year, a declaration which would not be without its effects in the future, as we shall see.

The annulment of the Laws of *Obediencia Debida* and *Punto Final*

In March 2001, within days of learning of the sentence given by the *Corte Interamericana de Derechos Humanos* (Inter-American Court of Human Rights) in the Barrios Altos case, which condemned Perú for the amnesty given to the perpetrators of massive human rights violations, Federal Judge Gabriel Cavallo declared the laws *Obediencia Debida* and *Punto Final* to be unconstitutional. This took place in the trial known as Simón, Julio in the case of the victims, José Poblete and Gertrudis Hlaczik. That sentence was confirmed by the various judicial breakwaters, until, in June 2005, the *Corte Suprema* (Supreme Court) did so too.

The social and political demands and institutional vicissitudes of 2001 – with people dead and wounded for good measure – gave rise to the government of Néstor Kirchner. Kirchner had the foresight to make his own an old dream of justice: that of the family members and human rights organizations, supported by significant sectors of Argentina's political milieu in the fight against impunity. He took office in May 2003 and gave unequivocal signs, such as the beheading of the military leadership and the dialogue with the human rights organizations. Left-wing legislators and Patricia Walsh – the daughter of the disappeared journalist and writer Rodolfo Walsh, who had been seen in the ESMA – had submitted projects with the aim of declaring the laws invalid through the legislative road. The Government decided to support the agencies' demand and endorse their project of annulment. In August 2003 the *Congreso de la Nación* passed the law by means of which the laws of impunity were declared irredeemably invalid.

While that was happening, about seventy soldiers were deprived of their liberty in order to be extradited to Spain. The deadline set out in the Extradition Treaty between Spain and Argentina was 1 September 2003 and Spain had to send the petitions for extradition before that date, or the soldiers would recover their freedom. And although that is what finally happened, that very same day CACCFBA's decision to reopen the two fundamental and symbolic cases of ESMA and the First Army Corps was made public.

The reopening of the trials

The CACCFBA, now composed of different members, was the organ which sat in judgment over the members of the military juntas in Case 13. In the same ruling of 1985 it had ordered that other trials be carried out in order to investigate the responsibility of other members of the military and security forces of lower rank than the commanding officers. The CACCFBA began with Case No. 450 (First Army Corps) and No 761 (ESMA). The first trials were undertaken by the CONSUFFAA. These trials were governed by the CJM which, among other things, forced the survivors to join a military unit so as to testify as witnesses before military courts. In many cases this made the situation of the witnesses worse and weakened their very testimony because many survivors found themselves prevented from narrating their experiences. In those trials dozens of officers and non-commissioned officers were called as suspects and progress was made in the investigation of hundreds of cases. The enactment of the laws of *Obediencia Debida* and *Punto Final* and their application by the *Corte Suprema*, closed them until 2003.

The reopening of the two cases by CACCFBA entailed handling the trials under civil procedural law with the involvement of civilian judges with jurisdiction over federal matters, thus excluding the previously dominant CJM.

After preliminary discussions between judges, the trials remained located in Federal Court No. 3 (First Army Corps Case) and 12 (ESMA). For the first time the witnesses could recount freely their experiences before civilian judges and prosecutors, and survivors and relatives filed as plaintiffs, thus taking part in the trials, with the power to propose and discuss measures and assist in judicial decisions.

A few days later, the *Cámara Federal de Apelaciones* (Federal Court of Appeals) in San Martín reopened the case of the clandestine centres of Campo de Mayo. Trials also reopened in other cities, including Córdoba, La Plata, Bahía Blanca, Santa Fe and Rosario.

Each trial will bear the imprint of the judges and courts in which it takes place. In the city of Buenos Aires, generally speaking, the trials made progress from the very start and despite many obstacles, debates, and certain legal complications. Something similar happened in La Plata. What made the difference was the existence of private plaintiffs and the activity of human rights organizations in each place. Where was little or no activity on the part of such organizations, the problems were greater. In many cases, judicial actors demonstrated their openness to the new times by limiting themselves to declaring the invalidity of laws and ordering the trials to be opened. But the activity of investigation and the call for military personnel to present themselves as suspects were almost nonexistent. This was the case in the cities of north western Argentina, or in places where the military presence is strong, such as Bahía Blanca, in the south of the Province of Buenos Aires.

Another distinction that must be made is that because of jurisprudential developments and the intense activity of the human rights organizations in the judicial forums, the courts recognized the authority of the latter to act in trials of human rights violations. When the cases of crimes against humanity were reopened, most of the agencies presented themselves as prosecutors, something which was accepted unanimously. This brought both the advantage of strong popular participation in the trials, and the disadvantage of weakening the legal debate, since most organizations lacked criminal lawyers and in many cases the resulting differences of opinion meant that the very accusations themselves helped delay the trials. However, it must be said that if the judgments advanced it was essentially because of the presence and activity of private accusations.

Among other proposals, the private prosecutors sought the annulment of the amnesties which had benefited the military officers in different cases. In every trial the judges reiterated the criteria adopted in other pronouncements, about the need to do justice and the invalidity of the laws of amnesty, which were contrary to international law. Thus, high-ranking officers found themselves being charged again.

A paradigmatic case was that of José Alfredo Martínez de Hoz, a businessman who headed the *Ministerio de Economía* during the dictatorship of Jorge Rafael Videla, and one of the people with the greatest responsibility for economic crimes, including the scrapping of the Argentine State, the weakening of the working class and the transfer of huge profits to the banks and financial institutions. Together with the dictator Videla and his Interior Minister, Albano Harguindeguy, Martínez de Hoz was charged in the case involving the kidnapping for ransom of the businessmen Federico and Miguel Gutheim, who had been forced into signing export contracts to the benefit of economic interests defended by the dictatorship. The amnesty from which they had benefited was declared unconstitutional and they were prosecuted for these acts. This resulted in other presentations of similar nature for investigating the direct relationship between the clandestine detention centres and economic objectives.

The most emblematic case was that of Papel Prensa, an enterprise vital to journalism, which controlled and still controls the paper trade. It had been transferred from its owners to the owners of the newspapers *La Razón*, *Clarín* and *La Nación*, in a shady deal involving members of the dictatorship, while the company's owners were kidnapped and tortured. In addition to laying bare the relationship between torture and abductions for economic crimes, the case of Papel Prensa brought to light the role of the media during those years. In the oral hearings which were carried out during 2010 it was demonstrated that the mass media had two positions on what was happening in Argentina: either they were silent, or they misrepresented reality, describing the kidnappings and murders as a "counterinsurgency operation" and giving the name "joint forces" to the task forces which were carrying out these crimes.

One case of direct complicity between the judges and the military occurred in the Province of Mendoza, where several judges said publicly they did not agree with the trials and some declared themselves, in a defiant tone, to be friends of the soldiers involved in the cases. When the opening of the proceedings became unavoidable, the judges actively took the side of the military, going as far as to order the release and "deprosecution" of those implicated in kidnappings and torture, arguing that insufficient evidence had been gathered. The case of Mendoza was aggravated when it emerged that, as officials of the court under the dictatorship, these federal judges had ignored the crimes of torture and rape committed against political prisoners. Not only was there complicity, but direct participation. They were denounced before the *Consejo de la Magistratura de la Nación* (CMN: Council of the Magistracy of the Nation), a body which judges the conduct of the judges. Some resigned their positions, while others, convinced and stubborn in pursuing a hypothetical war against terrorists, remained in their posts; they obtained support from some of their peers, which helped them to withstand the pressures not only of the human rights organizations and family members, but of the *Consejo de la Magistratura* itself, the *Cámara Nacional de Casación Penal* (CNCP: National Chamber of Criminal Appeal: made up of superior court judges and those immediately below the CSJN), and the judges who had to investigate the events for which these judges had been reported. The CMN reviewed the suspension of these judges, including most recently that of Attilio Romano, and the federal courts summoned them as being suspiciously close to the military ideology and therefore conceptually complicit in crimes against humanity, and the CNCP decided to separate them from prosecution. The obstacles kept increasing as the trials went on.

The case of the Campo de Mayo, for example, suffered many vicissitudes. Some of the accused proposed to the federal judge the invalidity of the reopening and of the law which had struck down the laws of *Obediencia Debida* and *Punto Final*. The federal judge, sharing the opinion of the public prosecutor and the complainants, dismissed these claims. The defendants appealed to the *Cámara Federal* (Federal Court) of San Martín, which judged in their favour and ordered the trial to be closed, arguing that the defendants had an acquired right to be favoured by the laws of *Obediencia Debida* and *Punto Final*. The prosecutor in the House, Pablo Quiroga, did not appeal against the closure of the case and had it not been for the human rights organizations, one of the most important trials would have been closed. Because of the appeals of the private prosecutors, the CNCP had to intervene and overturned the verdict and ordered the reopening of the investigation, a decision later upheld by the CSJN.

However, the biggest obstacle was seen in the very heart of the CNCP, the Argentine court of highest appeal in criminal matters and the one which has the task of reviewing all decisions of the courts in these oral trials. The ESMA case had hardly reopened when one of the defendants, Raul Scheller, appealed against the decision of CACCFBA, which had ordered the reopening. The Fourth Chamber of the CNCP, requested the submission of the proceedings, which delayed for two years a section of the case which had begun to be instructed after the judgment in Case 13. There were countless presentations and challenges against judges. Because of other arguments, other divisions of the CNCP, which consisted of four chambers, also intervened. In one, addressed by Trial Chamber I, one of its members, Alfredo Bisordi, tried the "criminal terrorist" Graciela Daleo, a survivor of the ESMA, and spoke contemptuously of the human rights agencies and lawyers. With a number of resolutions the CNCP also made clear its position in favour of the closure of trials and of giving every advantage to the military: amongst other things, they began changing their restrictive stances in favour of freedom in criminal proceedings, and saying that preventive detention was an exception, precisely in these cases. These actions taken together led to complaints against the judges of the CNCP before the CMN, which resulted in the resignation of several of its members. One of them, Alfredo Bisordi, today is the advocate of the commissioner Luis Abelardo Patti, who has been accused of multiple cases of torture, killings and kidnappings during the dictatorship.

Another obstacle encountered, mainly during 2009 and 2010, was the mass presentation of resignations and requests for retirement by judges who were oral court members who had to intervene in the trials.

Although the problems are not over, it can be said that, after the change in its members, in general the role of the CNCP now facilitates the organization of trials and the appointment of judges in various courts of the country.

The debate in the trials

Several oral hearings have been carried out in different parts of the country. Two trials began in the Province of Mendoza, and others in Córdoba, where the dictator Jorge Rafael Videla and the head of the Third Army Corps, Luciano Benjamin Menendez, were sentenced to life imprisonment. Still others have been carried out in the provinces of Santa Fe, Chaco, Formosa, La Pampa, Santiago del Estero, and in Mar del Plata, La Plata and San Martín in the Province of Buenos Aires. The year 2010 was, without doubt, the year of the oral trials for crimes against humanity.

In the city of Buenos Aires the trial of the clandestine centres Vesubio, Orletti, Atlético, Banco and Olimpo was completed, and that of the ESMA and Plan Condor and the systematic plan for the appropriation of children followed. In these trials, the origin of the plan of extermination by means of the various directives of the armed forces and their reception of the French doctrine of counterinsurgency has been proven.

A negative and significant landmark was the disappearance of the surviving witness Jorge Julio López in September 2006. López had testified in the trial conducted against one of the people with the greatest responsibility for crimes in the Province of Buenos Aires, Miguel Etchecolatz. The complete lack of information and the manner in which he disappeared have revealed the presence of sectors which will not tolerate the progress of the trials and which try to put pressure on witnesses. In fact, in addition to the lack of information, the disappearance of López generated in survivors a state of negativity and meant that several desisted from appearing or objected to appearing before the TOF for fear that the Argentinean State has not done enough to protect their integrity. There have been not a few people who, in the face of this fact, have spoken of their fear, especially those who had been forced into exile and continue to live outside the country.

The secret military regulations of 1968 – which predate the emergence of the armed groups – were incorporated into these trials. They were only made public a few years ago and abolished in 1995. From them it emerges that the armed forces anticipated eight years before the coup the methods which they later used. For example, the confidential *Reglamento RC-5–1 de Operaciones Psicológicas* (Psychological Operations Regulation RC-5–1) of 8 November 1968, signed by Lt. General Alejandro Agustín Lanusse, declares: "Method of Compulsive Action (page 14 item 2004): the method of compulsive action is any action which tends to motivate behaviours and attitudes by means of instinctive actions; it will act on the instinct of self-preservation and other basic human tendencies; the pressure urges the unconscious by means of compulsive action by appealing almost always to the fear factor, the psychological pressure which will engender anxiety; massive generalized distress will result in terror and that is sufficient to maintain the public in a state of innocence, in parenthesis, at the mercy of any subsequent influence; force will imply coercion up to the involvement of mental violence; in general this method will be promoted accompanied and supported by physical efforts or materials of the same tendency; strength and rigour will replace the instruments of reason, the technique of the physical facts and hidden media of psychological action are related to this method of compulsive action".

That is to say, although the trials had to wait many years, the passage of time also permitted more evidence to be gathered, other secret military documents to be discovered, progress to be made in the interpretation of legal criteria and some questions of fact to be decided which in some ways had a negative impact on the survivors, as discussed below.

As a result of the development of the oral trials, an interesting debate was generated about the different crimes committed in the clandestine centres. In particular, emphasis was placed on sexual violence applied against all the prisoners, especially women, who were often held as sex slaves or subjected to extortion through threats to other members of the family. While sexual violence was not carried out against women alone, it was the women who were encouraged by various state officials at the public and oral hearings to recount the sexual abuse and rape which they had suffered. While every clandestine centre had its peculiarities, the practice was spread throughout the country.

In addition to the limitations of all kinds, the survivors said they did not feel safe to testify about these facts before the judges of a State which for years had denied the disappearances, tortures and murders. With these trials a change of attitude can be seen, a gradually increasing confidence that testimony can be given in full freedom.

Since 2003 there has been a tendency to bring to trial those responsible in the lower ranks, in many cases those who had had direct involvement in the events. There are many obstacles, since we do not know the identity of a large number of involved parties, and because the personnel files usually contain falsehoods. This means that the testimonies remain the fundamental proofs which demonstrate crimes committed under the strictest secrecy. There are concerns: on the one hand, with the passing of time, because many witnesses have died; others have difficulty remembering, especially when it comes to faces or other physical signs.

The reflection which can be made on these trials is that during the government of Raul Alfonsín the goal was clear and the tools were effective: few perpetrators were prosecuted, those of the highest rank, resulting in accusations in few cases, which facilitated the work and the proof; and with courts which knew how to delimit their roles. In contrast, with the reopening of the trials in 2003, with the political will clearly demonstrated through the different messages sent out by the executive branch as well as the penalties set forth by the *Congreso de la Nación* (National Congress), and then the judicial decisions, the spectrum of defendants and victims multiplied without a clear goal, given the lack of sufficient proof. This situation found the different judicial actors without the tools necessary to undertake the colossal task proposed by the administrative and legislative branches. In the circumstances, it would have been appropriate to have adopted laws which would allow the powers of higher courts to be used by the lower courts in order to advance properly, preserving the evidence and above all the witnesses. Delays and procrastinations are incompatible protecting witnesses and carrying out justice.

The *Ministerio Público Fiscal* (Office of Public Prosecutions) created a research unit dedicated to these trials, something which permits an up to date survey of the status of the trials and ongoing collaboration among their officials. Added to this is that the *Corte Suprema* coordinates a commission of the different powers which also monitors the status of cases and serves as a forum for the discussion of the various problems. It must be said that the *Corte Suprema* has made important decisions which have established that the progress of these trials has become a policy of the state, and not just of the Government. However, there are some concerns, such as the fact that some defence attorneys, employees of the *Defensoría general de la Nación* (Public Defender's Office), have, as a defensive tactic, attacked not only the credibility of the testimonies of survivors, but the survival itself of the witnesses, accusing them of collaborating with the dictatorship.

It also generates some concern that some media organs, in particular the newspaper *La Nación*, have mounted a campaign to re-install the "theory of two evils" with the objective of negotiating a definitive closure of the processes to the benefit of the accused. Either they are looking for an amnesty or trying to equalize the responsibilities by highlighting some operations carried out by armed organizations during those years. The former is quite unlikely to be attained if the judicial pronouncements, the work undertaken by all actors and, crucially, the commitment of human rights organizations and the politically active sectors which support them are observed. That is why not only the progress of the trials but the existence of a communications policy which supports them and generates permanent debate in Argentinean society and abroad, remains vital. If justice, dissemination, protection and debate go hand in hand, the trials are guaranteed.

DANIEL EDUARDO RAFECAS

The Reopening of Judicial Proceedings for Crimes Against Humanity in Argentina

Introduction

It becomes clear from the social history of the West in the last century, and from the recent political experience of Argentina in particular,[1] that there have been many occasions on which the attacks of the police state broke down the levees which offered resistance on the basis of the rule of law

Thus, through the employment of an authoritarian and manifestly illegal power – what Baratta called the exercise of institutional violence – those impulses overwhelmed areas of rights and freedoms which had always been targeted and which until then had the protection of the law. These rights include, amongst others, life, dignity and personal freedom, the supreme

1 We should recognize that for much of the twentieth century, Argentina as a society had a long tradition of seduction by foreign authoritarian doctrines, and that during the 1930s and first half of the 1940s certain intellectuals and sectors of power also succumbed to the fascination caused by European fascist political movements. From this perspective, the profusion of Nazi ideology and iconography in the mid-1970s cannot come as too great a surprise; nor can the cruelty towards Jewish prisoners at the hands of the most sinister characters to have emerged from the armed and security forces throughout its history and in sites that came closest, in design and purpose, to those which functioned in the context of Third Reich. See in this respect, Rafecas, Daniel E., "La especial brutalidad antisemita del terrorismo de Estado durante la última dictadura militar en la Argentina", *Nuestra Memoria*, official publication of Museo del Holocausto Buenos Aires, nº 29, 2007, pp. 195–208.

values of any nation which wishes to belong to the international community, in the light of fundamental human rights enshrined in international charters which multiplied from the second half of the twentieth century.[2]

State terrorism and crimes against humanity in the case of Argentina

Let us examine the case of the most recent military dictatorship in Argentina. To the creators of the military regime, which they had set up in order to channel the enormous flow of state violence which they planed to inject into society, the catalogue of penal legal responses offered by the usurped rule of law was clearly inadequate.

The plan to be realized, that of prejudicing on a massive scale the fundamental legal rights of the citizens, faced a dilemma: whether, on the one hand, to change at will the formal legality regarding crimes, trials and punishments; or, on the other, to transfer the complete war machine of state power to the purest clandestinity, that is, to the most open illegality, so as then on that basis to be able to deploy an extralegal[3] or system-wide

2 For further details with respect to the historical, legal, penal and criminological aspects proper to this type of crime, compared to the Argentine case, see Rafecas, Daniel E., *La tortura y otras prácticas ilegales a detenidos*, doctoral thesis, Buenos Aires, Ed Del Puerto, 2010.

3 "The passing of the punitive function beyond the limits of the law, the Constitution and human rights is the norm in the case of societies in which, in fact or in law, democratic rules have been suspended [...], in which the dominant groups exercise, through state institutions or next to them, an action of repression [...] In these cases, the degeneration of the criminal justice system can arrive at extraordinary degrees of severity, in the presence of which it is more realistic to talk of an extra-legal penal system of extrajudicial punishment, rather than of the application of rules governing the legal justice system". Cf. Baratta, Alessandro, "Human Rights: between structural violence and criminal violence. For the pacification of violent conflict", trans.

criminal underworld.[4] The former solution was absolutely practicable due to the supplanting of the very same fundamental rule of the existing legal order, but it was the second, even more drastic solution, which was preferred.

And I reaffirm this note of open illegality, because the Argentinean government, despite the clear domination of the police state, maintained remnants of certain aspects of rule of law in non-vital areas.[5]

Thus it was recognized, for example, by the Federal Court of Buenos Aires on the occasion of trying the Simón case:

> In the domestic order criminal laws existed which typified and punished most of the conducts carried out by the accused [...] This circumstance demands, moreover, recognition of the existence of a legal order fully applicable to the unlawful conduct which developed during the period 1976/1983.[6]

In other words, we find, from late March 1976 in our country, Argentina, a new interruption of the constitutional rule of law, with almost all its internal spaces occupied by an authoritarian regime freed from all restraint and dominated by the executive agencies (military and security forces).

But in addition, as the hallmark of the state violence which occurred in Argentina in those years, the entire organizational apparatus of power (military, police, prison services, state security services) was arranged within a

---

Mauricio Martinez Sanchez, *Criminology and Criminal Justice System*, Buenoa Aires, F B Ed, 2004, p. 345.

4 Cr. Zaffaroni, E. Raúl, Alagia, Alejandro & Slokar, Alejandro, *Derecho penal – Parte General*, Buenos Aires, Ediar, 2000, p. 24.

5 Sancinetti and Ferrante describe it thus: "at the same time that in the law schools they were being taught, not without solemnity, the main guarantees of the state criminal law which Article. 18 of the Constitution supports, thousands of citizens were being dragged from their homes [...] without respect for their individuality, nor for their moral or physical integrity [...] and subjected to all sorts of horrible sufferings [...] they died in clandestine detention centres, or outside of them, and their bodies were thrown into the river or the sea or buried in mass graves [...] All this under the assumption, never brought to trial for elucidation, that these people or some of their relatives were endangering the national security". See Sancinetti, Marcelo A. and Ferrante, Marcelo, *El derecho penal en la protección de los derechos humanos*, Buenos Aires, Ed Hammurabi, 1999, pp. 109–110.

6 See: C.C.C.Fed., Sala II, causa n° 17.768, "Simón Julio s/ procesamiento", rta: 9/11/01.

single structure – in the style of the *Behemoth* described by Franz Neumann. It was liberated from every hindrance or restraint from the legal sphere, at least from the formal legality which would govern the political organization after the coup and until the restoration of the democratic system of government. This had a fundamental objective: the annulment of any vestige of political opposition or dissent, through illegal detention, torture and indiscriminate killing.

In *Derecho y Razón* Luigi Ferrajoli calls attention to the extent of the separation of the *ought* and the *is* of the punitive power of the state in our region at that time: "[t]he dramatic limiting case arises when the divergence between the normative level and the actual reality of legality reaches the terrible form which the military regimes of Latin America have experienced".[7]

In the same vein, Julio Maier points out – with quotations from the book *Nunca Más* among others – that while the legal regulations proper to the rule of law have failed to eradicate the old practices of the criminal prosecution bodies or of the State security agencies, who persist in ignoring in their actions these humane conquests, the fact is that in the recent past in Argentina the grossest forms have been "invented" in order to eliminate fundamental rights. These include completely avoiding the criminal process, punishing without it by means of imprisonment, torture and even death.[8]

Moreover, from the perspective of the State itself, those who usurped political power in Argentina provided those who carried out the arrests with a huge unified underground apparatus of power. They were given everything they needed to operate with impunity and in the greatest secrecy.

First, they were allocated the financial and logistical resources, derived from public funds, without which the enormous criminal enterprise could never have taken place.

And second, they were promised that the enormous discursive and media power at the service of the regime (through state or privately controlled information agencies and the silencing and prosecution of

7 Cf. Ferrajoli, Luigi, *Derecho y Razón*, trans. Perfecto A. Ibáñez, Madrid, Ed. Trotta, 1989, p. 764.

8 Cf. Maier, Julio B.J., *Derecho Procesal Penal, I Fundamentos*, Buenos Aires, Ed. Del Puerto, 2004 (2nd edn), p. 369.

independent and oppositional media) would be put into operation, so as to deny in the face of public opinion, foreign states and human rights organizations, everything relating to the illegal detentions, torture and other crimes against humanity perpetrated by this unleashed *Leviathan*. This promise was certainly fulfilled.

In other words, it was not with the tools of the exercise of the *formal punitive power* that the military regime in question carried out such illegal detentions, tortures and other crimes against those it considered is political enemies; rather it was through a premeditated widespread and criminal exercise of *clandestine punitive power* that they accounted for them. This methodology was kept secret by every means possible and, like any exercise of state violence freed from the restraints of the rule of law, immediately degenerated into state terrorism.[9]

We must remember here that the question of the secret maintenance of the power apparatus with the objective of committing, with pretensions to impunity, crimes which interfere with the life, dignity and freedom of the people, was not something unique to a particular regime. A similar strategy was undertaken by Nazism and Stalinism, amongst others.[10]

Every one of these regimes has respected the rule according to which "the more visible the government agencies, the less is their power, and the less known the institution, the stronger it will prove to be in the end [...] the real power begins where secrecy begins".[11]

9 A thorough analysis of the concept of state terrorism can be found in Garzón Valdés, Ernesto: *Derecho, Ética y Política*, Madrid, Ed Centre for Constitutional Studies, 1993, pp. 841–869: "when the government becomes the agent of indiscriminate or diffuse terror, it re-creates the conditions of the state of nature in which human life becomes 'nasty, brutish and short', to use Hobbes's famous formulation [...] the government abandons its role as executor of the laws to become a contender in the struggle for power. In this sense, state terrorism ends by undermining the very foundations of the justification of political organization" (p. 864).

10 Garzón Valdés defines as one of three characteristic components of state terrorism, the "illegal imposition of state-sanctioned measures banned by the officially proclaimed legal order (torture and murder, among others)". Nazism and Stalinism, among others, are referred to as examples (p. 845ff.).

11 Cf. Arendt, Hannah, *Los orígenes del totalitarismo*, trans. Guillermo Solana, Madrid, Alianza Editorial, 2002, p. 608.

To carry out its proposed objectives, any regime in which an unrestricted police state prevails forcibly removes its alleged political enemies from their spheres of belonging, whether family, social, cultural, or the circuits of social communication. It thus deprives them of all socio-legal significance: "the first essential step on the road to total domination". Arendt argues, "is to kill the juridical person in the man".[12]

Thus the citizen, both the natural and the legal person, becomes simply a *disappeared*, in relation to whom the holders of the clandestine apparatus of power (released from all limits by the ruling military leadership) had all the means necessary to either annihilate him or continue his illegal detention while transferring him from the clandestine criminal justice system to the formalized criminal justice system (legalization by the executive branch), or releasing him directly or permitting his exit abroad. This was clearly established in judicial proceedings relating to state terrorism in Argentina.

It is obvious that the widespread and indiscriminate perpetration of crimes against humanity against the purported enemies of the state during those years by the holders of the state's punitive power necessarily generated the emergence of radically new spatial areas[13] in which violence could be deployed without limits or external controls: "… a seemingly innocuous area [that] actually delimits a space in which the normal legal order is suspended and where whether or not atrocities were committed is not something that depends on law, but only […] on the police who temporarily act as sovereign".[14]

12 Ibid., p. 665.

13 Traverso argues that such camps are "a new phenomenon responding to a different logic" because in them the cessation of any connection to the outside can be verified, together with the suppression of identity and the complete loss of spatial and temporal references, amid conditions of extreme physical and psychological abuse, which distance it from the experience of mere prison. It is the irruption of the universe of the concentration camp (Traverso, Enzo, *La violencia nazi*, trans. Horrac Beatrice and Martin Dupaus, Buenos Aires, Fondo de Cultura Económica, 2003, p. 41).

14 See Agamben, Giorgio, *Homo sacer. El poder soberano y la nuda vida*, trans. Antonio Gimeno Cuspinera, Valencia, Ed. Pre-textos, 2003, p. 222.

The enclosures which had the characteristics of a concentration camp received in every state authority a particular name. Amongst us, that of *centro clandestino de detención y tortura* (clandestine centre of detention and torture) was imposed.[15]

15 Formed in the special case of Argentina with elements borrowed from the Nazi concentration camp, intermingled with the characteristic features of the *pozo* (den) or *aguantadero* (safe house) of the common criminal. This genetic crossbreeding is what distinguishes the clandestine detention and torture centre as an entirely new institution, distinguishable from the concentration camp characteristic of the Nazi regime. Thus, for example, the permanent *tabicamiento* (blindfolding) so as to prevent recognition of their captors or the absolute prohibition of speech, which did not exist in the concentration camp. Another distinguishing element is their visibility. The clandestine detention and torture centre was secret and endeavoured to remain concealed and invisible to the social environment; the concentration camp, by contrast, was highly visible, was placed at the centre of the criminal justice system and served the social function of intimidation towards those non-deviant elements and was thus indispensable to the stability and reproduction of the police state. The differences are even greater when the clandestine detention and torture centre is compared to the *extermination camp*: in the latter, their unambiguous purpose is none other than the mass production of corpses; the clandestine detention and torture centres are far removed from this, for the murders are carried out systematically, that is, as a rule the transferals take place outside of the centres: executions in open country, flights of death, etc. On this subject, the survivor of Mansión Seré and ESMA, Calveiro Pilar is clear: "[t]he secrecy surrounding removal procedures makes it one of the least known parts of the process [...] In a few cases, they were transported to prisons far from the camp, they were shot, bound and gagged, before proceeding to the burial and cremation of the corpses, or to discarding the bodies in public places so as to simulate fighting. But the method which was apparently adopted on a mass scale consisted in the camp staff injecting prisoners with soporifics and loading them onto trucks, presumably driven by personnel who were not part of the internal operations [...] Gagged, numb, handcuffed, hooded lumps, the packages were thrown alive into the sea ". Calveiro, Pilar, *Poder y desaparición. Los campos de concentración en Argentina*, Buenos Aires, Ed Colihue, 2004, pp. 38–39. Nevertheless, as appears from the title of the work, they call them concentration and extermination camps, cf. also p. 29: "[b]etween 1976 and 1982 340 extermination camps operated in Argentina, located throughout the country".

All institutions inspired by the universe of the concentration camp[16] reveal certain constants. In addition to the large number of victims who pass through them, there is the radical transformation of the perception of those held in them: invariably, they lose their status as citizens, people, human beings, to become objects as non-persons.[17]

Thus, in the context of the policy of state terrorism developed by the military dictatorship and the mechanism of the systematic disappearance of people, clandestine detention and torture centres (CCDT) have formed a vital piece of the repressive machinery. Arendt argues that these physical spaces specially prepared for captivity, torture and death are the true central institution of the organizing power imposed by the state terrorism.[18]

Thus, the existence of these enclosures with features of the concentration camp in Argentina in the mid-1970s, and the verified perpetration of thousands of unimaginably cruel and sadistic crimes against humanity in them, followed by the *transfers* for their subsequent physical elimination, have been the blackest page in our history as a country. Not just because of the fact itself of their existence, but also because they burst from the hand of state activity in the context of a supposedly civilized society, with the highest level of education in the whole of Latin America and similar cultural standards to those of Europe, at least in its major urban centres.[19]

In these compounds, the prejudicing of fundamental rights such as dignity and freedom is the rule. The levels of violence and terror inflicted on the victims have been of such a magnitude, and death has reached such a high level that it can only be said of them, as their common denominator, that in their womb "everything was possible".[20]

16 The common denominator of the material conditions – beyond the times and the regimes responsible – which are imposed in such sites or *spaces of non-law*, leading to systematic dehumanization of the prisoners held there.

17 Cf. Todorov, Tzvetan, *Frente al límite*, trans. Federico Álvarez, Mexico, Ed. Siglo XXI, 2004 (2nd edn), pp. 268–269.

18 Arendt, *Los orígenes ...*, p. 653.

19 In the same vein, see Sancinetti & Ferrante, who argue that from the start of the 24/3/76 coup, "the human rights violations at this stage had a generality, extension, planning and brutality previously unknown in the history the country", p. 102.

20 Thus in Arendt, *Los orígenes ...*, p. 652.

Finally, the establishment of secret detention and torture centres was also part of the anticipation of impunity for the aberrant events which took place in them. That is why the maintenance in secret of these sites was a central issue for its constant reproduction: the experiment of total domination in this class of compound depends on their isolation from the outside world.[21]

It permitted not justifying the arrests nor the *sine die* prolongation of the state of illegal privation of liberty. It permitted systematic denial of any information about the fate of subjects in the face of the formal requirements of judicial and human rights organizations. It made it possible not to bring the prisoners to trial and thus deprive them of every defence and thus to decide arbitrarily their final destination. It permitted isolating them from family and friends, putting pressure on them and torturing them because nobody would see or would ascertain the consequences.

The strategy of impunity would later count on symbolic links, not only during the period of the military regime but also once democracy had been reinstated in Argentina. Under military rule this included the enactment of the *de facto* Law No. 22,924 known as the "self-amnesty law" signed by the president, General Reinaldo Bignone on 23 September 1983, a month before the elections that restored democratic system in Argentina. After the return to democracy it was done through Law 23,492 *Punto final* and after the military uprising of April 1987, by means of Law No. 23,521 of *Obediencia debida*.

This was a question of concessions made by the nascent democracy in the face of the enormous potential for harm demonstrated by certain sectors of the armed forces at that time which were ready to rise up against the established power. This was due to the direct opposition of middle-ranking military officers to the convening of civil courts on account of their involvement in crimes against humanity during the last military dictatorship.

Indeed, the military corporation achieved its goal in the sense that the enactment of these laws almost completely put a stop to those investigations. This freezing lasted from 1987 until 2001, when, in an incipient way, the Federal Court began to take the path of reopening such criminal proceedings.

21 See Arendt, *Los orígenes ...*, p. 653.

Today both laws, after their formal repeal by Law 24 952 (BO 17/04/98), on the part of the same Congress which had enacted them, have been expressly declared void by Law 25779 (BO 09/03/03). Their obvious unconstitutionality has furthermore been consecrated by numerous courts including the *Corte Suprema de Justicia de la Nación* (Supreme Court of Justice of the Nation).[22]

The declaration of the unconstitutionality of the military pardons

Another of the legal obstacles Argentina faced in the process of seeking justice and truth with respect to its recent past, was the numerous presidential pardons signed by Carlos Menem in late 1989 and in 1990, shortly after assuming his first term as president.

Through a series of Executive decrees Menem appealed to the prerogative established in the Constitution. Not only did he pardon the military leaders convicted five years previously for crimes against humanity, but he also extended the application of the pardon to every single the military officer involved in every case being dealt with at that time in the country relating to the state terrorism carried out during the last military dictatorship.

Thus, hundreds of defendants were the lucky beneficiaries of President Menem's decrees of pardon. This act went down in history as the second great moment of consecration of impunity for these events, after the enactment of laws of *Obediencia Debida* and *Punto Final* a few years earlier by President Alfonsín.

22 See Guembe, María José, "Obligación de investigar y sancionar graves violaciones a los derechos humanos" in Abramovich, Víctor, Bovino, Alberto & Courtis, Christian (eds), *La aplicación de los tratados sobre derechos humanos en el ámbito local. La experiencia de una década*, Buenos Aires, Ed. Del Puerto/CELS, 2006, pp. 431–445.

Both these laws of impunity and Menem's pardons were resisted by a considerable number of federal high courts around the country, which even in those days attempted to show them to be unconstitutional so as to continue to proceed with the cases. However, all roads were closed when, in several *leading cases*, the *Corte Suprema de Justicia de la Nación*, with the membership it had in those years, upheld the constitutionality of both the laws of impunity and the pardons of convicted prisoners and those on remand.

It was thus that Argentina remained marginalized from the universal demands for the trial and punishment of crimes against humanity until 2001, when the first ruling by a federal judge, "Simón" was issued. From this point this tendency began to be reversed.

The "Simón" ruling in 2001 was the first crack to show in the dam of impunity which had been raised around these events. That crack has continued to expand from the point at which other judges began to do the same in their cases, when the federal chambers of the second instance ratified this unconstitutionality, and when finally, the wall broke definitively with the landmark ruling of the *Corte Suprema de Justicia de la Nación* where it was expressly stated that the pardons are unconstitutional (the "Riveros" of ruling, 13 July 2007).

In this important precedent, with the votes of the judges Lorenzetti, Highton, Maqueda and Zaffaroni, the *Corte Suprema de Justicia de la Nación* (Supreme Court of Justice of the Nation) declared the unconstitutionality of a 1989 presidential decree by means of which there had been pardoned, among others, the above-mentioned James Omar Riveros, who was the military commander of IV Corps and as such responsible for thousands of abductions and disappearances in the province of Buenos Aires.

At the time, a Federal Court, in dealing with the argument, was swayed by the "constitutionality" of that presidential pardon, but the Second Division of the *Cámara Nacional de Casación Penal* (National Chamber of Criminal Appeal) overturned the decision and declared the unconstitutionality of that decree, a decision confirmed finally by the highest court in this ruling which we are discussing.

In the Riveros case – and I follow here the summary made by the highest court itself – the Court stated that, because of their severity, crimes against humanity are contrary not only to the Constitution, but also the entire international community. For this reason the obligation incumbent on all States to throw light on them and identify the culprits also arises from international treaties and even *jus cogens*, which is the highest source of international law, and is not susceptible to being abrogated by any treaty to the contrary.

At that point, the *Corte Suprema* recorded its recent pronouncements in the cases of Arancibia Clavel and Simón, in which it declared the imprescriptibility of crimes against humanity and the unconstitutionality of the laws known as *Obediencia Debida* and *Punto Final* respectively.

It was reiterated in the decision, moreover, that after the reform of the Constitution, international human rights treaties have constitutional status and that by the will of the constitutional convention it has been desired that the international jurisprudence on the matter serve as a guide to interpretation by the judges.

On these juridical bases, the Court analysed international jurisprudence, in particular that of the *Corte Interamericana de Derechos Humanos* (Inter-American Court of Human Rights), which prohibits the use of statutes of limitations, amnesties or pardons.

It cited in particular the cases Barrios Altos and Almonacid of the *Corte Interamericana de Derechos Humanos*, regarding the scope and limits of *res judicata* and the guarantee against double prosecution for such crimes. It also mentioned various United Nations resolutions opposing the pardon.

This solution involved the majority of the Court, composed of judges Lorenzetti, Highton, Maqueda and Zaffaroni.

It is interesting to point out that in one of the two dissents from the ruling, Judge Carmen Argibay, did not share the solution with respect to the constitutionality of a pardon.

In this regard, she recalled that in this same case, the *Corte Suprema* itself had issued a ruling in 1990 which left firm a statement which had declared the pardon constitutional, all of which leads to the conclusion that it happened on the authority of *res judicata*.

From the point of view of this premise, and not without first noting that this pardon was considered unconstitutional for having been issued for the benefit of persons prosecuted and convicted, Dr Argibay said that *res judicata* has constitutional protection, is also recognized by various international human rights treaties, and is one of the pillars on which the rule of law rest. Leaving aside the disgust the consequences of a judicial decision taken seventeen years ago may cause, she argued, these considerations prevent a question being reopened which has been settled definitively and can not be revised without violating explicit constitutional provisions.

Apart from this dissent, and on the basis of the findings of the majority of the judges of the *Corte Suprema* of Argentina, it became clear in this ruling that the requirement of the international community under which all legal barriers to the prosecution and punishment those responsible for crimes against humanity should be removed, is supreme even in the face of a ruling in that respect emanating from the highest court of a state in the post dictatorial period.

In short, it is always preferable that the judicial power of the state itself retrace the path of impunity by means of the judicial remedies its own national law, than to arrive at the same conclusion through a secure condemnation of that State by the various international jurisdictional bodies which monitor compliance with the fundamental rights enshrined in human rights treaties both regional and universal.

Finally, it should be mentioned that President Menem, under the so-called slogan of the attempted *reconciliation among Argentines*, not only pardoned all those prosecuted and convicted for crimes enframed within the terrorism the state, including those most responsible such as Videla and Massera. He also pardoned the leaders of the leftist armed groups who were once condemned as responsible for attacks also carried out during those years.

The underlying message of Menem's policy on the subject was based on the discourse favoured by the representatives of the military dictatorship, who alleged, as a justificatory discourse of illegal state violence, the existence of "two sides". These equally matched, sides, the argument goes, would have disputed a "military conflict", a "war", in the framework of which, there would have acted not one but "two warring demons", in the context of which, the "excesses" were inevitable.

The other Menemist pardons directed at the leaders of the armed groups have been excluded in principle from the declarations of unconstitutionality. Because of this, there was no shortage of presentations to the courts, and even some fiscal ruling (in the case of Larrabure of the province of Santa Fe), which led to the enforcement of the category of crime against humanity so as to deprive these other pardons of effect.

Nevertheless, the highest levels of the Argentinean judicial system, especially the *Procurador General de la Nación* (Attorney-General's Office), have denied this possibility. They consider that at the time of the events in question there is no doubt that the concept of crime against humanity required for its formation, in addition to the *massive* and *systematic* elements, the *state* component, which for the cases of the armed groups cannot be satisfied. On the contrary, it is clear that these leftist organizations which chose the path of violence had as their main objectives of their activism, the State and its various representatives, in particular the armed and security forces.

The result is that the impediment to considering the crimes committed by these armed groups as crimes against humanity means a double lock on attempts to reopen such proceedings. These are, first, the existence of pardons not subject to cancellation, and, second, in those cases where there have been no pardons, the criminal statute of limitations due to the passage of time. It is now more than thirty years since the commission of the offences.

Notwithstanding this, we must not omit consideration in this context that the vast majority of the members of leftist organizations were punished by the "police justice" of the last military dictatorship. Tens of thousands were kidnapped and tortured and the majority of them were killed or remain in the condition of the disappeared. Thousands of others suffered years in prison, accused of a wide range of political crimes. And finally, tens of thousands of activists were forced to flee their spheres of belonging or forced to go into exile. Furthermore, many relatives, friends and close friends of these victims of political persecution suffered illegal state penalties too.

Perhaps these state actions should not be included in the account of the "police justice" of the Argentine criminal state? Military and police personnel decided to condemn tens of thousands of people to the penalties of the deprivation of liberty, torture, death, and forced exile for membership of, closeness to or sympathy with these organizations.

It cannot even remotely be said, on the strength of those pardons to a handful of the leaders of such organizations, that they have gone unpunished for their attacks. Contrary to what the negationists and relativists try to suggest, the degree of impunity of the perpetrators of state terrorism until the reopening of the trials in recent years is unequalled when compared to the persecutions widespread mass atrocities suffered by those who in those years were defined as their political enemies and the almost total absence of trial and punishment of those responsible.

The further evolution of Argentinean Justice since the "Riveros" ruling

From the time of the "Riveros" ruling and up to the present, there has been a formidable process of reopening of cases related to state terrorism in Argentina. To date, more than a thousand people have been accused, some of them have already been condemned and the majority are the non-participating witnesses in oral and public trials which will continue to be carried out.

In the case of the trial known as the First Army Corps case, over the last five years the courts have recognized a thousand victims, and 100 defendants, including Army and Air Force personnel, members of the security forces, intelligence and correctional services have been arrested and charged. These include all levels from the highest head (Videla) to those who tortured with their own hand.

The line of inquiry in which the existence of clandestine detention and torture centres known as Club Atlético, El Banco and El Olimpo,[23] were investigated, has involved 320 victims and defendants. For its part, the investigation linked to the clandestine centre El Vesubio has included 200 victims and ten accused. Without doubt, however, the most important and complex trial to have taken place in Argentina was that of the concentration camp of the ESMA (School of Naval Mechanics),[24] located in Buenos Aires, which encompassed some 600 victims and fifty accused, mostly members of the Argentinean Navy. It ended with the condemnation of seventeen repressors, the majority of whom were of high rank.

This forecast of progress in the cases and the imminence of trials is repeated throughout the country, in different jurisdictions. This has also been supported recently through the Supreme Court which, in February 2010, created a *Comisión Inter-poderes* (an "Inter-powers Commission") in order to expedite to the utmost the completion of these trials. This Commission is made up of representatives of the judiciary, the *Ministerio de Justicia* (Ministry of Justice), the *Congreso Nacional* (National Congress), the *Consejo de la Magistratura* (Council of the Judiciary) and the *Procuración General de la Nación* (Attorney General's Office), and is functioning optimally in solving every kind of problem which is presented.

23 All the judgments made in the context of this case can be consulted comprehensively and exhaustively in the official website of the *Corte Suprema*, www.cij.gov.ar, micro-site "Primer Cuerpo de Ejército". For more detail, especially in relation to the legal definition of crimes of torture and illegal deprivation of liberty, see Rafecas, Daniel E., *La tortura y otras prácticas ilegales a detenidos*, Buenos Aires, Ed Del Puerto, 2010, chapters IV and VI.

24 The ESMA judgment handed down on 26 October 2011 saw the condemnation of Alfredo Astiz, Jorge Eduardo Acosta, Ricardo Cavallo, Juan Carlos Rolón, Antonio Pernías and Adolfo Donda.

Genocide in the Argentinean case?

In the context of this country-wide reopening of criminal cases related to the investigation of the illegal detentions, torture and killings during the military dictatorship, a number of procedural actors have advocated the introduction of the legal definition of genocide in decisions and judgments related to these cases, so as to connote the context in which those crimes against freedom, dignity and life, were committed.

What was posed was the possibility of giving expression in judicial decisions, that is, in the communication circuit of the judiciary itself, to the reference to the *Argentinean genocide* which seems already to be to a large extent consolidated politically and in the media in Argentina.

That, without casting any doubt on the need to assign the status of crimes against humanity to the crimes which are accepted as proven in this type of court case, a condition which then ensured their imprescriptibility, as well as the other consequences envisaged by the legal system on the matter.

Even then, there were not a few private plaintiffs (and some prosecutors) who postulated that the crimes investigated qualify as committed *in the context of genocide.*

In this regard, it should be noted, first, that the plain or social sense of the meaning genocide is indeed broad and encompassing, and in this context coincides with the accusatory claims analysed here. Indeed, it is only necessary to go to the Dictionary of the Real Academia Española to see that it is defined there as "[e]xtermination or systematic elimination of a social group because of race, religion or politics".

Furthermore, we have witnessed in recent decades a generalization of references to the *Argentine genocide*, both by representatives of the victims of state terrorism and by referents of political or legislative agencies or legislative policy. This has undoubtedly been based on the influence which the work of renowned local sociologists such as Daniel Feierstein[25] or Marcelo

25 Cf. *El genocidio como práctica social*, Buenos Aires, FCE, 2007 and more recently, "La Argentina: genocidio y/o crimen contra la humanidad? Sobre el rol del derecho en

Raffin,[26] among others, has had in this respect. They are all advocates – in the field of sociology – of a definition of genocide which covers the events which occurred in Argentina during the dictatorship military.

However, the introduction of the term genocide into the language of the law requires a more detailed analysis of the issue, because it is a question of integrating a *normative* term into the jurisdictional circuit. To that end, any definition, any concept, must necessarily have a *formal source* of legal coinage, be it in domestic law or international law, in order to be received, and from there, generate the consequences which that same legal system provides for before its use.

What is specifically needed, then, for the purposes to which a large number of the private plaintiffs in these trials aspire, is, in first place, that we have some legal rules which have introduced the concept of *genocide* into our system.

And in the second place, that this juridical definition of *genocide* enables the framing of the episodes raised in these cases within this definition, in order thus to have acceded to what is requested. In this way the legal consequences projected – both material and symbolic – are legitimately claimed.

The first question is completely beyond dispute, for on 9 April 1956 Argentina ratified the text of the Convention on the Prevention and Punishment of the Crime of Genocide, adopted by the United Nations on 9 December 1948, and whose entry into force took place on 12 January 1951. It is an international charter which acquired constitutional status through the 1994 constitutional reform, because of its express provision in Article 75 inc. 75 inc. 22, CN 22, CN.

This definition has been confirmed more recently in the international concert of nations, through Article 6 of the so-called Rome Statute of 17 July 1998, which mandated the creation of the International Criminal Court, which Argentina joined on 8 February 2001.

---

la construcción de la memoria colectiva", in *Nueva Doctrina Penal*, 2008/A, Buenos Aires, Ed. Del Puerto, 2008, pp. 211–230.

26 *La experiencia del horror*, Buenos Aires, Ed. Del Puerto, 2006.

As a corollary of this initiative, on 9 January 2007 Law 26,200 was published in the *Boletín Oficial de la República Argentina* (*Official Gazette of the Republic of Argentina*). With it, the treaty which gave rise to the International Criminal Court is implemented in domestic law.

It is settled, then, that the first question, as to whether in Argentinean law we have any valid legal rule which allows the introduction of a normative concept of *genocide* in a hypothetical court ruling, must be answered affirmatively.

Let us now analyse the second question by determining whether this *legal* concept of *genocide* enables us to include within this definition the facts established in the judicial investigations.

It is clear that the letter of the UN Convention of 1948 excluded political groups from the groups protected by the Convention.

It must be added that, as well as being transferred to the Rome Statute, this narrow definition of genocide has also been followed more recently in both Article 4 (2) of the Yugoslav Statute of 1993 (ICTY, Decision 808), and Article 2 (2) of the Rwanda Statute of 1994 (ICTR, Resolution 995). This also comes through very clearly in the jurisprudence of both instances of the respective courts currently in operation.

For its part, the specialized doctrine on the subject of international human rights law is virtually unanimous in recognizing this genealogy,[27] and in accepting the exclusion of political groups from the framework of the Convention, and therefore of the Statute of Rome. This is usually accompanied by a note critical of such an exclusion, which is deemed arbitrary and unfortunate, motivated by political reasons mostly related to ensuring the rapid endorsement of the Convention, something has certainly been widely achieved.[28]

27 See for example, the analysis made by William Schabas of the evolution of the process and the negotiations which culminated in the ratification of the Convention, which led him to conclude that political groups were initially included within the list to be protected, and later excluded with the end of facilitating speedy ratification (*Genocide in International Law: The Crime of Crimes*, Cambridge, Cambridge University Press, 2000).

28 See the positions in favour and against this exclusion in Lozada, Martín: "El crimen de genocidio. Su renovada dimensión a 60 años de su construcción conceptual",

When the question is viewed from the standpoint of the twenty first century, the main cost of such a universal consensus has been without doubt, the exclusion of *political genocide* or *politicide* from the protection of the Convention, and thus the impossibility of legally defining as *genocide* around three quarters of the group conflicts which have taken place in the world since then. This, as I have said, has come under heavy criticism, especially in the field of international criminal law, from lawyers such as Albin Eser, Kai Ambos or Hans-Heinrich Jescheck among others.[29]

For example, Professor Natan Lerner has recently argued in this regard that "[i]t is clear that the Convention should be updated and, in the opinion of some, also extended to protect other groups than those currently covered by Article 2 of the text. Serious cases of the mass destruction of people defined by their social or political orientation has taken place and a strict application of the Convention does not permit its extension to such situations".[30]

Let me also quote the recognized expert Barbara Harff, who coined the suggestive term *politicide* to connote *political genocide*. In a recent paper she said in this regard:

> In the first place, the Convention [against Genocide] does not include groups of victims defined by their political stance or their actions in this regard. Raphael Lemkin (1944) coined the term genocide and then sought the support of as many states as possible to prepare a legal document prohibiting mass killings and establishing sanctions against the perpetrators. Because the first version of the Convention, including

---

in *Revista de Derecho Penal y Procesal Penal*, nº 6, junio 2009, Buenos Aires, Ed. Abeledo-Perrot, pp. 996–997.

29 See the citations in Feijóo Sánchez, Bernardo: "El Genocidio en el Derecho Penal Español (art. 607)", *Cuadernos de Doctrina y Jurisprudencia Penal*, Buenos Aires, ed. Ad Hoc, Año V, nº 8–c, p. 561.

30 Cf. "De Auschwitz y Nuremberg a Srebrenice y Darfur: la sexagenaria Convención contra Genocidio", *Persona y Derecho*, Ed. Univ. de Navarra, nº 58, pp. 45–70. The cited author adds that in this sense the Convention responded basically to the teachings of the Second World War and especially the Holocaust.

> political groups, was rejected by the USSR and its allies, the final version omitted any reference to political killings. The concept of *politicide* is used here to cover cases in which the victims defined politically [...].[31]

In this paper, Harff crystallized deep investigative work in which she identified as either *genocide* or *politicide*, or as both together, all acts that met such characteristics carried out between 1955 and 2001.

In the *genocides*, victim groups are defined by their perpetrators primarily in terms of their communal characteristics.

In *politicides*, on the other hand, groups are defined primarily in terms of their political opposition to the regime and dominant groups.

Both have in common the fact that the killings are never accidental or the result of individual actions, "but are carried out under the explicit or implicit direction of state authorities, or those who claim the authority of the State".[32]

Among the cases of *politicide*, Harff records the case of Argentina between March 1976 and December 1980, with a range of murder victims of up to 20,000 persons.

That said, so far we have dealt with the existing definitions of genocide internationally. But the truth is that for the purpose of channelling attempts to define the Argentine case as *genocide*, we could easily have referred to a local criminal law which deals with this crime.

For without prejudice to the full force of the Convention, nothing ever prevented the member States from categorizing *genocide* as a crime within their criminal codes, even going beyond the scope assigned by the International Charter, to encompass, for example, *political genocide* or *politicide* within the range of their territories.

31 Harff, Bárbara, "¿No se aprendieron las lecciones del Holocausto? Evaluando los riesgos de genocidio y matanzas políticas desde 1955", trans. Gabriela Pazos, in AA.VV., *Genocidio. La administración de la muerte en la modernidad*, ed. Daniel Feierstein, Caseros, Ed. Eduntref, 2005, pp. 172–173.

32 Op. cit., p. 174.

Moreover, the creation of criminal penalties which suppress genocide in the domestic legislation of the member States was expressly encouraged by the United Nations in its resolution 96 (I) of 11 December, 1946, in which "The General Assembly affirmed that genocide was a crime under international law and called on Member States of the United Nations to adopt the legislation necessary for the prevention and punishment of this crime".[33] And indeed, most States include the offence of genocide in their criminal codes. While most local lawmakers respected the scope assigned by the Convention for persecuted groups (race, ethnicity, religion or nation), as is the case of Article 607 of the Spanish Penal Code of 1995, Article 220 of the German Criminal Code or the Italian Law 962 of 1967, there is no shortage of examples of sanctions against genocide which went beyond this standard, and in all cases, thereby also projected the criminal protection of the political group.

On our continent, we can cite the case of Bolivia, which in Article 138 of its *Código Penal*, after defining the crime of genocide and determining as protected groups the national, ethnic and religious groups, states, "the author or authors, or other people directly or indirectly guilty of bloody massacres in the country, will incur the same penalty".

This reference is so wide as to undoubtedly cover the planned acts of destruction of groups due to political motivations. References which also refer to the protection of political groups are also found in the article 319 of the Paraguayan *Código Penal* (listing the national, ethnic, religious or social), Article 101 of the Colombian *Código Penal* (which, in addition to the four groups of the Convention, also mentions the political group, although it limited this to those groups "acting within the law") and Article 319 of the Peruvian *Código Penal*, which also extends to social groups in its definition of genocide. Finally we might mention Article 375 of Costa Rica, which covers groups of people based on "nationality, race or religious or political beliefs".

33 Cf. Robinson, Nehemiah, *La convención sobre Genocidio*, trans. Natan Lerner, Buenos Aires, Ed. Bibliográfica Omeba, 1960, pp. 111ff., p. 17.

Despite the recommendations of the UN for over 50 years, despite the widespread categorization in comparative legislations (even in our region) and in spite of the serious acts of state terrorism experienced in our country, it is regrettable that in Argentina we still can not count on a criminal classification which includes genocide in our criminal justice system. The possibility of formulating the Argentine case as a genocide in the legal sense from the perspective of domestic law appears, then, remote. In order to include political groups in the definition of genocide, a criminal offence which includes this crime would be required in a very fundamental way at the very least, and on this basis it would be necessary that the offence cover, among the groups targeted, *political groups*. In Argentina, we can count on neither one nor the other. So, as a sort of final survey of what has been reviewed so far on this subject, we can state the following:

First, that Argentina suffered during the last military dictatorship the force of state terrorism which led to the systematic persecution of victims for political reasons.

Second, that never in its history has Argentina sanctioned a criminal offence which represses genocide. Hence it lacks a locally produced normative provision related to this crime which can be applied to the case and, moreover, still less one which would be useful, in considering whether or not *political groups* are covered.

However, it is by going to the normative output of the international order to which Argentina adheres, that we can find a *legal* definition of *genocide*. This is a definition which emerges, in a harmonious way, both in Article 75 inc. 75 inc. 22 of the CN (the UN Convention against Genocide) and in Law No. 26 200 which ratifies the Rome Statute of the Permanent Court Building and International.

Finally, this *legal* definition of genocide, which has its roots in international law, is the only formal source of application to the case, in view of its historical omission in its treatment at the local level. It does not, however, cover political groups as possible victims of this crime.

It is from the logical linking of these findings that a negative response to this type of argument is arrived at. Although it has been proven that the matters under investigation are undoubtedly a *political genocide* or *politicide*, this kind of case has been excluded from the scope of international charters already made. Added to this is the prevailing legal orphanhood at the local level, and hence the judge is forbidden to change this situation, however laudable may be his reasons for doing so.

To do otherwise would not only be to work against the principle of legality enshrined in Article 18 of The Constitution in seeking a broad interpretation of treaty provisions. It would also provide a clear example of the appropriation of legislative powers by the court, which would defeat the republican scheme which governs us and would undermine fundamental procedural guarantees such as the right of anyone accused of a crime to *due process of law*.

In political terms, it is a question of giving up certain punitive desires prohibited by the full and effective enforcement of criminal and constitutional procedural guarantees for all defendants, including those involved in these processes. If it is true that these processes put in play the ethical superiority of the rule of law over the authoritarian state, then we must take care, under the administration of criminal justice, not to engage in situations which put on hold the direct and categorical devaluation of the latter, especially its arbitrariness and unpredictability.

Conclusions

In short, Argentina has managed – not without effort – to remove each and every one of the many material and legal obstacles preventing the progress of these trials, and thus, has travelled the always painful and difficult road of recovering the memory and bloody history of our recent past.

This was achieved through a firm state policy consistent across all three republican powers and sustained over time. By means of this policy it was able to move through a scenario in which, on a daily basis and with much effort, light was shed where before there had been darkness, the truth was discovered and justice ensured, always in the framework of respect required by the unrestricted effect of all the constitutional guarantees of the State Constitutional Law itself, from the state of innocence, passing through due process, to the strict principle of legality and guilt.

In short, with these trials, which I believe to be exemplary, Argentina, has been able to distance herself inexorably from the authoritarian model of the state which dominated the political stage for much of the twentieth century, and definitively consolidate a democratic culture and the rule of law, reaffirming the universal message against this type of heinous crime: "Nunca más".

CARLOS ROZANSKI

Crimes Against Humanity and Genocide: Origins and Meaning of the Prohibitions

How long would man survive on the Earth without law ? Not long. When the little monkey climbed down from the tree, the way of resolving problems with other little monkeys was without doubt the use of violence.

One of the important features common to man and animal is that both have been endowed with a so-called benign aggressivity which is eminently defensive, biologically adaptive and as such is at the service of life. This means that the brains of animals are programmed philogenetically to mobilize their impulses to fight or flee only when their essential interests are in danger: food, offspring, access to females. When this danger disappears, so too does aggression. But there is another type of aggression. This one is malignant and is not derived from the animal instincts and does not serve for physiological survival. This aggression is exclusively human and makes man the only living being capable of killing, torturing and destroying individuals of his own species without any sound biological or material benefit, although of course, many commit these acts also for some kind of profit, especially economic.

These differences, amongst other factors, make man and animal relate to the world in different ways. While animals do so by means of instinctively determined mechanisms, man does so by acquiring and assimilating objects (the process of assimilation) and relating them to other persons and to himself (the process of socialization). The principle of the evolution of the individual is the search for happiness. But happiness can never be achieved without the inclusion of this individual in a community. There the problems begin because the aforementioned processes of assimilation and socialization are not automatic nor are they produced naturally and spontaneously, but on the contrary, during their course necessarily generate conflicts. If man were, like the animals, a creature which solely reacted in the face of attack (benign aggression), the neighbour would represent a probable source of aid. But the rest of the community often constitutes for him a temptation to satisfy his own aggression, his inclination to exploit his fellow men, abuse them sexually, seize their property and even kill them. Similar trends, present to a greater or lesser extent in every human being, cannot but cause enormous difficulties in complying with that premise of inclusion in a community, essential to the achievement of any kind of happiness.

It is there that culture finds its greatest challenge. It must put a stop to these tendencies in men to attack each other and prevent violence impeding the realization of living in a community, which is the indispensable prerequisite of a dignified existence. Thus, the human being has from ancient times used norms which regulate coexistence, this being one of the most important resources culture has for putting up a barrier to these tendencies which without proper restraint would end up destroying it. Of course these normative limits, and in particular the repression organized by the penal systems, imply a new violence which often outweighs the harm done by the behaviours which the community censures and which, more often than not, are caused by the state itself. But, accepting that it would not be possible to coexist without norms, the challenge is to construct a society in which complying with the laws implies a greater social benefit than violating them. In summary, if in order to achieve happiness man needs, in addition to his personal evolution, his membership of a community, he will have to resign a part of his aggressive impulses in order to fit into the group. Thus Freud maintained that the civilized man has bartered a portion of his possible happiness for a portion of security.[1]

It is obvious that this renunciation of the primary impulses was not and will not be easy. There will always be individuals who are not disposed to resign any of their aggressive tendencies and will try to satisfy their emotional and material desires without taking into account the harm which this satisfaction occasions. There will also be those who, in spite of complying punctually with the sacrifices imposed by culture by means of norms, do not receive in return that portion of "security" for which they resigned their

1 S. Freud, *El malestar en la cultura*, Madrid, Alianza Editorial, 2006.

primary impulses. In both cases the responsibility of the community leaders is enormous. In the first hypothesis, establishing a legal system which represses those behaviours considered harmful but which does so from a three-dimensional perspective under no circumstances represents, either for the transgressors or for the society, a greater harm than that caused by the transgression. In the second hypothesis, the life of the community is driven and administered with such honesty that those who comply with the rules of the game feel the least possible amount of frustration. All of this is linked to the need to put up a barrier against violence, to put a stop to the destructive tendency which is present in every human being.

When impunity is an established phenomenon in a society it is proof of the failure of the directing class, especially when it comes to sanctioning those who have committed the most horrendous crimes, whose maximum expression is genocide. In that sense, when those who kidnapped, tortured, disappeared and killed people on the part of the state perceive that they will not be sentenced, or that the risk of being sentenced is minimal, they not only have an incentive to continue or start again their crimes – when there was a democratic period in between – but rather constitute in addition an example to common criminals who experience that impunity as a model to be imitated. On the contrary, when societies manage to confront with sincerity and energy the violations suffered, the result not only is different, but offers the majority of the members of that society the enjoyable feeling that a future is possible in which essential rights are respected. As will be seen, the trajectory of the Argentinean ruling class is in this sense a clear example of this.

The Argentinean State in the face of the Violations of Human Rights in the Period 1976–1983

A rapid summary of the evolution of the different attitudes of those who represented the state after 1983, when democracy was re-established, will allow us to understand the complexity of the process after the last dictatorship and the alternatives which were presented for the future. In 1985 the so-called *Trial of the Military Juntas* was carried out. In it, Jorge Rafael Videla was condemned to life imprisonment, perpetual and absolute disqualification from holding any public office, supplementary costs, and dismissal from office. He turned out to be guilty of numerous homicides aggravated by malice aforethought, illegal privations of liberty aggravated by threats and violence, repeated tortures, and repeated tortures followed by death, and robberies. Likewise, and with different sentences, other members of the Military Juntas were also condemned. In the now final and unappealable decision, it had already been demonstrated with the weight of double jeopardy, that during those years there had been carried out in the country a systematic plan of kidnappings, tortures, disappearances and deaths.

Notwithstanding such legal progress, however, the following year, the *Congreso de la Nación* (National Congress) sanctioned the law of "*Punto Final*" (Full Stop) and in 1987, that of "*Obediencia Debida*" (Due Obedience). These meant the beginning of a trilogy which would be complemented after 1989–1990 with the amnesties granted to the commanders previously condemned by the law, dictated by the then president, Menem. These three decisions impeded for more than twenty years the judgment and eventual sentencing of those responsible for the widespread violations of human rights which took place in the period from 1976 to 1983. Then, in 2003, the *Congreso de la Nación* declared irredeemably null and void the above-mentioned laws (by means of Law 25.779). By doing so, they opened the road to what is undoubtedly one of the most significant pronouncements which the *Corte Suprema* (Supreme Court) has taken, its declaration that the laws of impunity are unconstitutional. This finally permitted the carrying out of the current trials for mass violations of human rights, in one of which a definitive and now unappealable sentence has already been dictated (Case 2251, Etchecolatz).

Another interesting fact is that in the year 1998, the Federal Chamber of La Plata declared that "the right to the truth" was a question which had not been covered by the then current laws of impunity. This decision signified the beginning of an unprecedented practice in the world which was known as "the trials for the truth", which was carried out initially in La

Plata. In these proceedings, although they did not count upon accused nor even eventual condemnations, the right of the victims of state terrorism and their families to know the truth of what happened during the military dictatorship was recognized.

The stages which followed the reestablishment of democracy emerge clearly. They consist of an encouraging start, with the performance of justice, then a period of impunity, with the enforcement of unconstitutional laws, and finally, of the full force of the institutions, organized around a common slogan of the society, namely that of the prosecution of those found responsible for the violations of human rights committed in the period from 1976 to 1983.

Crimes Against Humanity

The idea of "crimes against humanity" was mentioned for the first time in the Prologue to the Hague Convention of 1907 and latterly has been used in different international instruments in which the concert of the nations has gradually consolidated the firm decision not to tolerate the impunity of those acts considered to be crimes against humanity. In this context, the generalized and systematic attacks against a civilian population, the common threshold of crimes against humanity, has its structural base in an apparatus of power organized by the state. This establishes a functional system maintained in a collection of orders which are disseminated in a descending hierarchical scale and which most of the time generate the segmentation or fragmentation of the executive functions by those who participate in the organization.

At the same time, it must be recorded that the primacy of international law over Argentinean domestic law in the question of human rights began to be affirmed in our country many years ago. The first paradigmatic case in this context was the one resolved by the *Cámara Federal de Apelaciones* of La Plata in the demand for the extradition of Franz Josef

Leo Schwamberger, a Nazi criminal, the author of crimes in the concentration camps of Krakow, who had escaped to Argentina after the end of the war.[2] The specific situation was that the crimes against humanity for which the German courts demanded extradition, were proscribed according to Argentinean law. A similar dilemma arose years later in the face of the request on the part of the Italian government for the extradition of Erich Priebke, another criminal responsible for the massacre of the Ardeatine Caves which took place in Rome, bringing about the deaths of 335 Italian civilians. As Leopoldo Schiffrin points out, in both cases preference was given to the law of imprescriptibility, which was considered to be the limit of the rules of the domestic law.[3]

In the Schwamberger case, there was no extradition treaty with Germany, while in that of Priebke, the problem arose that the extradition treaty with Italy required that the crime which motivated the demand was not prescribed in either the legislation of the requesting country or that of the requested. The solution which won the majority in the *Corte Suprema* (Supreme Court) was to establish that the extradition treaties ought to be interpreted in the light of *jus cogens*, under which the crimes against humanity are imprescriptible. In the same decision it was stated that "the application of international law is recognised by the legal system" in virtue of being prescribed by Article 118 of the National Constitution, and that the constitutional convention received directly from the postulates of international law on "offences against the law of nations".[4]

On this subject, the crimes *iuris gentium* which our highest court cites as recognized in our legal system through Article 118 of the Magna Carta, were defined in the previous century by Diez de Medina as "those

2 http://www.elpais.com/articulo/agenda/Josef/Schwammberger/criminal/nazi/elpepigen/20041205elpepiage_2/Tes.

3 L. Schiffrin, "La primacía del derecho internacional sobre el derecho argentino", in *La aplicación de los Tratados Internacionales de Derechos Humanos por los Tribunales locales*. Buenos Aires, PNUD. Del Puerto, 1998, p. 115.

4 That is why the application of international law in the national jurisdiction is obligatory according to the content of Article 41 of Law 48. This development arises from considerations 38, 39, 49, 50 and 51 of the judgment of the Corte Suprema in the previously mentioned Priebke Case. Ibid., p. 117.

which make their perpetrators enemies of humanity".[5] For his part, Germán Bidart Campos, commenting on the previously mentioned vote on Schiffrin, points out, with respect to the human rights contained in international law, that "they are part of the common juridical consciousness of the world (at least of that which is usually dubbed civilized). If Argentina wishes to remain enrolled (or return to enrol herself if she ever disenrolled) in the civilized world, she has to abide by *ius cogens and to the general principles of international public law, a field in which, we say again, human rights have today an undisputed place*".[6]

On this subject, several reflections are in order. The Organic Charter of the Nüremberg Military Tribunal defined crimes against humanity as "murder, extermination, slavery, deportation or politically, racially or religiously motivated prosecutions.[7] At the same time, the Convention on the imprescriptibility of war crimes and of crimes against humanity, adopted and opened for signature, ratification and adhesion by the General Assembly in its Resolution 2391 (XXIII) of 26 November 1968, establishes in its first article the imprescriptibility of crimes against humanity. The principle of the pre-eminence of Human Rights within International Law over the domestic law of each country is firmly established in the international community on the basis of the Vienna Convention on the Law of Treaties. This was approved by Argentina in 1972. It is signalled in Article 53, entitled "Treaties conflicting with a peremptory norm of general international law (jus cogens)", which establishes:

> A treaty is void if, at the time of its conclusion, it conflicts with a peremptory norm of general international law. For the purposes of the present Convention, a peremptory norm of general international law is a norm accepted and recognized by the international community of States as a whole as a norm from which no derogation is permitted and which can be modified only by a subsequent norm of general international law having the same character.

5 N.P. Sagües, *Los delitos contra el derecho de gentes en la Constitución Nacional*. Edt. 146, p 936, Buenos Aires, Derecho Internacional Público, TEA, 1955.

6 EL DERECHO t. 135, p. 329.

7 Alberto L Zuppi, *La prohibición "ex post facto" y los crímenes contra la humanidad*, ED 131–765.

The *Convención Interamericana sobre Desaparición Forzada de Personas* (Interamerican Convention on the Forced Disappearance of Persons), approved by Law 24556 (of constitutional rank on account of Law 24820), considers that this systematic practice constitutes a crime against humanity. In turn, the Rome Statute of the International Criminal Court adopted in 1998 and promulgated as Law 25390 in 2001, lists in its Article 5 the crimes which are within the competence of the court. Point b) indicates crimes against humanity as those which are listed in Article 7 and amongst them are a) Murder [...] e) Imprisonment or other serious privation of physical liberty in violation of the fundamental norms of international law; [...] f) Torture [...] i) Forced disappearance of persons.

For its part, Article 29 states: "The crimes within the jurisdiction of the Court shall not be subject to any statute of limitations". With respect to this, it is worth recording what was said by the international tribunal for former Yugoslavia in the case of Endemovic:

> Crimes against humanity are serious acts of violence which harm human beings by striking what is most essential to them: their life, liberty, physical welfare, health and / or dignity. They are inhumane acts which by their extent and gravity go beyond the limits tolerable to the international community, which must perforce demand their punishment. But crimes against humanity also transcend the individual because when the individual is attacked, the whole of mankind is attacked and denied. So what essentially characterizes crimes against humanity is the concept of humanity as victim.[8]

The *Corte Suprema de Justicia*, in turn, overwhelmingly prescribed the principles signalled in the international law of human rights. Thus it established the imprescriptibility of crimes against humanity, in the Arancibia Clave case in 2004 and defined them, expressing that it:

> corresponded to qualify the behaviour of Arancibia Clavel as a crime against humanity, for the group of which he was part had as its object the persecution of the political opponents of Pinochet, through killings, forced disappearances and torture (of whose character there is no doubt) with the acquiescence of state officials. Indeed, in accordance with the text of the Rome Statute which in the resolution appealed is

8 Cited by the C. Nac. and Corr. Sala 4°. 28/2/2003, G.H.A. JA 2003-III-378.

> cited only in its Article 7, all possible forms of intervention in this kind of event are covered. Thus, not only are "traditional" forms of participation included (Article 25, inc. 3, aps. A, b), but it expressly mentions the contribution "in some other way in the commission or attempted commission of the crime by a group of people with a common purpose" (Article 25, inc. 3 °, ap. d), where such contribution is made "for the purpose of carrying out the activity or criminal purpose of the group, when one or the other involves the commission of a crime within the jurisdiction of the Court" *(ap. d, supuesto i)*. (Conf. CSJN – "Fallos": 327, pp. 3312).

At the same time, on 14 June 2005 the *Corte Suprema de Justicia de la Nación*, pronounced sentence in the Poblete case, resolving definitively the legal obstacles in the way of judging the crimes of the dictatorship. Thus it declared the invalidity and unconstitutionality of the laws of *Punto Final* and *Obediencia Debida* because they go against international norms which have constitutional status. The CSJN highlighted:

> In conclusion, in the decade of the seventies, that is, at the time of the events under investigation, the domestic legal system contained (international) rules which regarded the forced disappearance of persons as a crime against humanity. These norms, as evidenced in numerous international, regional and universal instruments, were in force for our country, and integrated, therefore, into domestic positive law, not only because the Republic of Argentina had participated voluntarily their process of creation, but also because, in accordance with the most authoritative national and international opinion of the doctrine and jurisprudence, these rules boasted for the time of the events the character of universally valid law (*jus cogens*).

Consistent with this, the *Corte Interamericana de Derechos Humanos* (Interamerican Court of Human Rights) established, in the case of *Almonacid Arellano vs. Chile*, that crimes against humanity can be committed in times of peace as well as during war. With respect to when they were committed, the Interamerican Court recognized that "crimes against humanity include the commission of inhuman acts, such as assassination, committed in a context of generalised or systematic attack against a civilian population. It is enough that one illicit act such as the ones mentioned above be committed within the context described, in order to produce a crime against humanity". It also signalled that "crimes against humanity go beyond what is tolerable to the international community and injure humanity as a whole".

In the first trial following the annulment of the laws of impunity (the Etchecolatz Case), it emerged clearly again in the sentence – unappealable today and with the authority of *double jeopardy* – that in the Argentinean Republic there existed a systematic plan of kidnappings, tortures and disappearance and extermination, contrary to human dignity, which according to the above mentioned doctrine and jurisprudence, qualifies these events as crimes against humanity.

The Genocide

In the mass violations of human rights, the role of the words with which society refers to what happened, take on a particular importance. Although language is essential to every community because it permits communication between its members, the social and judicial framing which gave rise to these violations is decisive when it comes to transmitting history and afterwards in integrating it with the memory of those peoples. In the Argentinean process, as has already been pointed out in the previously mentioned sentencing of Etchecolatz, "to recognise that in Argentina there took place a genocide is an ethical and judicial necessity". This is because it makes the relation between law and truth inseparable. Whenever the law manages to reflect reality, justice will fulfil its commitments. In this sense, in the question of judgments of crimes against humanity, the recognition of an historical "truth", such as the mass violations of human rights, acquires a decisive importance for the construction of collective memory. I will return to this later.

The effective sentencing of someone responsible for mass violations of Human Rights satisfies an important part of the demand for justice on the part of the citizens of whatever democratic state, but not the whole of that demand. That sentencing of a specific person must include those essential concepts which describe what happened in this class of event and most especially the true context and finally naming them under appropriate denominations which form part of the cultural heritage implicit in the International Law of Human Rights. It is just not a question of one or more words in the dictionary, but of nothing less than the way in which the stories of what happened are communicated. This must be done, not on the basis of an interested vision which deforms or minimizes them, but from a broad and comprehensive perspective which guarantees that this transmission to future generations reflects the truth, guaranteeing that the atrocities which they caused will never be repeated. What took place during the 1970s was without doubt a genocide, and thus it is right to name it so. A brief overview of the history of the subject will enable us to understand the question better.

After the Second World War, discussion began at an international level about what was the most adequate definition of the concept of genocide. This discussion, which continues to this day, passed a milestone in the Convention for the Prevention and Punishment of the Crime of Genocide sanctioned by the United Nations in December 1948. That Convention has in turn two antecedents which cannot be overlooked when explaining why what passed in Argentina should be described as a genocide. Thus, in Resolution 96 (I) of 11 December 1946, as a consequence of the events experienced due to Nazism, the United Nations invited its member states to promulgate the laws necessary for the prevention and punishment of genocide. In this context it was declared that:

> Genocide is a denial of the right of existence of entire human groups, as homicide is the denial of the right to live of individual human beings; such denial of the right of existence shocks the conscience of mankind, results in great losses to humanity in the form of cultural and other contributions represented by these human groups, and is contrary to the moral law and to the spirit and aims of the United Nations. Many instances of such crimes of genocide have occurred when racial, religious, political, and other groups have been destroyed, entirely or in part.

It then continues, pointing out that: "The General Assembly, therefore, affirms that genocide is a crime under international law which the civilized world condemns, and for the commission of which the authors and their accomplices – whether private individuals, public officials or statesmen, and whether the crime is committed on religious, racial, political or any other grounds – are punishable". In the transcription which was made, it emerges clearly and is of utmost relevance that in the resolution cited, the international community, horrified by the knowledge of the crimes committed by the Nazis during the Second World War, did not hesitate to include the concept of genocide those "political groups, and others" in the first paragraph transcribed and then those of "political or any other grounds".

The second antecedent which ought to stand out is Article 2 of the first draft of the United Nations Convention for the Prevention and Punishment of the Crime of Genocide which signals that:

> In this Convention, genocide is understood as any of the following deliberate acts committed with the purpose of destroying a national, racial, religious or political group, for reasons based on racial or national origin, on the religious beliefs or on the political opinions of their members: 1) killing members of the group, 2) harming the physical integrity of members of the group, 3) infringing the norms or conditions of life of members of the group with the aim of bringing about death: imposing measures intended to prevent births within the group.

As can be seen, the inclusive nature of both the political groups and the political opinions of their members was maintained in the draft. However, due to political circumstances prevailing in that epoch in several states, the Convention sanctioned in 1948 defined the figure in the following way:

> genocide means any of the following acts committed with intent to destroy, in whole or in part, a national, ethnic, racial or religious group, as such: a) Killing members of the group; b) Causing serious bodily or mental harm to members of the group; c) Deliberately inflicting on the group conditions of life calculated to bring about its physical destruction in whole or in part; d) Imposing measures intended to prevent births within the group; e) Forcibly transferring children of the group to another group.

In this new drafting, it can be appreciated that both the political groups and their political motivations were excluded from the new definition. From then on an interesting question – especially with regard to what happened in Argentina during the military dictatorship – was opened about whether the dozens of thousands of victims of that state terrorism fell within the so-called "national group" alluded to in the Convention. I understand that the affirmative answer imposes itself and that there is no impediment to the categorization as genocide the events which took place in our country during the period in question. The above affirmation proceeds from the analysis which follows and results from the use of the most elementary logic. As was stated at the beginning, it was already proven in the sentence of the historic case of the trial of the Junta that the mechanism of mass destruction was organized by those who themselves called the it the *Proceso de Reorganización Nacional* (Process of National Reorganisation). Thus, in this case, 13/84 in which the former members of the Military Juntas are condemned, it is stated: "The system put into practice – kidnappings, interrogation under torture, clandestine and illegal deprivation of liberty and, in many cases, the elimination of the victims – was substantially identical in the whole territory of the nation and prolonged in time".

It is exactly on the basis of this acceptation both of the facts and of the responsibility of the state for them, which, as I understand it, the process of the "production of truth" begins, without which there would only be retreats and impunity. It is obvious that during all those years this process was subject to a huge number of factors of pressure whose denial would be naive and in many cases interested. Nor is it admissible to ignore that the misrepresentation, the trivialization and even the denial of what happened, result from the intention not only of securing impunity but also, and in particular, of continuing to support the regional economic project which was one of the principal reasons for carrying out the genocidal processes of the 1970s. This economic project, obviously, has been clearly unmasked and begun to be reversed on the basis of the processes of democratization which fortunately are currently being experienced in Latin America. The characterization of the events which took place in the period from 1976 to 1983 as crimes against humanity for the reasons mentioned above, does not preclude and much less enter into the analysis of whether these events were isolated or part of a larger project

With respect to the division the Argentinean territory into different zones and sub zones of operation, and the hundreds of clandestine detention centres, the sociologist Daniel Feierstein points out the following:

> One of the elements which calls the attention in these events is the exhaustive nature of the planning. The extermination was carried out with a speed and precision which denote years of conceptual development and prior learning. The perpetrators did not deprive themselves of applying any of the mechanisms of destruction of subjectivity from previous genocidal or repressive experiences. The Argentinean concentration camps constituted a compendium of the worst experiences of the Nazi concentration camps, the internment camps of the French in Algeria or the practices of US counterintelligence in Vietnam. To the figures of torture through "electric shocks", the "submarine" (submerging the victim's head systematically in a bucket of water almost to the point of causing asphyxiation), the introduction of rodents into the interior of human bodies, the humiliation and daily denigration of prisoners, abuse, beatings, overcrowding, and hunger, were added some features specific to the Argentinean experience. These included the torture of prisoners in front of their children, or the torture of children and spouses of prisoners in front of their parents or spouses, and illegal appropriation (and delivery to military families) of many children of the "disappeared". What a competition of horror! The Argentine genocidaires evaluated and utilized the most degrading treatment of every previous genocidal experience with a level of sophistication which overcomes doubts about possible improvisation or about a spontaneously arising hatred [...].[9]

As to whether what took place in our country should be framed within the concept of the "national group" according to the wording that Article II of the Convention finally took, an affirmative response is already anticipated and the reflections of the author cited are illustrative of the particular case.

> the characterization of "national group" is absolutely valid for analysing the events in Argentina, since the perpetrators are out to destroy a particular section of the social relations in a state in order to produce a change substantial enough to alter the life of the whole. In view of the inclusion of "in whole or in part" in the definition of the 1948 Convention, it is clear that the Argentinean national group has been annihilated "in part" and a sufficiently substantial part as to alter the social relations within the nation itself. The annihilation in Argentina is not spontaneous, it is not accidental, it is not irrational: it is the systematic destruction of a "substantial part" of the Argentinean national group, with the objective of transforming it as such, to redefine its way of being, social relationships, fate and future.[10]

9 D. Feierstein/G. Levy, *Hasta que la muerte nos separe. Prácticas sociales genocidas en América Latina*. Buenos Aires, Ediciones Al margen, 2004, pp. 63, 64.

10 D. Feierstein/G. Levy, op. cit., p. 76.

I understand that from everything stated it appears undeniable that we are not confronted with a mere series of crimes but rather with something significantly greater which should be called "genocide". But it should be clarified that this cannot and should not be interpreted as indifference to the significant differences between what happened in Argentina and other exterminations, such as the first genocide of the twentieth century, carried out against the Armenian people from 1915 and which had more than a million victims, that of the millions of victims of Nazism during the Second World War or the slaughter of one million persons in Rwanda in 1994, to cite some obvious examples. It is not a question of a competition about which people suffered more or which community has the largest number of victims; it is one of calling by their correct names phenomena which, even with contextual differences and occurring in different times and places, show a similarity which ought to be recognized. It is that, as Feierstein concludes on giving the reasons why the distinct historical processes can be named in the same way: "to use the same concept implies postulating the existence of a thread which points to a technology of power in which the 'negation of the other' is taken to its ultimate limit: their material disappearance (that of their body) and symbolic disappearance (that of the memory of their existence)".[11]

The importance of calling things by their names

Relevant here is a brief allusion to the sense and utility of – from my point of view – naming correctly, without euphemisms and above all without concessions, what happened in Argentina as a result of the terrorism of the state. During the course of the first trial held in connection with the repeal of the laws of impunity (the Etchecolatz case), different situations could be observed generated by the juridical oddity of judging events which had occurred three decades previously. One of the most obvious is linked to the multiple victimization to which the convened witnesses had been

11 D. Feierstein/G. Levy, op. cit., p. 88.

subjected. Reliving the pain of the sufferings endured, both by the direct victims of these events and by those who were family members or loved ones, or because they had shared captivity with those victims, cannot pass unnoticed by either the justice system or by the rest of the state which is obliged to elaborate some kind of adequate response. In that sense it is well known that one of the greatest allies of impunity is the passage of time. Witnesses who die, witnesses who are not able to return to relate the horror or who do not feel secure to do so. To them all, our legal system gives a series of adequately studied safeguards which requires review of dogmatic concepts elaborated for traditional criminal assumptions, but not for crimes against humanity and genocide.

There is a regulation of the *Código de Procedimientos Penal* (Code of Penal Procedures) which permits us to exemplify clearly what has just been said. Article 384 says with respect to oral and public hearings:

> Immediately the President / Chair person shall proceed to the examination of the witnesses in the order he considers appropriate, by beginning with the offence. Before declaring, the witnesses will not be able to communicate amongst themselves nor with other persons, nor see or hear nor be informed of what is happening in the court room. After declaring, the president will resolve whether they should be held incommunicado in the waiting room.

It is obvious that the legislator who at that time drafted the norm transcribed above, never remotely imagined that, in the country in which this regulation applied, there would be carried out thirty years later trials in which the presence of these witnesses and victims would be required. Much less that during these years, these victims and other witnesses would – as did in fact happen – have founded organizations with the aim of demanding justice for the violations of the human rights of those affected. It is absolutely obvious that during these decades the persons in question spoke amongst themselves and with third parties of the events which had occurred. Nor is it less obvious that many of these persons were partners or couples who during these decades lived together and even slept in the same bed. To say to any of these persons that they will be "incommunicado" during long periods of waiting in the waiting room is not only absurd, cruel and unjust, but moreover today is illegal. That is because it is contrary to what is laid down by Article 75 inc. 22 of the Constitution which accords higher legal status to the Conventions on Human Rights, a regulation obviously superior to the *Código de Procedimientos* referred to above.

However, the question is not so simple. For this truism, contradiction and injustice to be avoided, judges are needed who understand the question this way. Judges are needed who have managed to overcome their training, which has been merely dogmatic and in many cases consists in the mechanical application of norms, even of those such as the previously noted Article 384, which defies, in cases of mass violations of human rights, the most elementary common sense. In turn, prosecutors and plaintiffs must not only recognize the problem, but must moreover have the training and above all the energy to confront where appropriate those judges who refuse to do what is right in the name of some juridical construction which in force for some, but never for judges who apply the current paradigms in unconditional defence of human rights.

It is precisely the new paradigms in the field which force us to rethink the methods, practices and fundamental arguments with respect to the true context in which these events are judged and to adapt accordingly at all times these practices to what is ultimately just: respect for the dignity of every one of the witnesses and parties who attend the courtroom. Equally illustrative of this is the foundational ruling handed down by the *Corte Interamericana de Derechos Humanos* (Interamerican Court of Human Rights) in the first sentence issued to a member country of the *Sistema Interamericano de Derechos Humanos* (Interamerican System of Human Rights). The CIDH pointed out in the case of Velazquez Rodriguez:

> The State has a legal duty to reasonably prevent violations of human rights, to investigate seriously with the means at its disposal any violations which have been committed within its jurisdiction in order to identify those responsible, to impose the appropriate sanctions and to ensure the victim adequate compensation. In certain circumstances it may prove difficult to investigate acts which make attempts on the rights of the person. However, it should be undertaken seriously and not as a mere formality condemned beforehand to be ineffective.[12]

12 Court I.D.H. Case Velázquez Rodríguez, Sentence of 29 July 1988, Series C No. 4. Para. 172, 174, 177.

These wise affirmations, above all with respect to the need to be serious in the investigations, do not refer to being serious in the field of violations of human rights. It is neither more nor less than to investigate the truth, to respect and apply the superior regulations of a nation, which as in our case, obliges the adaptation of all the legal procedures to the challenges generated by these new judgments. This includes without doubt setting aside any rule whose implementation affects basic rights but is the product of a legal reality which was valid at the time of its approval but which is absurd when judging crimes against humanity in the context of genocide. To take care of these new paradigms, to decide not to apply rules contrary to the *Constitución Nacional* and also to call everything by its name, is part of that challenge produced by the new legal reality. This must necessarily be extended to the different stages of education and most especially to the universities, for it is there that those officials and magistrates responsible for implementing the norms are going to graduate. No less instructive is what Feierstein recently identified in this regard:

> The Argentine case can be thought of, complementarily, as one of the most synthetic experiences and achievements of this "reorganizing genocide" as a model of the destruction and refounding of social relations. Even as a social process which explicitly suggests the character of the practice through its self-designation as the "Process of National Reorganization", a novelty in relation both to other military dictatorships and previous genocidal processes.[13]

While I personally believe that the idea of a "reorganising" genocide defines very clearly what happened, it is not just a question of the name with which the events which took place in our country are described. From what Feierstein says, it appears indisputable, as has already been said, that we are not dealing with a mere succession of crimes but rather with something significantly larger, and this must always remain clear. Christian dela Campagne wrote that "the twentieth century introduced the absolute evil that is genocide. It also invented a most insidious practice, so as to allow us

13 D. Feierstein, *El genocidio como práctica social. Entre el nazismo y la experiencia argentina*, Buenos Aires, Fondo de Cultura Económica, 2007, p. 356.

accommodate ourselves. This consists in trivializing evil, relativizing it or degrading the words used to designate it".[14] This brutal denunciation in terms of what it means to relativize evil or degrade the words with which we describe it, is, as this author points out, another way of permitting a society to "accommodate" itself to this phenomenon. This also means thinking of it as less serious than it was and even of not thinking about it at all.

It should be added that, in many cases, it is not only that this is used to trivialize evil acts as a defence mechanism by some members of society in order to convince themselves that these horrors did not take place or that they were not so serous; it is that this often conceals evil intentions. It is a case of sectors which are either linked directly to the authors of those crimes, who they wish to protect, or are connected by their own ideological affinity with that which led to the killings, and who strive daily to make the population believe that the crimes have been magnified by the families of the victims or by the survivors. They disqualified all of those who had the least resources, trying to shift responsibility for what happened to the victims who, according to these arguments, caused with their own actions the reactions of those who in this view had no choice but to repress them. It is clear that in order to justify such arguments, they not only must deny the magnitude of the horrors, but when the crimes become evident, call them "excesses". To conclude this section it is enough to point out that in the case of genocide as a phenomenon intolerable to the universal juridical consciousness, the designation of every phenomenon which, as in the Argentinean case, is eligible to be called by that name, is to my mind a further step towards better and more serious investigations and ultimately towards obtaining the truth.

14 C. dela Campagne, *Banalizacion del mal, acerca de la indiferencia. Un estudio sobre el genocidio*, Nuova Vision, 1999.

The Genocide and the irradiation of Terror

In a play written before the last military dictatorship a well-known dramatist made a leading character say, "For every one who we touch, a thousand are paralysed with fear. We act through irradiation". In societies which have suffered mass violations of human rights, and in which the perpetrators of genocide have necessarily resorted to terror as one of the main tools to facilitate their actions, to become consciousness of this irradiation is the first step towards elaborating it and counteracting it. Neither the one nor the other is easy. This is because the irradiation, permeating the society as a whole, generates consequences which are maintained throughout many years and the duration of these effects depends on the level of consciousness about what happened and the decisions which are taken in order to deactivate it. The prejudices, the phrases fabricated for the occasion and the interminable distortions of history are the biggest traps for that elaboration of what happened. And this elaboration is so important for the collective health that this undertaking must be a true politics of the state in the field and not merely the product of individual initiatives or of non-governmental organizations. This is so, not because their struggle is unimportant: thanks to them and their demands the state of impunity which reigned during so many years in the country has been reversed. Rather it is that this enormous work is not sufficient on its own to ensure the full force of the current paradigms in the field of human rights, but requires a state which supports and spearheads with all its power, this work of elaboration. The consequences of the irradiation of terror in our society are uncommonly extensive.

Loss of empathy: Empathy is the possibility of putting yourself in the place of the other, or, as the indigenous proverb puts it, *caminar con los zapatos del otro* (to put yourself in the other person's shoes). A society whose members find it difficult to put themselves in the place of the other is in serious problems. The widespread terror of the periods of mass human rights violations undermines this possibility of feeling empathy for the neighbour and contributes to the formation of extremely selfish citizens who have a high level of resistance to understanding, and even suffering, for the pain of others.

Insensitivity to injustice: Sensitivity is the capacity which the senses have of capturing the world which surrounds us. The greater our sensitivity, the more aspects of reality we can understand. In this process, at the same time, our subjectivity usually selects those things which unconsciously we do not want to capture and then we act as it they haven't happened, even when they take place before our eyes. Individuals with little empathy, who have been pierced by the irradiation of terror, frequently become numb to injustice. They can pass by many situations of injustice, and look the other way.

Anomie: Finally, the person who is neither capable of putting themselves in the place of the other, nor sensitive to the pain of the other, finds it difficult to take notice of the norms which the society in which they live establishes as regulations of behaviour. Needless to say, that anomie ranges from not stopping at red lights to refusing to accept the reality of recent history. Not to mention prosecuting and punishing those responsible for the serious crimes committed in those periods. The three consequences pointed out are sewn together in their synthesis, shaping a significant number of insensitive citizens, who lack the slightest ability to take the place of their neighbour and are very little willing to comply with the law.

It is possible, however, to recover these qualities. There can be no doubt that the terrible consequences which state terrorism generated in the citizenship has not only marked several generations, but as has been said before, runs through the entire society today. In turn those representatives of the state, committed to the struggle for human rights and aware that, until the disastrous consequences of the genocide have been recognized and elaborated, it will not be possible to adequately educate the new generations, started out several years ago on the complex road on which we walk today. This road, on which the Argentinean Republic is an example to the world, integrates fundamentally four inescapable conditions for creating a better society: to know the truth, do justice, redress and have memory. A short analysis of each one of these will perhaps enable us to understand better what we have so far noted.

Truth

The first condition necessary for preventing new atrocities is knowledge of the truth of what happened, without distortions and above all without concealments. In this respect, it has been proven today with the force of double jeopardy that there existed in the region a systematic plan of kidnappings, tortures, disappearances, and the death of thousands of persons and that this plan was elaborated and executed by the state itself. This was proved as of 1985 in the trial of the Military Juntas and this knowledge has been enriched in the course of the previously referred to "Trials for the truth". From that foundational trial of the Military Juntas (later indefectibly tarnished by the amnesties which were subsequently granted), as well as the trials without penal sentence, emerged the truth of one important part of what happened under the terrorism of the state. However, it was clearly demonstrated that the truth was not enough. And it was not sufficient because the truth is *static*: its knowledge is important but cannot establish the modifications in reality which would be detrimental to the sensation of impunity which reigned on the basis of the previously mentioned laws of *Punto Final*, *Obediencia Debida* and finally of the amnesties. In order to undermine such a state of affairs, something *dynamic* is required, with a force and a power sufficient enough to awaken in the citizenship those feelings of solidarity and sensitivity to injustice, which, as has been said, have become lethargic, if not lost, thanks to the irradiation of the terror suffered. Only justice can provide this dynamic.

Justice

Justice is dynamic because it investigates and analyses a situation which has already passed and finally resolves whether crimes were committed during this period and whether it is fitting to hold anyone responsible for them. This mobility is what enriches the knowledge of the truth and gives meaning to rights as the very producer of the truth and at the same time to justice as the producer of a modification of that historical reality of transgression and crime, which is translated into an adequate sanction for its authors. In cases of mass violations of human rights, the contrary, the lack of justice, is the most powerful source of new violations, because there exists no better incentive for the perpetrators of genocide than the impunity of their predecessors.

Reparations

Functioning justice is productive in turn of reparations. Crimes against humanity generate in their victims harms which are almost always irreversible. In fact, with respect to those who died, the obviousness of what has been said does not need comment. But, with respect to those who have survived, the question is neither so clear nor so definitive. Concerning the scale of harm, the writings of Jean Améry, the Austrian philosopher who was tortured by the Gestapo and then deported to the concentration camp of Auschwitz, are significant: "Whoever has been tortured continues to be so [...] Whoever has suffered torments will not be able to find a place in the world, the curse of impotence will never be extinguished. Faith in humanity, already shaky with the first blow, then demolished by torture, will never be recovered".[15] Améry committed suicide in 1978. In that so often irreversible process of pain there exist alternatives which sometimes, just sometimes, can alleviate such suffering.

As a counterpoint to what happened to the above mentioned philosopher, something said by the mother of a disappeared Argentinean is illustrative. The woman had participated with her white headscarf, characteristic of the *Madres de Plaza de Mayo* (Mothers of the Plaza de Mayo), in the different hearings of the trial of Miguel Etchecolatz. After the reading of the sentence in which the person named was condemned to life imprisonment, she stated, resting her hands on her breast: "I suffered oppression for 30 years ... now it has gone". It is difficult to find a more opportune example of the refreshing effect which justice can have, even if thirty years late. The difference between impunity and active justice is in many cases

15 P. Levi, *Los hundidos y los salvados*, Barcelona, El Aleph Editores, 1986.

the difference between life and death. It is so, at the very least, among the victims who relive their suffering on a daily basis in the face of the inactivity of a state which does not respect their pain and their just demands, and those who can rest without that tightness in the chest, which without exception accompanies the victims who have not received reparation for their martyrdom.

Memory

As has already been noted, sensibility is the capacity which the senses have of capturing the world which surrounds us. The impression produced in us by what is perceived is memory. Memory, finally, is the foundation of the identity of a community. It is because of this role which memory has in the growth of a society and above all in the decision of its members not to repeat the atrocities of the past, that the state has the obligation of honouring, stimulating and preserving it. It must not be forgotten that in our case, it is the state itself which kidnapped tortured, raped, disappeared and killed. This is also the same state which, under the watchful gaze of the organizations which defend human rights and which maintained alive the memory during thirty years, now favours the prosecution of these crimes and is to honour and preserve the memory of what happened.

This distinguishes the Argentina of today from the rest of the countries of the world. Even years later, this society has the consciousness and the energy not only to look for the truth but also to judge, repair and promote memory as the principal antidote to the barbarism lived. Far from a spirit of vengeance, its object is a peaceful society which looks forward but with full awareness of its past. The Nobel prize of Guatemalan literature, Miguel Ángel Asturias, wrote with reference to the victims of his country: "The eyes of the buried will close together on the day of justice, or will not close at all".[16] If they do not have justice, the murdered will remain with their eyes open wherever they are. Only when justice is done can they rest in peace.

16 M.A. Asturias, *Los ojos de los enterrados*, Buenos Aires, Editorial Losada, 1979.

ANA OBERLIN

The Process of Justice for the State Crimes Committed in Argentina During the Last Civil–Military Dictatorship: The View of a Lawyer Representing Victims and a Militant in HIJOS

The appearance of HIJOS as part of the human rights movement in Argentina: The context of impunity

Formed in the year 1995, HIJOS (*Hijos e hijas por la Identidad y la Justicia contra el Olvido y el Silencio*: Sons and Daughters for Identity and Justice against Forgetting and Silence) is a political organization that struggles for human rights. When this collective emerged, there already existed the *Madres* and the *Abuelas de Plaza de Mayo* (the Mothers and the Grandmothers of the Plaza de Mayo) and various other human rights organizations in Argentina, which had been born before or during the regime. These organizations fought to put an end to the impunity of those responsible for the mass violations of human rights committed during the last civil–military dictatorship (1976–1983). This impunity had been established by different actions and omissions of the democratic governments which came after the pro-coup elements.

Before the year in which HIJOS appeared, a series of events occurred that had a marked impact on the struggle of the human rights movement in our country. In what follows I will briefly describe the principal landmarks, so as to permit understanding of the context in which this organization arose.

In the closing stages of the dictatorship, on 23 March 1983, the regime dictated the so-called *ley de autoamnistía* ("law of self-amnesty"). The objective of this regulation (No. 22,924) was the de-responsibilization of the authors, participants, accomplices, instigators and accessories after the fact of the mass violations of human rights which had been perpetrated by the Armed Forces of the State, together with a large group of civilians, against the Argentinean people.[1] Although it was several months before the military left power, which happened in the December of that year, the dictatorship was already dying and the dictators were paving the way to avoiding legal penalties for the serious crimes they had committed.

The first president after the end of the dictatorial regime was the Radical Raúl Alfonsín. On assuming the presidency he sent a bill to Congress to the repeal the above mentioned law. A week after the presidential bill arrived at the Argentinean parliament, the military "self-amnesty" was abolished by means of Law 23,040. This was the first law sanctioned by the brand-new deputies and senators after the re-establishment of democracy.

In order to confront the crimes of the dictatorship, Alfonsín decided on a strategy of truth and limited criminal responsibility.[2] The strategy of truth was carried out by means of the creation, on 15 December 1983, of CONADEP, a commission of notables whose object was to investigate the events which had taken place during the dictatorship. This institution

1 In Article 1, the law declared the following: "The penal actions arising from offences committed with terrorist or subversive motivation or purpose, from 25 May 1973 to 17 June 1982 are declared extinguished. The benefits granted by this Law extend also to all the facts of a criminal nature carried out on the occasion of or in connection with the development of actions designed to prevent, avert or put an end to the terrorist or subversive activities in question, whatever their nature had been or whether legal rights had been injured. The effects of this law cover the authors, participants, instigators, or accomplices and includes related common crimes and crimes with a military connection".

2 For an analysis of the strategy of truth and limited criminal responsibility of Alfonsín's government and the tensions with the human rights movement, see Font, E., "Confrontando los crímenes del Estado. Poder, resistencia y luchas alrededor de la verdad: las Madres de Plaza de Mayo" in *Criminología Crítica y Control Social*, vol. 2 (2000), pp. 51–106.

produced the famous *Nunca Más* report, which documented some 9,000 cases of violations of human rights. After nine months of work, the report was presented on 20 September 1984.

At the same time, the strategy of limited criminal responsibility was based on an attempt to make the Armed Forces "cleanse itself" by putting on trial in military tribunals those members of the different Juntas which had held power. This strategy broke down because of the absolute refusal of the Armed Forces, which did not carry forward trials of those responsible, who they instead protected systematically.

Thanks to an article introduced into the discussion of the *Código de Justicia Militar* (CJM: Military Justice Code), the previously existing limited possibility of civil judicial intervention in cases which fell under military justice, was extended. Thus, the option of going before non-military judges was added in the face of unwarranted delays, without the need to arrive at a definitive sentence in order to do so. This made possible what was knows as the Trial of the Juntas which took place before the National Court of Appeals in Criminal and Federal Correction Matters of the Capital Federal.

The Trial of the Juntas, also known as Case 13, did not include every documented case, but was used as a selection mechanism for paradigmatic cases. Of these, 281 ended up being tried. At the same time, only those with the greatest responsibility, that is to say the members of the different Military Juntas which had usurped power from 24 March 1976, were prosecuted. Between 22 April and 14 August 1985, the public hearing of oral proceedings was held and 883 people presented their testimony. On 9 December sentence was given, condemning Jorge Rafael Videla and Emilio Eduardo Massera to life imprisonment, Roberto Eduardo Viola to seventeen years' imprisonment, Armando Lambruschini to eight years and Orlando Ramón Agosti to four. On the other hand, the defendants Omar Graffigna, Leopoldo Galtieri, Jorge Isaac Anaya and Basilio Lami Dozo were not condemned because the judges conceded that they were unable to prove the charges against them.

Alfonsín's strategy of truth and limited criminal responsibility also failed because the human rights movement was far from satisfied with judging only the Juntas and promoted trials against the middle-ranking and direct executors of the crimes. After the ruling in Case 13, the next step was to advance on these responsibilities. To that end criminal proceedings began to open up throughout the country, involving hundreds of defendants and thousands of victims. Although these trials progressed at different rates, depending in good part on whether or not the judges who carried them out had colluded with the dictators, there were some two thousand trials in the course of which a large body of evidence was produced.

This situation caused increasing unease in sectors of the Armed Forces and their civilian accomplices and was the source of a series of episodes aimed at destabilizing the democratic government. Faced with this pressure, Alfonsín intervened personally in 1986 to make Congress sanction the first of the two laws of impunity, Law 23,492, known as the Law of *Punto Final* (Full Stop). This intervention was consistent with his strategy and imposed a mandatory period of sixty days for trying those accused of crimes against humanity committed during the military government. As a result, the human rights organizations and lawyers committed to the search for justice found themselves obliged to redouble their efforts in order to try to include the greatest possible number of cases and evidence in this limited period of time.

Even after this huge concession, the military pressures continued and Easter 1987 saw the largest military uprising. In this there took part for the most part young officers, known as *carapintadas*, led by Lieutenant Colonel Aldo Rico. In response, millions of people demonstrated in the streets throughout the country in order to oppose the uprising and support the democratic regime.

In spite of this enormous popular support, Alfonsín negotiated with the insurgents the crippling of the trials against military personnel for violations of human rights committed during the dictatorship. This capitulation took concrete form in the second law of impunity, the Law of *Obediencia Debida* (Due Obedience), which carried the number 23,521. In this a presumption of *iuris et de iure* – that is to say, without admitting proof in contrary – was established. As a result of this concession almost none of the crimes committed by those acting as commanding officers, junior officers, NCOs and enlisted personnel of the Armed Forces, security forces, police and prisons, would be punishable as their authors had perpetrated their acts in virtue of *Obediencia Debida*. This same presumption, although with different scope, was applied also to superior officers who had not acted as commanders in chief, heads of zones, sub zone chiefs, and the heads of security forces, police or prisons.[3] In Article Two of the law, however, the crimes of rape, child abduction and concealment or substitution of marital status and extensive appropriation of property were explicitly exempted.

The fundamental consequence of this law was the immediate de-prosecution of the majority of those accused in the criminal cases which were then in process. Although, as pointed out in the previous paragraph, there were crimes which were not covered by this law, the reality was that no case continued its course and all judicial progress was blocked in a scandalous way. This implied a serious institutional retreat and meant a major setback for the combative Argentinean human rights movement.

In order to complete the closure of the construction of impunity which for almost twenty years benefited those responsible, the president who succeeded Alfonsín, Carlos Saúl Menem, of the Partido Justicialista, pardoned those who had been convicted in the preceding years. Between 7 October 1989 and 29 December 1990, this benefit was conceded to the 220 military men who were then serving sentences. This permitted the liberation of the few prisoners, who from then on returned to walk freely through the streets of our country.

This is the context in which HIJOS joined the human rights movement: with those guilty of one of the worst massacres which had occurred in Argentina at liberty, a situation which was apparently irreversible. Without doubt, the public appearance of this collective signalled the entrance of a new generation, youths of about twenty years at that point in time, who joined the struggle which was being carried forward by the human rights organizations.

HIJOS is composed not only of the children of the disappeared, assassinated, former political prisoners and exiles, but also by those who feel an

3 Although it clarified that those who had had a decision-making capacity or had participated in the elaboration of the orders would not be punishable if their case were not resolved judicially within the thirty days of the promulgation of the law.

identification with the objectives set out by this organization. These were basically centred on three axes: Memory, Truth and Justice. While these objectives are interrelated, in this work I am going to concentrate on the third of them, Justice, and on my point of view as a lawyer and a member of the organization with respect to the process of trial and punishment which is occurring today in our country and which had as its antecedent the contents of this section.

The *escraches*, Trials for the Truth and international authority: preparing the ground for the current state of the judicial process

The search for justice for the crimes of the dictatorship was always a very important aim of the human rights movement in Argentina and it did not abandon its efforts in the face of the previously mentioned setbacks. In the case of HIJOS, the concept is even included in its name: Sons and Daughters for Identity and *Justice* and against Forgetting and Silence. The emphasis given to justice is related to the historical moment of the emergence of the organization, when the bloc of impunity was so solid that it seemed impossible to achieve the demanded Justice and Punishment, the historic slogan of the Argentinean human rights organizations.

Having arisen at a point when the institutional channels were blocked, HIJOS carried forward a series of innovations with the aim of achieving the repudiation of this situation on the part of society. Thus through HIJOS, a new form of protest was created: the *escraches*. These demonstrations were characterized by the use of music, colourful disguises and dance, and contrasted strongly with the first mobilizations at the start of the return to democracy which were understandably more solemn.

The *escraches* consisted of a process which began by identifying the places where those who had acted as repressors were currently living, so as then to spread knowledge in the zone as to who they were and what crimes they had committed and, finally, to identify their houses in a public act. For the most part, the members of the task forces which were active during the dictatorship had used aliases during the commission of their crimes in order to avoid identification and thus to procure impunity; to locate them therefore required prior work to verify that they had been identified correctly. Once the place where they lived was known, a tour was made of the area, telling the neighbours who these persons were and what crimes they had committed. In the majority of cases these criminals were unknown, because they were camouflaged within the society and carried on lives which in the view of the rest were "normal". Moreover, the people participating in the *escraches* found out not only the names of their victims, but what jobs they had done, what organizations they had been members of, where they had been taken, and as much information about them as possible. Finally, the *escrache* culminated in an action in front of the house of the repressor. The walls were painted to identify the place with the aim of letting everyone know that there resided there someone who had committed serious crimes and who enjoyed impunity because the democratic institutions of the state had not fulfilled their role adequately.

These demonstrations became highly visible and were repeated in the majority of the cities of Argentina. The results were successful in nearly every case: several repressors had to move because, once aware of their crimes, their neighbours no longer greeted them in the street, did not want to share the lift with them or raised demands in the residents' committees that it should be suggested to them that they moved. In addition, as a form of political expression, the *escrache* was used and appropriated by social, political and trade union organizations for other demands than those which originally motivated them.

In addition, other groups simultaneously generated highly creative protests with the same objective of preventing immunity for these acts. This resulted in an increasing social acceptance of the need to judge those responsible for these crimes and in an increased rejection of these crimes and their authors, generating the basis of what years later would be consolidated as a new stage in the prosecution of justice.

This political strategy was developed parallel to a strategy which we can consider more formal, linked fundamentally to the field of judicial power both at home and in other countries of the world. As a collective, HIJOS decided at the national level to participate, as far as this was possible in each region,[4] in the attempt to achieve the reopening of the trials.

In this process, which was pioneered by CELS (*Centro de Estudios Legales y Sociales*: Centre of Legal and Social Studies), and to which other organizations later adhered, important milestones were constituted by the so-called *Juicios por la Verdad* (Trials for the Truth) and the trials which took place abroad with the aim of bringing to justice the members of the Armed Forces and security forces for their illegal actions during the dictatorship in Argentina. In the latter, the members of HIJOS of other countries also participated, collaborating extensively in the international campaign for justice.

The so-called *Juicios por la Verdad* were a *sui generis* form of criminal trial which had the limited aim of finding out what had happened to the people who were disappeared or assassinated during the military dictatorship, but not of the punishment of those responsible. This limited form of trial was unavoidable as the impunity laws in effect at the time prevented the progress of fully effective criminal trials. But the existence of these trials permitted the collection of a large body of evidence which has been transformed into the sustenance of current criminal proceedings and which has permitted knowledge of the identities of many of the victims and of several perpetrators.

Meanwhile trials were also taking place simultaneously in other countries and had an impact on the process which was unfolding in our country. Thus in several European countries trials were carried out against Argentineans guilty of acts of genocide. This resulted in the arrival in the country of demands for the extradition of repressors and generated a certain amount of pressure at the local level because it was necessary to give an answer to these requests and this in turn deepened the social discontent at the lack of prosecution of these criminals. It also influenced several

4 HIJOS functions as a national network and has different regional organisations throughout the country. The network meets annually and takes decisions which will be carried forward, to the extent that this is possible, in each region.

resolutions by supranational organizations which, in general terms, showed our country that to permit impunity for the crimes of the dictatorship implied the international responsibility of the Argentinean state.

The unconstitutional nature of the laws of impunity: the new step in the process of Justice in Argentina

As a consequence of the advances mentioned briefly above, on 6 March 2001 the judge Gabriel Cavallo declared the laws of *Punto Final* and *Obediencia Debida* to be unconstitutional. The resolution was given in response to a presentation by CELS which had for many years been building up a serious dispute in the courts with the aim of modifying the context of impunity. The declaration of the unconstitutionality of a law implies only that that law, being contrary to the Constitution, will not be applicable to the case investigated in the trial in which it is declared, but has no general scope and only means that it will not be employed in the case for which it was issued.

Anyway, Cavallo's decision was imitated by other investigating judges throughout the country. This resulted in the opening of new cases which had not previously been investigated and the re-opening in various parts of Argentina of cases from the eighties which had been obstructed by the laws of impunity.

This new stage was intensified on 25 March 2003 when Néstor Kirchner assumed the presidency and gave his explicit support to the judicial process which was beginning to extend itself on the basis of the first declarations on unconstitutionality. On the first 24 March of his presidency, he went so far as to make the Military College take down its pictures of the known repressors: Jorge Rafael Videla and Reynaldo Benito Bignone. As this was the anniversary of the military coup, this gesture caused unease within the Armed Forces and had great symbolic weight. He also resolved that the buildings of the *Escuela de Mecánica de la Armada* in the Ciudad Autónoma de Buenos Aires and of La Perla in Córdoba, should be used as cultural spaces and taken out of the hands of the Armed Forces. These were paradigmatic places of the repression and famous as clandestine centres of detention and extermination.

Simultaneously, the judicial declarations of unconstitutionality mentioned at the beginning of this section, which had began in such a fragmented and isolated way, were developing strength and being replicated throughout the country. Eventually on 14 June 2005 the *Corte Suprema de la Nación*, the highest organ of judicial power, confirmed Cavallo's decision. In our country the lower judges have a duty to comply with the doctrine which this court imposes, except when new reasons appear which modify them, hence the importance of the resolutions of the *Corte Suprema* judges. On the basis of this resolution, a huge number of cases was opened up in different federal courts.

Today, those responsible for the mass and systematic violations of human rights during the period of state terror are being judged in nearly every jurisdiction. Many of these trials have reached the critical stage of criminal proceedings, the oral hearing.[5] The year 2010 ended with 110 persons condemned, having been found culpable of a range of crimes. These include members of different armed forces and security forces and, to a lesser extent, civilians, and their crimes embrace homicides, illegal deprivations of liberty, applications of tortures, illegal searches without a warrant, robberies, the abduction of children and one case of rape.

HIJOS has participated in several of these trials as an organization in the role of the plaintiff promoting the trial; in others it represents, through lawyers who are members of the organization, individual victims. Moreover, while in some trials these activities have not been taken on formally, it also cooperates by supporting the witnesses and their families during the most important moments. Its participation in ongoing cases in different parts of the country has allowed the group to develop a broad and critical vision of the process of justice which is being carried out.

5 In Argentina the federal penal process – which is applied in these cases in which the Federal Justice intervenes – is divided into two parts: the stage of instruction, in the charge of a judge, whose object is to find out what happened, who was responsible, and to gather the proofs which will be the basis of the second stage, the oral hearing. In this the accused are judged and a sentence dictated.

The limitations of the current stage of justice: what is missing

Without doubt, the road being taken in Argentina gives an example to the world of what ought to be the judgment of those responsible for mass violations of human rights. Moreover, major advances have taken place with the new or reopened judicial investigations and light has been shed on issues which were previously completely unknown to the victims and their families. In spite of this, certain points which should be identified in order to address the current state of this new stage.

A central item is, as previously indicated, the existence of many criminal proceedings in different jurisdictions, in which disparate criteria of penal prosecution of these crimes are applied. An example of the disparity of criteria is that some investigating judges investigate crimes organized according to the victim; others do so organizing them according to the person accused; others according to repressive events; others according to the clandestine detention centre; and still others by the circuit of repression, in which various clandestine centres are included.

This situation arises from the fact that when the new stage began there was no clear and uniform definition of the criminal justice policy which could be adopted in order to carry out these trials. This lack is principally due to the fact that the two state actors involved which ought to have planned this policy, the judicial power of the nation and the *Procuración Nacional*,[6] did not do so; this has had many negative consequences.

The causes of such a blunder can be found in two principal factors. The first is caused by the state of apathy and collapse in which the judicial system of our country was found ten years ago when these trials began to be activated. (And I consider that it still is in this condition today.) In order to change this situation, new positions were assigned throughout this

6 The first of these, because in our country the criminal justice system adopted is mixed and in the first stage, that of instruction, is eminently inquisitorial and it is the examining magistrates who design the investigation. As for the Procuración Nacional, the role of prosecutors is to carry forward the accusations and they had to unify the criteria at the national level, which they did not do until very late in the process, in 2008.

period, both in courts and in tribunals of oral instruction, and in attorneys' and public prosecutors' offices, because the majority of the accused used the public system of defence provided by the state. The problem is that in many cases these new positions were used in order to hire family members and assign them to tasks other than those for which they had been created. Nevertheless, the allocation of special resources to these trials has benefited the progress of the processes and the difference has been noticeable from an early stage.

The other factor which should not be overlooked is the direct connivance of some judges and criminal service functionaries who have deliberately prevented – and continue to prevent – these trials from moving forward, delaying the procedural steps and fragmenting the cases in such a way that the timelines have become even longer. This has given rise to a number of complaints to the *Consejo de la Magistratura* (Council of Magistrates), to the dismissal of some judges and to the presentation of petitions to the Attorney in the cases where prosecutors have been reluctant to do their work properly. Equally, as we are dealing with highly corporate institutions, it has not been easy to make headway in the proceedings against magistrates and other judicial functionaries.

To the two points indicated above, it is necessary to add one more issue: the lack of specific training for the functionaries of the criminal justice system. These functionaries had previously been used to dealing with other classes of crime and lacked, in many cases, the sensitivity necessary to intervene in these proceedings. Evidently, these judicial processes are different from those habitually dealt with by the judicial system. This is primarily due to their greater complexity – the number of victims and defendants, their social repercussions, the years which have elapsed since the acts took place, and their institutional importance, amongst other things. There are also features which should be allowed for, such as possible connecting factors between cases, because in some cases the victims were transferred to different jurisdictions around country and / or through the actions of the defendants in different zones.

The existence of these multiple trials has as one of its most negative consequences that the witness-victims are summoned to give testimony on more than one occasion and in different jurisdictions. On each occasion, those who are summoned are questioned about fragments of what they have experienced. This is another thing which goes against the victims,[7] who are obliged to relive the horror over and over again; it is an abysmal procedural technique which also prejudices the trial since it gives leads to forgetfulness and generates waste of state resources.

In turn, the fact that the investigations into the violations of human rights which are currently in process are being judged in such a mistaken way has another negative consequence. The fact that they have been divided into thousands of trials rather than organized by means of a single large trial – or at the very least through several major trials – means that there are many cases which are not investigated. This is because the repression had a high level of coordination and interaction between its actors, in spite

7 On 3 September 2007, testifying at the trial where the accused was the priest Von Wernich, Adriana Calvo, one of the most important referents of the Asociación ex Detenidos (Association of ex-Detainees), whose case was Case No. 1 in the Trial of the Juntas, said, "that all the witnesses who testified in the trial will do so again, first in the upcoming trial against von Wernich, and the same witnesses will then testify in each of the lawsuits against each one of the other repressors involved". She noted the number of repressors identified (135), and with proof that they were in the Brigade of Investigations of La Plata, as an example. She wondered how many more trials, how many other testimonies, how many repressors will have died and how many survivors will be included, and how many more witnesses will disappear like Julio López; she asked that no more trials be conducted against only a single repressor, no more trials for only a few crimes, that genocide not be treated as the sum of isolated crimes. She noted that with one trial a year, there are twemty-nine camps [of the Camps Circuit] which will have to wait thirty more years, and even so, they will be multiplied by ten. She added that this is the third time she has declared in this Court [TOF 1 of La Plata], and that it is perhaps the fifteenth time she has declared and asked that they exempt her from telling the whole story again [the motive for which had already been cited], that there was no right to be treated in this way, and asked to declare only that which referred to Elena De la Cuadra [the motive for which had been quoted]. That she first declared in August 1984, when the case of Pozo de Banfield was initiated, and the secretary of the court is present. And that for twenty-three years she has been reiterating her story. She highlighted the physical and mental effort, and more, because last year Julio López was there and today he is not, and his kidnappers enjoy impunity".

of the fact that in appearance the distinct task forces have acted independently. From this feature derives the fact that in many cases the victims passed through different clandestine detention and extermination centres, located in different geographical locations and run by different armed and security forces.

As a result of this, where, as in the majority of cases, there are no specific complaints which would permit the incorporation of the crimes into some of the possible jurisdictions, cases are not always formed from these victims, and the crimes go unpunished. This brings with it a high level of frustration for relatives and victims who are unable to find answers within the democratic institutions to their reasonable demands for justice. In addition there can sometimes also be an overlapping of investigations, which results in judicial weakening and a waste of completely inadequate state resources.

With regard to the perpetrators of these crimes there are some difficulties relating to the passing of time: because the prosecution is taking place thirty years after the crimes were committed, many of those culpable have died or are found in impaired health, which means that they manage to gain impunity again. On the subject of health problems, this kind of "biological impunity" is used as a deliberate strategy on the part of the defence lawyers. Thus, the lawyers often try to remove the defendants from these trials by exploiting the decline in health they have suffered with the passing of the years – we are always talking of people of more than 50 – which might not always go so far as to imply immunity from prosecution.

Lamentably, in the majority of cases this device is passively accepted by the judges who leave out of the trials those accused of aberrant crimes, although this exclusion is not merited by the sufferings caused. To this is added the existence of grave suspicions of corruption with regard to the doctors who formed part of the *Cuerpo Médico Forense de la Corte Suprema de la Nación* (Forensic Medical Corps of the Supreme Court of the Nation).[8] It was they who generally undertook the forensic medical

8 These suspicions even gave rise to the intervention into the Cuerpo Médico Forense (Forensic Medical Corps) and severe criticisms on the part of the Minister, Carmen Argibay. See: http://www.pagina12.com.ar/diario/elpais/1-116322-2008-12-08.html.

tests which the judges used in order to decide whether or not to continue with the trials with respect to the unimputable suspects. This has resulted in the undue exclusion of some of those responsible and configures a new form of impunity detrimental to the process.

Another important issue when looking critically at this process is linked to the non-application of all the legal precepts which ought to frame these events in the offences established under the Criminal Code of the country. It must be emphasized that the legal precepts which are used and the criteria of their legitimacy vary according to the jurisdiction concerned. This depends on the discretion of each magistrate and brings about a lack of equality. Among the differences in ways of framing these events, some judges deliberately refuse to charge certain crimes.

Beyond the removal of several offences which can be considered of minor or low importance, the most serious examples are those of omitting the figure of torture when it was not, or could not be, proven that there had been torture in the most ordinary sense of the term – the passage of an electric current, immersion of the head in water, beatings, amongst the most well known. Other examples are not framing the disappearances within the crime of murder and not charging for the sexual crimes committed against detainees of both sexes.

On the basis of the point of view prevailing in the development of international human rights law, the deplorable conditions to which the kidnapped and abducted were subjected must be considered as encompassed in the crime of the application of torture. In the majority of the clandestine detention centres there occurred one or more situations which fall outside the more widespread idea of torture previously mentioned, but which without doubt constitute this crime. Amongst the more common are: to remain deprived of vision (which is known as *tabicamiento* or *blindfolding*); with the hands and feet tied, chained or handcuffed; receiving little or insufficient food; naked or semi-naked, which increases vulnerability exponentially; deprived of medical assistance; without being permitted to use toilets or to bathe for days at a time; sleeping on the floor, lying or sitting; deprived of their identity, which was replaced by a number; without contact with their families and the outside world; unable to be in the sun for even a few hours during the day; kept in confined spaces which did not permit the least movement, which obliged them to be cramped; listening to the torture, beatings and rapes of other people in the same position; receiving continual verbal abuse.

Without doubt, subjection to these conditions of confinement constitutes the crime of the application of torture and ought to be understood as such by the judges when it comes to framing these acts within the pertinent crimes. But this does not occur in every jurisdiction. It depends on the judge involved, who decides in a completely arbitrary way whether or not to apply the legal penalty in question.

Another kind of penalty which the judges are unwilling to use is that of homicide in the case of persons kidnapped and later disappeared. Even though it is nowhere established as obligatory, some judges erroneously demand the appearance of the corpse in order to impute the crime. Such a requirement turns out to be a form of negation or, at least, a profound ignorance of how the action of repression functions in our country. The central mechanism used by those who carried it out, the disappearance of persons, had several ends. Amongst these there can be distinguished – in addition to generating terror and imposing perverse doubts on family and friends – the concealment of the traces of the crime, by disappearing the bodies, with the objective of procuring future impunity. Paradoxically, the action of these judges rewards those who deliberately effected these disappearances with the objective of eluding the penal consequences of their crimes.

Moreover, it is now more than thirty years after these events occurred: it seems offensive not to recognize that the persons who passed through the centres of detention and extermination set up by the dictatorship, without being seen afterwards outside of these places set up especially as a machinery of annihilation, have been killed. At the same time, it has been thoroughly proven in recent years that the fate of the disappeared was death. This has been shown by the recovery, fundamentally through the work undertaken by the *Equipo Argentino de Antropología Forense* (Argentinean Forensic Anthropology Team) on a vast quantity of the remains of disappeared persons who were buried clandestinely. In penal terms, the difference is not unimportant, because at the moment of sentencing, not to apply the crime of homicide implies the impossibility of condemning the perpetrators to life imprisonment, the maximum penalty possible in our country. This is not possible if only kidnappings and tortures are applied, even if they are sentenced for thousands of cases. And in these cases, because of their characteristics, the facts are, moreover, demonstrated.

The origin of the non-imputation of the third group of crimes has to do with different questions from those analysed previously, which coincide with an incorrect evaluation of the facts and their isolated analysis, outside the context in which they took place. This is the refusal of the judges to advance with the investigation and punishment of the crimes against sexual integrity committed by the members of repressive groups and suffered by male and female detainees. These crimes took place in a generalized form in nearly all the clandestine detention and extermination centres set up in our country, and were carried out by members of every force and also by civilians and form a differentiated repressive practice.[9]

The sexual violence to which women and men were subjected cannot be addressed as though they were individual crimes produced by the perversion of their authors, without disregarding a significant part of the plan of annihilation and degradation of the subjectivity of the detainees, which was carried out in our country. This is different from the non-imputation for homicides in cases of disappearances and tortures with respect to the conditions of captivity, in that the root of this refusal has other aspects. Sexual violence, in general, is treated as being as being of lower rank with relation to other existing crimes, without distinguishing between whether it was indeed committed in the context of a clandestine detention centre or today, and this has its origins in the sexist and discriminatory understanding of gender which the judicial power reproduces.

In spite of the mass nature of the production of these crimes, there has only been one sentence for sexual violation. The general tendency of the

9 For a detailed analysis of the point, see: "Violencia de género y abusos sexuales en centros clandestinos de detención. Un aporte para la comprensión de la experiencia argentina", produced by Lorena Balardini, Ana Oberlin, and Laura Sobredo; on behalf of CELS and the Centro Internacional para la Justicia Transicional (ICTJ) as part of a book on the process of justice for the crimes of the last military dictatorship in Argentina.

judges is either to disregard and ignore them, or to erroneously subsume this class of offence under the figure of the application of torture, invisibilizing a specific and deliberate practice. This has negative consequences for the victims, who in the majority of cases believe that these crimes have been the ones which have most traumatized them and seek a separate penalty for them, regardless of progress with other charges. This results in frustration and must be addressed by the penal system, like other crimes suffered, as the different treatment accorded to them is wrong.

A form of closure: the value of the trials

I consider the criticisms outlined in the previous section to be necessary because they give a deeper insight into the process and into what changes work. That said, the present period has an unprecedented value both for the victims and the rest of society.

In the majority of cases, the victims are beginning to see the face of reparative justice for the first time. Despite being late, fragmented and somewhat limited, as indicated earlier, these trials have produced a major symbolic change in the place occupied by the victims who have lived through years of being negated, maltreated and challenged by the judicial power, where access to justice was systematically closed for twenty years. Somehow, these trials have once again put things in their proper place. Those who suffered these events are sitting in the place which witnesses have in criminal proceedings and must be heard by judges, the other parties and the public. In return, the defendants are located – in many cases for the first time – in the dock, answering very serious allegations in the context of respect for every constitutional guarantee established by the process.

In this sense it is also important to highlight two highly significant and important changes between the trials of the eighties and those which are in process now. On the one hand, the narratives which appear in the current trials are much richer in detail with respect to the experiences and sufferings of the witnesses. This is something which was addressed in an almost tangential form in the trials during the return to democracy, because in those years the evidence centred on what had happened to others, and above all on what the disappeared had suffered. In a way, the need to establish the figure of disappearance and to prove the plan of extermination – which today is completely accepted – during the eighties, is displaced now by the story of individual subjugations and experiences. In this, undoubtedly, the passing of time has had an influence and has permitted social and individual modification of the perception of what occurred and has set up a context which enables the entry of more personal narratives.

On the other hand, in the current stories both the survivors and the families of the disappeared or assassinated make explicit the political identities of the victims, even when they were members of armed organizations. During the trials of the eighties, these identities were nearly always kept hidden. The main reason for this was the force and centrality of the so-called "theory of the two demons" which equated the mass and systematic violence of extermination of the population effected by the terrorism of the state, with some actions allegedly perpetrated by guerrilla organizations. This produced fear in the witnesses, who had in their minds the thought that allowing these identities to come to the surface could result in judicial prosecutions or suffering refusals and discriminations and thus felt compelled to deny them.

Socially, moreover, these trials imply the highest exercise of collective memory. The existence of these trials, and the great media significance which they have, brings as a consequence a debate about the dictatorship, about the inheritance it has left us, about the repressed generation, and about political systems and liberty, which is extremely healthy for a democratic system.

That is why, although there are no ideal trials and we remain aware that we still have a long way to go, this process of justice currently taking place in our country is extremely positive and shows that perseverance in the struggle, as taught from the beginning by the *Madres* and the *Abuelas*, has its fruits. In short, these trials make clear what we knew from the outset and that is that the impossible only takes a little longer.

VERA VIGEVANI DE JARACH

The Role of Testimony as a Tool for the Creation of a Political Project

"Silence is health": this was the "advice" given to the entire society during the years of the civil-military dictatorship. In reality it was not a simple warning, but rather a form of intimidation, an ongoing and latent threat. It should be said that, in reality, when the terror was established, the greater part of the population fell silent. And, unfortunately, it was directly or indirectly complicit in what was happening. In some cases, it explicitly showed itself to be allied to the execution of those sinister plans of bloody repression and massacres which resulted in a real genocide designed to eliminate any form of opposition or resistance to *de facto* power. In itself, what was intended was the prevention of the realization of those social and economic changes which constituted the common project of a generation whose goal was to achieve a better, more just world, with equal opportunities for all and with full respect for human rights within a framework of full democracy and full freedom. Nevertheless, we recognize that not everyone complied with the mandate of Silence. Or, rather, that there was also a silence of quite a different nature and depth. It was a silence which, in truth, it sounded almost like a cry, and was repeated systematically every Thursday from 30 April 1977 in the Round of the *Madres* of the Plaza de Mayo. In that silent round the *Madres* always demanded answers, clarifications of those tragic disappearances into the Nothing. They asked always the same painful question: "Where are our children?".

It should also be pointed out that, in the face of the general silence of the national and foreign press, in the face of the silence of the diplomatic world and that of the majority of foreign governments, there were some important exceptions. These distinguished themselves by showing that, sometimes, in the darkest moments of history, ethical commitments also emerge, in which impulses of solidarity prevail, making truly courageous gestures and giving rise to brave strategies of open or clandestine resistance. Throughout the last century several different forms of generous defiance and rebellion have been recorded, which start and advance from different social environments in defence of freedom and human rights. History makes us aware of them and today, after a long time, it is memory whose mission it is to dispel the shadows of the half-truths and generalizations which can lead to unjust or biased assessments.

This has been possible largely thanks to the witness testimonies, one of the important sources of direct experience, coming together of course, with the documents, files and a number other contributions which can enrich historical knowledge. Great documentary value also derives from the Law which illuminates the truth in the development of the trials of those guilty of crimes against humanity committed during that period. It all comes together, finally, in the building of bridges of memory. We aspire to make them endure over time because we hope they will help achieve the desired *Nunca Más*. Hence we feel a symbolic and reflective duty to allay a worrying doubt: that with the passage of time, everything or much will gradually be denied and that the project of burying the memory of the past and consigning it to oblivion or misrepresentation will succeed.

We know, in this respect, that the key lies in the stubborn will to testify. The most suitable instrument is the word. We hope that, spoken or written and supported by the strength of the documents, the word will always record what should not be forgotten. We express this hope without ceasing to assume our commitments as witnesses of what each person has lived personally in addition to the many dramatic analogies which unite the numerous voices in a similar narrative. In any case, it should be noted that there are ever more forms of expression which offer us new strategies for memory for the future. They can break the wall of indifference and denial and even the attempts at impunity which still remain in certain sectors.

Particularly active and valuable in this field are expressions in the visual arts, theatre, literature, film, and the media in general, as well as didactic efforts in all spheres of education. Other forms of memory emerge in public spaces, from Memory Forests or Memory Parks to monuments and the maintenance of sites which in themselves raise awareness of what happened, such as those in which the kidnapped were imprisoned secretly, and are now open to today's visitors and those of the future. Seminars and meetings dedicated to remembering and reflecting on the events are other ways of marking and focusing the past with the active memory of what those crimes were: kidnapping, torture, killings, "disappearances". New initiatives of memorial and homage to the victims of this genocide and to the dreams and the ideals which inspired their lives emerge all the time. The totality of these efforts could perhaps be summarized in the slogan which for a many years the Madres chanted together with the people accompanying them, "*Presentes, ahora y siempre*" ("Present, now and forever"). Thus is our goal: that presence which marks a continuity with the past. From that point our journey begins.

"Present, now and forever"

Clearly this slogan refers to the thousands of victims of the ferocious repression carried out by the civil–military dictatorship. In other words, the regime which, after being established on 24 March 1976, kidnapped, tortured and killed thousands of people, attempted something which had never occurred before in the country: erasing any trace of the crimes committed, crimes which for years have been defined as "crimes against humanity". In order to carry out this extermination they availed themselves of various nefarious methods of "disappearance". The bodies were buried in mass graves such as "NN", thus removing their identity, or victims were thrown still alive, barely numb with an injection of pentothal, from planes, into the Rio de la Plata or the Atlantic Ocean, in the atrocious "flights of death". The clandestinely-held prisoners thus assassinated had previously experienced the hell of captivity in different sinister places, some in large and genuine concentration camps and others in smaller but no less terrifying sites scattered throughout the country.

With their "disappearance" the civil–military regime wanted to erase everything, from their journey through life to their very names. It did not succeed.

Although it did indeed exterminate thousands of lives, on the whole of young people between fifteen and thirty years old, they failed to erase their memory; nor will it succeed in erasing their place in the collective memory of society and we are also confident that history will show respect for them and pay them homage. We vindicate the meaning they gave to their existence, characterized by the desire to contribute to a project of changes which, they hoped, would lead to a fairer world for all. A better world. It will be recalled that the dictatorship took the lives of those who in the vast majority of cases had been devoted with passion to the cause of social transformation. It believed that by massacring them and hiding the evidence everything would be wiped out and erased forever, but their stories are present here in a history which is still being written and will continue to be written. Neither their names nor their faces will be forgotten, because we will remember them. And we will also remember those life commitments and ideals.

What seemed like broken utopias and blighted aspirations remain in reality open roads which a society with a strengthened democracy can travel, or in other words, a world with justice and equality of opportunity, and without poverty, without exclusions, with health and justice for all, marked by a strong civic consciousness of the possibility of participating and acting within the channels which democracy really offers. It is the best system of coexistence so far known and, although perhaps imperfect, it is always perfectible without ever resorting to violent means, and with peace and freedom as guarantees of harmonious coexistence. It is this which, along with the memories of the past, we want to transmit above all to young people, highlighting the strategic assets which may be at hand: among the first is public education. In any case it means always defending each and every one of the Human Rights. This is what the continuity of those projects means for us *Madres* of Plaza de Mayo and clearly explains the meaning of "present, now and forever".

It is an expression which links together different subjects, because it contains and summarizes those demands which for so long we marched for with aching footsteps, accompanied by the various organizations set up in defence of human rights. These are our objectives: Truth, Justice and Memory. It is worth reflecting on the meaning of each of these goals, so as to see how they intertwine and interconnect in a trajectory which links the past with the present and both with the possible future. This trajectory, moreover, encourages every effort to ensure that *Nunca Más* (Never Again) can anything like that terrible chapter in our history be repeated here or anywhere else in the world. To this end we have learned, among other things, that it is worth searching carefully in the contexts of the past which could give rise to it, uncovering, perhaps, both symptoms and preventive powers.

With knowledge and reasoning there may always be in society early warning systems capable of detecting in time something which could repeat itself, take notice of it and never, ever again, be indifferent or resigned to silence. This, of course, means taking into consideration and respecting today's methods and approaches and, above all, recognizing the value of the search for consensus in an egalitarian and collective context, a search which is invaluable for what it brings in terms of prior discussion and reflection as opposed to top-down strategies and any form of rigid orders. We see how democracy is growing and spreading. There is a continuous process of learning and this is true of all generations.

Light on the truth

I think that when talking about and discussing the light of Truth we must always bear in mind not only the circumstances in which this terror was able to establish itself, but also the reasons which motivated it. In other words, it is necessary to establish what interests and objectives led the state to organize such a horrific violence of repression. We then discover that it was a civil-military relationship based essentially on the economic interests of a particular social class which encouraged the coup through which the armed forces helped to install it in power. It wanted to thwart in this way any attempt at change promoted by a political activism whose ranks were swelling noticeably. Composed largely of workers and students, but also of professionals and intellectuals from reformist and progressive spheres, these groups were generally united by a common desire to restore an authentic representative democracy with popular participation through voting and the empowerment of political parties. It should be noted that Argentina had previously suffered several military coups which interrupted other brief periods of democratic life, always with analogous intentions of maintaining the "status quo" of self-interested economic systems and models. And in each interruption of democratic normality the Armed Forces turned out always to be the same indispensable actor, allied decisively in the achievement of this goal.

It is a reality which I experienced personally when, in 1938, in my native Italy, the fascist regime passed its race laws. My family, being Jewish, was in danger, but we managed to escape the worst, just in time, by taking refuge in Argentina in March 1939. Argentina welcomed us with opened arms, and also, upon arrival, we discovered a wonderful thing: freedom and democracy. I understood this well, despite being a girl of eleven years. It had nothing to do with the racist and totalitarian fascism of Benito Mussolini. There was a civilian government and the president, Roberto Ortiz, had been elected by popular vote. But we knew that there had been a military coup, that of Uriburu in 1930, and soon there was another. Argentina experienced six in the course of the twentieth century. And the periods of civilian rule and democratic context were few.

There were another five coups and that history is part of what I experienced in exile as I went through the various stages of my life in this beloved land. My childhood having been cut off early (I was expelled from primary school due to the racial laws), all the rest of it in Argentina was confronted with successive realities, historical events. And the dramas. Of those five coups, the last, of course, was the most tragic because of its terrible consequences. No previous dictatorship had been quite as hell bent on mass extermination, the physical removal of any person suspected of being an opponent and defined generically as a "subversive". The strategies which accompanied the cruel repression were of such magnitude that the silence demanded did not take long in becoming established. The state of terror demarcated a shocking atmosphere of helplessness, hardly broken by those few examples of resistance. The silence expanded in concentric circles which went beyond the national, stained in a way which seemed – and still seems – to me like a progressive poisoning capable of producing habituation to violence and "disappearances". The wounds which all this provoked were not only limited to the family, friends and comrades of the victims, survivors and exiles, but have also left marks, indelible traces, on the whole of society.

Hence the need to uncover the whole truth, to cast light on every aspect of those events, and also the demand for justice. And when the truth is confronted, another need immediately emerges, that of establishing bridges of memory to the younger generation. The road of Truth, then, leads to Justice and from both of these to Memory. The transition to Justice must be completely transparent and ensure flawless and absolutely fair convictions. It is worth mentioning that the many trials now under way in several cities are being conducted with the utmost impartiality. The historical events are clearly focused, which means that the truth is unquestionably clarified for everyone, both those who were already aware of it and those who have so far doubted or denied it. The story picks up the valuable support documented in the court hearings. Important material will also emerge within the general context of recent Latin American history in which there has been no shortage similar events, marked by similar networks complicit in repression within several countries, and therefore of interest worldwide.

This logic of commitment to memory has long been recognized in academic work, in the world of scholars and, in general, in the most diverse ways a kind of activism against forgetting. It is in this field that the testimonies become valuable vehicles, but always with an awareness of their own limits. It is not sufficient to allude to the thousands of "disappeared" and all the other victims of repression: the political prisoners, exiles and survivors of the clandestine detention centres often carry with them the heavy charge of feeling – unjustly – guilty of having saved themselves. Nor is it sufficient to testify in court hearings by expressing that grief, those feelings, along with the demand for justice. There is one further mission: to provide evidence of the painful experiences themselves and the recognition of the ideals which guided the victims until their lives were taken from them.

It is important that this testimony also comprises what it meant in everyday life, in the psyche, in the feelings, in every aspect of life, that individual and social drama, and, in parallel, the role the organizations for the defence of Human Rights, the few but essential exceptions of solidarity and resistance, the events until the fall of the regime, because everything flows into the collective memory we are trying to build. I saw, heard, and met many of these witnesses over the years and I think that each one brings a part, a portion of the story itself, which is still incomplete but which we can hope to complete step by step. I refer to the fact that the majority do not yet know the whole truth about the fate of their departed loved ones. I also believe that it would be necessary to stimulate reflection on general and particular testimony, my own too.

Testimony, role and limits

We are confronted with a past which is not passing away and with the continued presence of voices which try to deny or reduce the liability of those who gave the orders to repress and who, in executing these orders, tortured and killed, trying, in every case, to hide these crimes against humanity in the mists of uncertainty. In the face of this reality, we should try to shed light on what happened, using the various channels which are emerging for this purpose. We are referring to the different types of evidence, the testimonies contributed by the courts, in front of judges, and those which, in contrast, are systematically collected in major oral and audiovisual archives alongside the extensive documentation which has been preserved.

With the return of democracy and in course of time, they appeared urging us insistently to be reconciled, to set aside the past. "Enough", they said, "stop looking into the past, now take care of the future" and we responded promptly "it is because we are thinking about the future and because we do not want those events and those horrors to be repeated, that we give our testimony insistently and with perseverance". In the judicial sphere, of course, the voice of the witnesses assumes a key role by becoming in some cases the very proof of the crimes committed.

Following the annulment of the laws of impunity and the amnesties, trials were opened in Argentina and established throughout the country. In each of these trials witnesses appeared before the judges with the firm desire to contribute to the elucidation of the facts. It is certain that they never did so in a spirit of vengeance as some nostalgic supporters of the regime claim, but driven by a moral and civic duty to confront the difficult responsibility for uncovering the past in front of judges, lawyers and public opinion as a whole. They also faced some of the defendants themselves when they agreed to be present at the hearings, a fact that is not always the case given by the various difficulties in the establishment of the trial.

When anyone has to give testimony in a trial, in the time prior to their giving their statement we refer to this snare which is the presence of the repressors in the courtroom. For my part I usually compare this critical moment with the most important examinations which anyone may have had to face in their life. This, no doubt, would in any case be the most difficult and most necessary. There are possible analogies with the great examinations which require full maturity on the part of the student. What is demanded is absolute honesty together with a capacity for narrative and an analytical approach to their own thoughts and experiences, in the attempt to overcome the deep sorrow of incurable wounds which continue to bleed. This need exists at both the personal and the collective levels. I maintain that after testifying one feels liberated from a great burden, such as when taking off a rucksack after a long walk. One also feels emptied, as is the case after a particularly difficult examination.

This liberating feeling was also confirmed for me by a companion of the *Madres de Plaza de Mayo Línea Fundadora* (Mothers of Plaza de Mayo Founding Line), Haydée Gascía Gastelú, the mother of Horacio, who, like my daughter Franca, was a student of the *Colegio Nacional de Buenos Aires* (National College of Buenos Aires). This school had 106 victims among its students, as can be seen on a sculptural plaque which pays homage to them in the central patio. This is the patio, which is full of students during breaks and which brings them together for other activities, one of which is precisely to record, by means of special events, what was experienced by the school itself during those tragic years. Within the student framework itself, this is a valid and constructive way of not failing to cross the Bridge of Remembrance. What happened to Haydée after testifying in a trial is significant. The trial is related to the Massacre of Fatima, one of many abominable deeds committed during the dictatorship. Upon finally learning of the sentence which condemned some military officers and at the same time, declared the innocence of one due to lack of sufficient evidence, she felt all of a sudden confronted with a crossroads and I myself began to reflect upon this unexpected situation. How should we continue after this partial legal victory?

The question was raised again of how to fully maintain the personal commitment of Haydée and of other Mothers of Plaza de Mayo, always keeping in view the threefold axis of goals, Truth, Justice and Memory, foreign to any spirit of mere revenge, and, yes, in favour of the hope of the *Nunca Más*. In the case of Haydée, the court judgment was added to the fact that, thanks to the work of the forensic anthropologists, the remains of Horacio had been identified, buried as NN in a communal grave, and that had been certainly a victory to celebrate. It had, furthermore, allowed the family to pay their final respects to their child with a moving rite in the Church of Santa Cruz and afterwards take the ashes to the family tomb. The question which was born and which she launched was, "And now what?" But, immediately the answer also sprang up: "Keep going", or continue on our path. This is also, I would say, a civic and social commitment, driven by the will to honour the memory of our children as well to honour their dreams and ideals, and that so solid project for a more just world.

In this context it is clear that we are addressing in particular the young people of new generations as it is for them that we build these "Memory Bridges". We do so with the confidence not only that we will be heard and understood but that there will be, in response, a commitment to continue to persevere on this course. So, as Mothers and as witnesses, we are aware of our responsibility, which is almost a mission. Hence the biggest effort is rightly made in the courts, taking into account that the development of trials and their resolution in the judgments, in the sentences given, is a very important contribution to the historical construction of a collective memory which is duly recognized by society and has become truly instructive. Reflection has also led to the correct perception of our limits. We must recognize that our perceptions cannot be absolutely impartial, even though we try hard to be. Our expressions, gestures and words will translate the traumatic lived experience; our pain will emerge every time our memory reopens those wounds which never really close.

As an activist responsible for memory, at those moments I usually point out the need to listen to other voices, to consult documents, review the filmed and recorded material. This also substantiates an often raised demand that the trial hearings be filmed and distributed, in addition to being maintained as a valuable material which can be always available to be reviewed. As a means of dissemination I am referring in particular to television as a immediate medium for monitoring the trials by public opinion. The filmed material may also be a very useful teaching tool in schools and, moreover, could be stored in libraries and video libraries in the future. Most of the ongoing trials are filmed but not broadcast on television. In some cases moreover there were courts which had denied the access to the filmings, something which led the Government to pass a law which clarifies the obligatory nature of these filmings.

In any case, for students in schools today there is a vast reservoir of information. This covers not merely the reading and the consultation of documents in the existing archives and the sight of many films which deal with these questions, but also guided tours of clandestine detention centres which have been converted into deeply meaningful places of memory. All the arts have played an expressive role; they have contributed much and continue to do so. That is, there is no shortage or lack of ways of getting closer, knowing, understanding.

All of this strengthens and inspires, with perseverance and courage, anyone who must bear witness. Courage is necessary because, unfortunately, there have been no lack of threats and indeed one case of a "disappeared" witness, that of Jorge Julio López, so it is necessary to overcome fears and hesitations. His disappearance happened following a trial in the city of La Plata, and under conditions of full democracy. We continue to call for the "appearance with life" of this witness who survived his first forced "disappearance" but we have been unable to find out anything about him after the second. And several years have passed already. These threats currently impose the need to protect witnesses who testify in court. Protection is provided by the state and must continue even after declaration and it is not just a question of physical but also psychological protection in the case of the survivors who carry the burden of terrible and traumatic experiences. In some cases it is also a question of people who, having passed through several places of concentration, have to testify in other trials, which means repeating such painful experiences.

Justice advances in any case. We worry about its slowness but we recognize its great value, we recognize its gradual progress. Amongst us, the families of the victims, the oldest often think that perhaps they will not see the end of these trials, that perhaps they will not see justice in their own cases. But we continue to follow, one step at a time, this path which is essential to uncovering the truth and judging those guilty of so much horror. What we ask is that an attempt is made to unify some of the trials which have a similar character or present certain analogies.

The newspaper *Página 12* has continued to record systematically invaluable everyday information, in the detailed chronicles of a number of its journalists. Other media have devoted very little attention to the subject. To give a numerical idea of the work and the rhythm of justice, a single example will suffice: in 2009, 67 prosecutions were instituted, resulting in thirty-two convictions. This work was further intensified and this accounts for the fact that impunity has been vanquished and we believe that there are guarantees that there will be no turning back. The mega trial for the crimes committed by the ESMA, which is considered the symbolic case among the hundreds of clandestine detention centres because it received several thousand victims, has seventeen defendants and nearly a thousand witnesses. It is known that almost 400 clandestine detention sites were scattered throughout the country and this means that there are currently trials in many cities.

As the *Madres de Plaza de Mayo Línea Fundadora*, we have set ourselves, among other things, the task of accompanying the witnesses to the hearings, which are painful and traumatic experiences. They really need not only the warm support we can give, but also that of the whole of society. The accumulation of trials, and the fact that some witnesses are called to testify in several cases, accentuate the psychological burden which has to be sustained. In fact, professional counselling becomes directly necessary. Some experts in the field believe that in the judicial sphere twenty years may be needed to complete these trials, because of, among other things, the huge number of papers, records and proofs to be examined. Since many of the family members are already at an advanced age, it is logical to think and fear that many of them will not – nor will we – be able see the conclusion of this process of justice. Nevertheless we know it is our duty to take part, both with the testimonies, and with our presence at the hearings. This in addition to the apparently inevitably slow progress of justice.

In the light the continuing receipt of threats, it is worth noting that there are provisions to grant protection to witnesses, but that this is not accepted in all cases by the parties concerned, as it means a surveillance which conflicts with the normality of the daily life of any citizen. This inconvenience is overcome by recognizing how important it is for everyone to do justice. In general we can say that this protection and psychological support are indispensable, above all when it comes to witnesses who are survivors of the concentration camps. It is they who, inevitably, remembering and recounting the events experienced, face the bloody reopening of wounds which have left indelible marks. They have experienced and remembered the pain personally. To this pain of the loss of their companions, is added that of the unjust burden of feeling guilty for having been saved. These witnesses understand the relevance of their contribution and bear the trial with fortitude and courage. They do so with the consciousness, moreover, of the threats, and in the face of the reality of the intimidation which some have received and the notorious case of the disappearance of the witness Julio López after testifying in one of the most important trials in La Plata.

There was even the theft of documents relating to the repression, carried out at the headquarters of the *Secretaría de Derechos Humanos* (Ministry of Human Rights) in this city, an action which was also seen as a threat. Fortunately it was not repeated, but the threats in different forms, do not stop. All of this has been confronted decisively, while disappointment and sadness are frequently expressed over the great silences maintained by the news media about the precise conduct of the trials. Few words are dedicated to it, and not the detailed chronicles which society would need. In this we see a continuation of that painful silence on the part of the press which accompanied us throughout the dictatorship. Let us not forget to mention of some characteristics of that silence, since we have as our fundamental objective the attainment of the goal for which so many years had animated our path: the universal *Nunca Más*.

We are going, then, to pay particular attention to the silence which had, unfortunately, a crucial role in helping the regime to keep quiet about the different events and aspects of its repression. At the same time, we must recognize and stress the importance of the few but courageous acts of resistance which joined with our own, acts which, in some cases, were the exact exceptions to the general silence. We owe them recognition and honour because they meant, indeed, running many risks in those days of terror. They can remain as examples of the highest civic and human endeavour.

Silence, yes, but not everyone fell silent

What began to make itself visible as resistance were our rounds in the Plaza de Mayo. They soon became almost a folkloric aspect of the city centre opposite the Government House, the Casa Rosada. Thus they saw us on Thursday afternoons as they passed by. They were those who for the most part watched from the "other side", with an air of manifest indifference. They were those who said of us, "they are just a bunch of crazy people". "That's right", we clarified, "we're mad with pain because they have taken our children". "Tell us where they are" we demanded. Our grief was answered with indifference and silence and not the solidarity we demanded. The press followed suit: it kept quiet. I think the mass information media of that period were, in truth, mass media of disinformation. The same was true of foreign countries and their diplomatic representatives, with very few exceptions, such as Sweden which moved itself for one single disappeared person from that country or the Italian Consul Enrico Calamai who managed to save a few people. The Silence of the other countries was a result of the economic interests which they had in Argentina, which were apparently more important than human lives.

At any rate it is necessary to remember those in the media who dared to break the silence. In addition to the underground press, there was an English language newspaper, the *Buenos Aires Herald*, which reported on the kidnappings and published some of our *Habeas Corpus* demands, which were rejected systematically by the law. Its editor, Robert Cox, who has recently been made an honorary citizen of the City of Buenos Aires, used the pages of his newspaper to denounce what no one else denounced. Perhaps they let him do so in the belief that few, apart from some North American and English people, would read it. But they were wrong. The truth is that this news broke through the siege, leaving the country by means of foreign correspondents and some international news agencies but without thereby managing, in any case, move to their respective governments. This information, together with other materials gathered secretly by organizations for the defence of Human Rights, also came to appear in two local publications, the daily *Noticias* and the weekly *Descamisado* ("Shirtless") until their distribution was severely repressed. The illegal news agency, the ANCLA (*Agencia Noticiosa Clandestina Latino Americana*) was invaluable, thanks to the courageous work and the abilities of its organizers, Horacio Verbitsky and Rodolfo Walsh. Courage was also shown by some other journalists who, faced with media directors who impeded publication of news about what was happening, gave the information to the agencies and foreign newspaper correspondent. In this way "something" was carried out of the country.

An exemplary figure of strength and courage was certainly that of Rodolfo Walsh. His famous *Carta Abierta* (Open Letter) took stock of the reality of crimes and disasters caused by the dictatorship in the year after the 1976 coup; it was also distributed clandestinely by his wife after he was murdered. Today it is read in the schools as an example of great courage and clarity of analysis. But at that time there was not even the slightest mention of Walsh in the two major Argentinean newspapers, *La Nación* and *La Prensa*, although they had accommodated the writings, the literary work, of this remarkable writer and journalist in the past. Once again proving their courage, the only newspaper which dedicated a note to him was the aforementioned *Buenos Aires Herald*. The assassination of the writer was a direct "response" of the regime to the famous *Carta*. A military "gang" from the ESMA committed the crime which the authorities wanted to pass off as suicide. They said that Walsh had taken his life at home waiting for them to come and look for him after having written that open letter, an assertion which has to be completely rejected since the journalist was living in hiding and no one knew where. In fact, on reaching the exterior, the *Carta Abierta* had the impact it deserved.

Resounding facts concerning the press of the time are the arrest of the editor of the newspaper *La Opinión*, Jacobo Timerman. Timerman was saved by international pressure but after having experienced, like many others, the repressive violence in a prison cell. He later recounted that suffering in a seminal book of great evidential value, published in several languages. *La Opinión* had been an example of the great renewal of journalism, and was known throughout the world. And there were victims of the dictatorship among its journalists. In fact about 90 journalists "disappeared" in Argentina at that time.

The silence of the news media had to do both with the undeclared but actual systems of censorship, with the "review" by the regime of the news which came out of the country and, of course, the terror imposed on the entire society. In the case of journalists this often meant a self-imposed censorship in addition to the strict orders they were given by the owners of newspapers, magazines, radio and television. With regard to the media of foreign countries, with few exceptions, the silence lasted until the 1978 World Cup Championship which was hosted that year in Argentina. In addition to their reports on the matches, the sports commentators who came in large numbers to Argentina noted down some comments about what had happened and what was happening: the terrible events of the dictatorship. They talked to the *Madres* of the Plaza de Mayo and listened to other voices. This news was different from the exaltation of sport and helped break the silence.

It came too late, however, because thousands had already become victims. From time to time, however, some foreign newspaper took care to focus on the drama which was happening both in Argentina and elsewhere in Latin America. And it will suffice to give as an outstanding example, the performance of a French newspaper, *Le Monde*, whose local correspondent kept sending news which the paper published and which many of its faithful international readers also read, step by step.

One special case which accounts for how the silences were handled has to do with the story of an Italian journalist, Giangiacomo Foá, correspondent of the Milan newspaper *Il Corriere della Sera*.

The long period of silence maintained by this newspaper under the influence of the P2 lodge and its leader, Licio Gelli, while under the management of the company Rizzoli, is remembered today in Italy as a truly shameful fact. This occurred because the "venerable teacher" Gelli, a recognized partner of the Argentinean dictatorship, operated as a official business manager representing Argentina in its dealings with Italy. He did so using an Argentine passport, a false document made in no less a place than the ESMA. In the *Corriere* Gelli dictated his orders so as to prevent injury to the interests of the Argentine regime with which he collaborated or, for whom he was, as he defined himself, their spokesman. The manufacture of the false passport is mentioned in the testimony of Victor Basterra, one of the survivors of the ESMA.

Giangiacomo Foá managed to carry out with courage and professionalism his task of providing information to the Milan daily. He did so until, under the influence of Gelli, the company warned him to leave the office in Buenos Aires and called for silence on Argentina. Foá, however, continued to report from Rio de Janeiro and send articles about the tragic Argentine realities which the newspaper promptly failed to publish. He also obtained a list of the "disappeared" of Italian origin, and was eventually able to get the newspaper to publish it on the very day that Gelli's influence collapsed with the newspaper's change of ownership. Its publication caused an uproar and from that moment a good part of the press in Italy began to deal with the tragedy of the "disappeared". Moreover, in the following weeks a sort of competition was sparked off among Italian newspapers to tell everything which had happened and was happening in Argentina. The silence was broken and finally also the news sent by the Italian news agency ANSA, which until then had been systematically dismissed by the newspapers, began to be published. Foá's bravery earned him widespread popularity at the time; unfortunately he died shortly after at a very young age.

With respect to Italy in the early days of the dictatorship, when lives could still been have saved, the then Ambassador, Enrico Carrara, closed the doors of the Embassy. He thereby prevented the relatives of "disappeared" of Italian origin from directly presenting their dramas, their situations, their demands, something which, perhaps, might have led to concrete actions of solidarity.

From this dismal picture, however, we must rescue the noble figure of the then Italian President Sandro Pertini, who tried repeatedly to save his compatriots who had been kidnapped or were in danger of being kidnapped. He was unable to arouse decisive actions or responses, always due to prevalence of the economic interests over humanitarian. Indeed the Italian system prevents the President from taking the big decisions. These remain with the head of the Council of Ministers, the "premier", and it was there that the collusion was rooted. Everything changed a few years later but, obviously, by then it was too late. This is to emphasize once again the need to act in time when human lives are at stake, to show solidarity while "something" can still be done. Pertini will not be forgotten by those who were welcomed by him with deep affection and we know that he tried in vain to help us, his inability to do so being a bitter disappointment in his life.

The panorama of the other countries was similar. Even the Vatican, from the figures of the Nuncio Apostólico, who in those days was Pio Laghi, to the highest prelates (also with a few courageous exceptions in this sphere), failed to respond to the insistent demands of the families of the "disappeared" even though among them were priests and nuns who had enlisted in Catholic social movements, set up by the Church in the Third World. And to continue with other negative examples, even the Soviet Union did not engage in helping members of the small Argentine Communist Party who had fallen as hostages, victims of the dictatorship. Silence and apathy were the answers we had and it is not possible to forget them. By contrast, there were cases in which, thanks to courageous actions taken in time, it was possible to liberate prisoners already legalized in prisons and at the disposal of the Executive and, in exceptional cases, save some who had been abducted and taken to clandestine detention centres, anterooms generally of death. We must remember and recall that there were righteous people who risked their own lives to save others. Unfortunately, however, the balance always weighs on the side of the lack of solidaristic action.

Those of us who today bear our testimony in different areas and want to build truly valid bridges of memory, must pay homage and point out as examples the figures of those beings who were able to act with dignity and courage against the grain of that whole indifferent, silent majority which was also somewhat functional to the prevailing state terrorism.

With regard to my particular interest addressed to secondary school students, my most exciting experience has taken place in the National College of Buenos Aires, the school my daughter went to; there I organize competitions on human rights issues and also managed to put together exchanges with some high schools in Italy. To give an example of what is at stake in these exchanges, I will mention the last one which was undertaken in conjunction with the high schools of Italy. The purpose was to develop a common theme: that of migration in both directions, Italians to Argentina and Argentineans to Italy. It focused above all on the often injured Human Rights of migrants who are subjected to marginalization, exclusion, discrimination and sometimes racism. The value this has had for my particular case will be readily understood. It was precisely because they were attempting to carry forward similar objectives of achieving justice and a better world, that there were over 100 victims of the dictatorship among the students at the National College of Buenos Aires. Today, by contrast, with the maturation of the Democracy we retrieved more than thirty years ago, the ideas and the dialogue, as well as the student movement in defence of human rights are respected. Furthermore, in many cases it has entered directly into the curriculum.

The phrase which a student at a secondary school in Turin wrote to me some years ago, after having listened to me, always resounds powerfully in my ears and I usually repeat it: "*The only thing which can guarantee Nunca Más is that never again is there any indifference*". This is in fact the cornerstone of all preventive measures and the fact that the prescription comes from young people shows that our efforts are worthwhile and we can be hopeful. Since this is a question, moreover, of efforts shared with every agency which continues to concern itself with Human Rights in Argentina, this hope is strengthened and encourages us to believe that, looking towards the future, there are indications which give us back the importance of the dreams of our children. They give us a glimpse of a continuation of their road: the goals to be reached not only for Argentina and Latin America in general. They are for many other regions of the world. Perhaps for the world as a whole.

What matters is the transverse nature of this work of memory in the future and there is always an ideal time to establish the aforementioned inter-generational "bridges". This is when our need to narrate corresponds, on the other hand, to the visible need expressed in questions, to listen. There, in the middle of the "bridge", is where we understand each other and unite in a common project, a shared progress. Only in this way can the many violations of human rights, the wars, poverty and hunger, social injustice, really be left "behind" and, side by side, we would defend resources, protect our planet, and confront the diverse ecological problems in the context of liberty for all.

Yes, they are perhaps still utopias, but some utopias can become realities if we all strive after them with full commitment and intelligence. Thus, in this plan of action, memory suggests instruments of different types, almost all of them linked in some way to education, but we will cite some examples which endorse symbolic support: monuments, works of art, literary expression, music, theatre. The sites of memory created in places where the most sinister events occurred in various parts of the world have a very strong, very significant role. The very trees, forests, squares and commemorative trails, as well as thematic reviews of cinema and television, free consultation of audiovisual archives and collections of factual texts are all important aids to memory, which sometimes become very popular protagonists for reviewing the paths of history. There is no shortage of sources, nor lack of the means to access them; it is enough to spark an interest in the consultation, the will to know, to learn and understand where the failures and the complicities were, and also to take into account some fine examples of resistance and solidarity.

In the face of the will of the repression to erase all traces of its crimes, deleting the names of its victims, erasing their life stories, reminders have been established at many sites in recorded lists of names and historical reconstruction through images, documents, stories. A newspaper, *Página 12*, has published promptly, on a daily basis, reminders of the dates of kidnappings and "disappearances". Everything may seem difficult and complex and nothing is easy, indeed, but, as Judge Carlos Rozanski of La Plata said, on being given a prize for being a "Teacher of life", summarizing everything in three words: "If one can".

PART IV

Memory and Democracy

MARINA DI FRANCO

Gaps in Memory and Political Silences

In Argentina the evocation of state terrorism invokes automatically the armed forces and last military dictatorship. This is entirely undisputable if it is considered that the military as an institution was responsible for a murderous enterprise based on the forced disappearance of persons, and was responsible for a dictatorship which seized power in 1976 with the aim of reshaping the nation.

However, this memory tends to establish, by default, a split between the dictatorship on the one hand and the years and the governments which preceded it on the other. At best, it is typically noted that the clandestine repression began with the Triple A, a paramilitary organization created by José López Rega, Minister of Social Welfare in the Peronist government prior to the coup, and especially active from the beginning of the presidency of María Estela Martínez de Perón from mid-1974. Another antecedent which is often cited as an example of the military "rehearsals" before 1976 military is "Operation Independence", carried out by the Armed Forces in the province of Tucumán from 1975 onwards. However, as will be argued in these pages, the authoritarianism and repressive and disciplinarian practices began long before 1976; they were carried forward not only by means of clandestine practices but, fundamentally, as a systematic official policy of the democratic Peronist governments between 1973 and 1976 and enjoyed the support or indifference of various political sectors with institutional responsibility.

The invention of the past

The image of the military dictatorship as an absolute fracture in the course of the recent history of our country is real and is the result of the brutal social, political and economic break produced by that government. However, this was also a retrospective construction consolidated during the first post-authoritarian period as a result of the needs of multiple actors (starting with the two main parties: the Radicals and the Peronists), which assigned to the dictatorship a sphere unconnected with the rest of the political dynamics of the previous decades. The first fundamental fact of that retroactive construction was the creation of a "taboo" surrounding the repression carried out by the Peronists in the years of democratic government (1973–1976). No doubt this silence was not new, and had been the subject of older tensions. For example, during the dictatorial years some exile circles tended to omit from their international campaigns public condemnation the fact that repression had begun before 1976.[1] Within the human rights organizations too, references to the repression mention the year 1975 only sporadically, and even then the agents seen as responsible were always the Armed Forces and the Triple A associated with López Rega, detached, of course, from both the Peronists in the government and from the political parties in general.[2]

In any case, the construction of the break around 24 March 1976 was not resolved in the earliest post-authoritarian years and ended up being defined in the political decisions and negotiations of that first moment of

1 See, for example, Franco 2008.

2 According to Nadia Tahir, the human rights organisations originally argued that the sole responsibility for the repression lay with the military. This reading began to be modified from the time of Menemism, when the participation of Peronism and the government of Isabel and the restoration of the repression began to be invoked. Amongst the newly responsible appeared the figure of Lúder, but also Balbín and the UCR. (Nadia Tahir, "Les associations de victimes de la dictature: acteurs politiques dans l'Argentine de 1976–2007", Universidad Paris IV-Sorbonne, under the direction of de Miguel Rodríguez, thesis in progress).

the political recreation of the democratic illusion. When the CONADEP, created by Raúl Alfonsín, expressed its intention to investigate the crimes committed before 1976, the Radical president rejected the idea that the investigation should touch on the responsibilities of Peronism and other political forces in general.[3] At the same time, the law of *Reparación Histórica* (Historical Reparations Act) was passed as a result of an agreement between Alfonsín and the former President, Martínez de Perón. This exonerated her from criminal responsibility for any offence committed before March 1976 because she had been removed from office by an "act of military rebellion". The arrangement also covered members of the three branches of the Armed Forces, and in connection with the Triple A, stated that since the organization had begun to function before the presidency of Perón's widow and the people involved were dead, "Isabelita" had no responsibility.[4]

Among the evidence of the profound breaks constructed in the early years of democracy there is also the new legitimacy of human rights discourse and the dilution of the formerly natural and valid explanations for violence. Thus, the reality of the "war" and the "subversion" in unquestioned and valid use in the years before the military dictatorship, gave way to other all-explaining figures: "victims" and "genocide".[5] From the start of the eighties the difficulty encountered by human rights organizations, some leftist forces and the exile circles in disarming the notion of "war" and establishing the legitimacy of the categories of "genocide", "victims" and "crimes

3 E. Crenzel, *La historia política del Nunca Más*, Buenos Aires, Siglo XXI, 2008, p. 232, n. 167. According to Malamud Goti, Alfonsín's strategy was to avoid widening the responsibilities to include Peronism and the trade unions of the right in order to circumvent an "alliance between the trade union and military corporations".

4 Law 23.062, 23/5/84 (BO, 19/7/84). For an analysis of the political conjuncture which defined the passing of the law, see Verbitsky, "El pacto Alfonsín-Isabel". *Página 12*, 11/2/2007.

5 I have addressed in detail the political and media circulation of the idea of war and subversion in Franco in *Un enemigo para la nación. Orden interno, subversión y guerra (1973–1976)* (forthcoming). Because many of the issues raised tangentially in this paper are taken from that more extensive publication, I am obliged refer to it frequently.

against humanity", was directly linked to the weight these images had in the universe of military ideology, in the military organizations themselves and, more widely, in the social circulation of representations of violence in the years before the dictatorship.[6] The result of that juridical effort succeeded in breaking up the discourse of war and of political conflict so as to make it possible to think of the victims as legal persons affected in their most basic right, the right to life. The Trial of the Military Juntas in 1985 also contributed substantially to this development; its closing argument had as one of its main axes the dismantling of the war argument and the construction of the figure of the victim devoid of any political or activist connotation.[7] Thus, the construction of the "innocent". "depoliticized" victim, subdued by an authoritarian military regime, which was consolidated in those post-authoritarian years, permitted the splitting of the dictatorship from the political conflicts from which it had arisen. In other words, the victimization was also necessary in order to make the military regime absolute and separate it radically from the rule of law which had preceded it between 1973 and 1976 and followed it from 1983.[8]

Thus, although Alfonsín had been harshly critical of the repressive state policies during the democratic years of the 1970s,[9] the 1976 break was tacitly affirmed by his government's policy of investigation and justice starting from 1983. Thus, the matrix which constituted the passage from the authoritarian state to the rule of law was the construction of a binary opposition between dictatorship and democracy. The former was associated with violence and "human rights violations" committed by the armed forces. The latter, by contrast, was associated with the political and legal condemnation of these violations and the recognition of the victims. The

6 See, in particular, the argumentation of de Vezzetti, 2002, about the discourse of war.

7 See the analysis of the statement of the public prosecutor Julio César Strassera in Lvovich & Bisquert.

8 Without doubt, the succession of military coups and the political instability of Argentina during the twentieth century prevent location of the dictatorship as a parenthesis, but at least its repressive uniqueness was remains clear.

9 On the positions of Alfonsín between 1973 and 1976, see M. Franco, ibid.

violence itself was no longer conceived of as part of politics and become instead a form of *mal radical* ("radical evil": Nino, 1997) which democracy had purged in its act of refounding itself.

In short, the hushing up of Peronist participation in repression, of the widespread repressive consensus which accompanied the final stage of democracy and the "forgetting" of the collective appeal to the military forces to carry out this task, has been an essential part of a narrative which consolidated itself between 1983 and 1985. In those selections from memory our entire contemporary narrative of the recent past has been constructed. At present the criminal cases concerning acts of repression prior to 1976 and those which involve the responsibility of civilian actors in the clandestine repression have begun to open a gap in the monochord memory of the past. Nevertheless, there are still many steps to be retraced.

1973–1976: some neglected issues

Part of that retracing of steps obliges us to review the short period of democracy in the 1970s: this was the defining moment the of the consolidation of the road to state terrorism. The brief three-year period was marked by the presence of Peronism in power and by two other simultaneous and concurrent political scenarios: first, the prevalence of internal conflicts within the governing force in national politics and, second, an extensive process of social mobilization and left-wing political radicalization. The most visible facet of the latter was the growing presence of political-military organizations of an insurrectionary nature, among the most visible the ERP-PRT (*Partido Revolucionario de los Trabajadores-Ejército Revolucionario del Pueblo*: Revolutionary Workers Party-People's Revolutionary Army) and the *Montoneros*. These groups had arisen in the context of the authoritarianism, the political proscription of Peronism and the military repression of the 1960s. As result, with the reestablishment of a democratic context, the government and the political leadership thought their armed activities would cease. However, these groups continued and deepened the escalation of violence, in part because their project was not the democracy which the new institutional framework could offer, but a project of radical and revolutionary transformation inscribed on a regional and epochal scale.

The constitutional period in question began in May 1973 with the presidency of Héctor Cámpora, who owed his position to the fact that Perón was banned as a presidential candidate. His government began with two key acts: the annulment of the repressive legislation imposed by the previous dictatorship of the *Revolución Argentina* ("Argentinean Revolution": 1966–1973) and the release and the pardoning of the political prisoners who had arrested during those years, a good number of whom were members of the armed revolutionary organizations which had emerged during the late 1960s.

However, after a few weeks in office and once electoral constraints had been lifted, Cámpora resigned and new elections were held. With almost 62% of the vote, Perón governed between October 1973 and June 1974. After his death, he was succeeded by his vice president and widow, María Estela Martínez de Perón. But long before this, during the brief interim government of Raúl Lastiri (July–October 1973) which preceded the assumption of Perón, a slow escalation of state policies of an *authoritarian, disciplinarian and repressive* nature began and this would continue during the government of the General and then of his widow. These policies were expressed at a number of highly coordinated levels: a) government policies of a formally legal character, many of which, however, suspended and systematically violated the rights enshrined in the constitution; b) paramilitary or clandestine policies; and c) intraparty politics mixed with government decisions of national scope.[10]

10 The analysis which follows concentrates on the problem of state violence and the authoritarian process. Thus we can conscientiously leave on one side the social, economic and sectoral conflicts which were also especially serious in the years studied and which form a part of the history indispensable for understanding the road to the coup d'etat. For more information on this period, see: L. De Riz, *La política en suspenso 1966–1976*, Buenos Aires, Paidós, 2000; J.C. Torre, *El gigante invertebrado. Los sindicatos en el gobierno (1973–1976)*. Buenos Aires, Siglo XXI, 2004; M. Svampa,

For chronological reasons we shall begin with the intraparty level as it was the first to emerge in 1973. In those years, Peronism was permeated with irreconcilably conflicting projects and tendencies. In a very schematic way it could be said that, on the one hand, there was the "revolutionary tendency" consisting of youth groups, armed organizations, a militant wing of trade unionism, intellectuals and various forces from the left who had joined Peronism in the preceding years, and who advocated a *patria socialista* ("socialist homeland"); and, on the other hand, there was a broad and heterogeneous right, formed by the majority trade union tendency and some party-political sectors of a fascist, nationalist, and anti-communist persuasion, later linked to López Rega and the security forces. These different forces all contended for the legitimacy of incarnating the true Peronism and its leadership.[11] In any case, for the traditional sectors of Peronism embedded in the highest state and party leadership, building a new power project involved the "cleansing" of the leftist youth sectors: in previous years these had been functional to the political and electoral process but, once the institutional situation had been normalized, they were seen as potential threats to the desired new Peronist order.

Thus, from half way through 1973 there began a major intraparty offensive to oust the radicalized sectors from the spaces of state and party power. Probably the famous "Massacre of Ezeiza" on 20 June 1973 when Perón returned to the country, is the best remembered expression of these internal conflicts. Soon after, in October, the same Perón officially announced the "cleansing" of Peronism of any "Marxist" and "subversive infiltration" so as to "eliminate" the "pathogens" which had declared internal "war" within the movement.

"El populismo imposible y sus actores, 1973–1977", in Daniel James (ed.), *Violencia, proscripción y autoritarismo (1955–1976): Nueva Historia Argentina*, Volume IX, Buenos Aires, Sudamericana, 2003, pp. 381–438.

11 For a discursive interpretation of the conflict, see Sigal, Silvia & Verón, Eliseo, *Perón o muerte: los fundamentos discursivos del fenómeno peronista*, Buenos Aires, Legasa, 1986.

> The groups or sectors which in each location operate by invoking adherence to Peronism and General Perón must define themselves publicly in this situation of war against the Marxist groups and should participate actively in the actions which are planned to carry forward this struggle.[12]

This call, made from the Casa Rosada and before all the provincial governors, unleashed a genuine McCarthyite style persecution within the main political force in the country. Taking into account the party-political and government framework to which we referred above, throughout 1973 and the whole of 1974 the "cleansing" was channelled simultaneously at a number of levels: first, through intra-party actions which affected even the most local and smallest areas of Peronist political action; second, through the official policies of the government; and, third, through armed paramilitary activities. In the strict sphere of the party itself, all provincial parties were intervened in, activists were expelled, the party's internal structure reformed and the youth sectors systematically dislodged. But, as Peronism also boasted control of the state apparatus, the "purification" also appeared directly through government policies.

This leads us to the second level of the above-mentioned analysis: the official policies carried out between 1973 and 1976. Officially and legally, the Peronist government launched various measures aimed at the social and political disciplining of their opponents – many of them rank and file members of Peronism itself – through increasingly repressive policies. Thus, for example, the working of the institutions was altered in various provinces through federal intervention or by forcing the resignation of the legally elected authorities with the aim of expelling those officials considered sympathetic to the Peronist left. This systematic practice was carried out between November 1973 and October 1974 in cases where the provincial governors were close to or had the support of sectors of the Juventud Peronista (JP: Peronist Youth), for example in Salta, Mendoza, Santa Cruz, Buenos Aires and Formosa.[13]

12 "Restricted document", Peronist Supreme Council, *La Opinión*, 2/10/1973.

13 Beyond the federal interventions or the forced renunciation of governors, all the provinces and their administrative structures were obliged to "purify themselves" and were affected by the expulsion of functionaries considered to be "Marxists".

In many other areas of national life similar policies were imposed. To take just a few cases: on the grounds of the continued violence of the guerrillas, all penalties under the Criminal Code were substantially hardened (even further than the legislation introduced by the military dictatorship of 1966) and policies were created to ensure "national security" through the suppression of "terrorism" and "subversion". Under these designations were included armed actions by the Guevarist and the Peronist left, with particular emphasis on the former, whose priority targets were, moreover, the security forces and military installations. However, as we shall see, the notion of "subversion" was extended to describe a variety of phenomena and actors. In parallel, the systematic restriction of different rights led to the permanent suspension of constitutional freedoms and guarantees.

In the sphere of work, for example, a series of legislative measures tended to reduce the space and the political feasibility of more the combative trade unionism which had emerged in the late 1960s. Power was centralized and concentrated in the national Peronist trade unions, and union democracy was cut substantially, as was the right to strike. These laws permitted intervention in and the suspension of the official trade union status of many trade unions, created legal frameworks for the arrest of non-Peronist union leaders and substantially limited strikes and conflicts the factories. In the university field, moreover, which was very much under the control of the Juventud Peronista (Peronist Youth), laws restricting the kind of university and political life proper to those houses of study were imposed, education authorities with openly fascist roots were put in place, all universities were intervened in and student centres closed. In the sphere of the freedom of expression and information, finally, an accelerated process of censorship of the press and television and prohibition of books and materials considered "subversive" began early in 1973.[14]

14 The list of policies is not exhaustive and only intended to give an overview of the different areas affected by the official disciplinarian and repressive policies. In the sphere of the workplace there was the interference of the *Ley de Asociaciones Profesionales* (Professional Associations Act: November 1973); the *leyes de prescindibilidad* (laws of dispensability: October 1973 to August 1974) and the *Ley de Seguridad* (Security Act: September 1974); in the universities, the *leyes de prescindibilidad* (laws

These official policies were accompanied by their illegal side, i.e., the action of armed paramilitary gangs belonging to other sectors of the right and of Peronist trade unionism. This was devoted to the assassination of and permanent menacing of sectors considered to be leftist opponents, whether within or outside of Peronism. No doubt the best known was the Triple A vigilante force organized by the Ministry of Social Welfare through its high authority and Peron's personal secretary, José López Rega. Between 1973 and 1975, the Triple A included among its victims of hundreds of young Peronist activists, trade unionists who did not belong to the official unions, political opponents, congressmen and senators, lawyers for political prisoners, intellectuals, artists, etc. The action of these groups worked in "solidarity" and in conjunction with the intraparty and governmental policies already mentioned. For example, the brutal repressive action of these gangs was exercised against students and teachers in the university environment already affected by the laws which restricted the functioning of the educational sector; many newspapers were damaged by governmental pressure and censorship; dozens of journalists were assassinated or threatened and numerous editorial offices were attacked with bombs; trade union officials and militant workers in sectors affected by the new trade union laws were killed; some of the governors and functionaries dismissed by federal interventions were then killed or disappeared before 1976.

During Perón's government different security policies aimed at the control of "subversion" and the disciplining of a number of specific environments were launched, but the repressive climate significantly hardened

---

of expendability), the *Ley Universitaria* (University Act: March 1974) and that of Seguridad (Security). In the sphere of liberty of expression, government advertising in various media was discontinued; foreign news agencies were prohibited from disseminating information about Argentina (August 1973); the entry and circulation of numerous books was prohibited (October 1973); and partisan publications were censored: *El Mundo* (September 1973 and March 1974), *El descamisado* and *Militancia* (April 1974), *El Peronista* (June 1974) *Noticias* (August 1974) and *La causa peronista* (September 1974); and the commercial media: *Crónica* (December 1974), *La Opinión* (February 1975), *Radio Rivadavia*, among others.

after his death, as did both the paramilitary violence and the action of the guerrillas. All of this formed an unstoppable spiral of violence and political crisis which encouraged the most extreme solutions on the part of broad political sectors. From that point on the state's repressive policies were reinforced significantly and were oriented directly to the "battle" against "subversion" for which the Armed Forces were convened. In that sense we can say that the government of Perón's widow, heavily controlled by the Peronist right, meant a quantum leap with respect to such policies, but this hardening is inscribed in a previous and ascending tendency going back to mid-1973. In that early process both the internal struggle within Peronism and the repressive policies against the armed militancy of the left were articulated under similar ideological focuses.

The politics of security after Perón's death in September 1974 began with the enactment of the *Ley de Seguridad* (Security Act), aimed at "the suppression of terrorist and subversive activity" with the aim of "eradicating subversion in the country", "within the bounds of the law".[15] Shortly afterwards, in November, a state of siege was decreed which would not be lifted until 1983. From then on, both provisions created the basic legal instruments of repression in terms of the suspension of all constitutional guarantees, the establishment of the legal limbo of the new offences, and thus the unlimited expansion both of the universe of the dangerous and of the power of the state over it.

From 1975 the provisions were oriented to establishing new operational arrangements so as to formalize, above all, the use of the armed forces in repressive actions. However, the military corporation had already been in use in internal conflicts for several months, albeit neither openly nor systematically. This official call to the Armed Forces, supported by the majority of the dominant political actors from 1975, was accompanied by the increasing pressure on the government on the part of the pro-coup section of the army. Thus from the February of that year, authorized by

15 María Estela Martínez de Perón, *La Nación*, 27/9/74; Law 20.840, 28/9/74. The force of this law would be reconfirmed by the Military Junta after 1976 with the sole addition of a minor clause.

the executive, the armed forces began actions in Tucumán resulting in the so-called *Operativo Independencia* (Operation Independence) which launched the first clandestine detention centres. In fact, a large number of the disappeared from Tucumán were recorded in the period prior to 1976. Months later, the government extended the military intervention throughout the national territory for the purpose of "annihilating subversive activity". By then, the official argument considered the following to be "subversive": workers' protests, student activities, criticism of the government in the commercial press, and all forms of political opposition and social mobilization. These were answered by applying the Security Act and the state of siege. A large part of the traditional and dominant political actors (institutional political parties of the centre and the right, Peronist unions, employers' organizations, newspapers, and the Church) also joined in this reading of the problem of "subversion", considering it to be one of the greatest national evils.[16]

During 1975, the "counterinsurgency" legislation continued to increase, concentrating all repressive authority in the Armed Forces and the Executive. They even came to contemplate the imposition of capital punishment and the establishment of emergency zones under military authority, issues which were discussed in Congress without actually gaining definitive sanction. Many of these measures had been in effect during the dictatorship of Onganía and were restored again or discussed during the democratic Peronist government, not just at the proposal of the Executive but also with the acquiescence of numerous political groups in parliament.[17]

16 Towards the end of 1975, for example, a large part of these actors were talking about "factory subversion" or "industrial guerrillas" (see Franco, forthcoming).

17 The only partial exceptions in the parliamentary arena were the centre-left parties, grouped in the Alianza Popular Revolucionaria (Popular Revolutionary Alliance): the Partido Intransigente (Intransigent Party), the Partido Revolucionario Cristiano (Christian Revolutionary Party), the Partido Comunista (Communist Party) and Unión del Pueblo Argentino (Argentinean People's Union: UDELPA). For a detailed analysis of this legislation and the debates and parliamentary positions of the different blocks, see Franco, forthcoming.

As to the final year, 1975, the permanent crisis of Peronism in power, its inability to lead the political process and the complete failure of the corporate economic and social agreements which Perón had implemented, made the coup a possible "exit" demanded by many sectors in the face of the "power vacuum" and economic "chaos" and violence. The growing autonomy and pressure of the military did the rest.

However, and this is the question we wish to emphasize, that military pressure does not explain the repression instituted long before the coup, and nor is it explained by the simple action of the gangs led by López Rega and the power of the Peronist right. The disciplinarian and repressive politics was a state policy introduced gradually and systematically from mid-1973. It did not happen in a deliberately Machiavellian way, but as slow sliding of state policies in the face of the declared needs of intraparty "order" with the aim of stopping the social and political mobilization of the 1970s, something which was seen as a national threat. In this context, the actions of the guerrillas fed the spiral of violence in general and created the necessary climate which the government used to justify these policies. Thus, institutional and democratic legality was progressively unravelling through the very government policies which were supposed, precisely, to protect it.

Towards a more complex memory of state terrorism

What has been said so far does not mean that no specific weight should be given to the institutional rupture of the 1976 coup and the establishment of a repressive system articulated and systematized on a national scale under military responsibility from the March of that year. To emphasize elements of the long political process which marked the road to state terrorism does not diminish the seriousness of the actions taken by the military corporation. Therefore, it is not a question of taking away responsibility, but of changing the focus to illuminate, *also*, the governmental and civilian actors involved in the construction of the authoritarian process prior to the military dictatorship. Similarly, to talk of escalating state repression does not diminish the historical responsibility of the armed organizations of the left for feeding the unstoppable spiral of provocation. In turn, this does not mean that their actions justify the repression which struck both them and the forms of social mobilization of that time.

With regard to the democratic government of the years 1973–1976, it can be said to have been characterized by a slow drift toward authoritarianism *from within and through the institutions of the democratic system itself.* This was not the result of the actions of certain sectors in power or some parallel or clandestine practices, but a systematic policy of the State, ideologically linked to the national security policies of the military dictatorships and 1966 and 1976. This doctrine assumed the existence of an enemy of external origin, the "Marxist subversion", which was within the national borders and, as a true cancer, had to be eliminated because it represented a threat to the continuity of the nation.

This conception of national security had first been established by the dictatorship which began in 1966, and ten years later was also the ideological support of the dictatorship in 1976. But while it is usually said that both military dictatorships were imbued with this doctrine, two things are forgotten. The first is that part of the politics of the Peronist government of those years was based on similar conceptions of national security (although they were not an organic part of that military doctrine). The second is that Peronism established important continuities with both dictatorial regimes in terms of its conceptions and repressive practices against the radicalized political movement. In fact, as we have seen, the intraparty policy of "cleansing" Peronism was not too far removed from the conception of internal adversaries.[18]

18 A key piece of information to which little importance has been given is that in 1973 the government of Cámpora revoked all previous repressive legislation with the exception of the founding Decree-Law of the government of Onganía: the *Ley de Defensa Nacional* (National Defence Act) of 1966, which established the fundamentals of the theory of national security. This law was not revoked and was in fact invoked repeatedly in order to support the repressive legislation applied by Peronism between 1973 and 1976.

However, unlike Videla or Onganía, Peronism was a democratic government and its first act was the annulment of the previous repressive legislation and a commitment to restoring lost democratic institutions. This institutional framework was then rapidly and progressively undermined by the authoritarian policies which violated rights and eventually involved the reinstatement of much of the repressive provisions of the regime of Onganía and Lanusse.

It could be argued that the degradation of democracy was not new, but had formed part of the political practices of the democratic regimes which preceded Peronism. These practices had begun with the electoral exclusion of Peronism and were followed by the security laws which were used in different circumstances and for several decades from 1955 at least. This is true, but the Peronism of the 1970s brought this logic to its extreme through a government based on a "contradictory and complex relationship between democracy and authoritarianism".[19] Thus it is incumbent on the political actors of the period to take greater political responsibility for having authorized the path of repression which was closely related to the terrorism of the military state. These actors include both the Peronists and the opposition and the various sectors which sustained the escalation of repression.

However, the perspectives which recognize that the repression began before 1976 have so far concentrated almost exclusively on the Triple A, that is to say, only on the clandestine and illegal side of the phenomenon. This focus has masked the severity of the institutional destruction which had taken place before that date. This partial remembrance of the past is not a "forgotten" element of memory, but the result of a collective historical process. It was something which was debated within certain political sectors and has served to obscure the enormous political responsibility which devolved much farther and long before the Armed Forces realized their last coup.

19 Rico (pp. 187–188) explains the particular functioning of the constitutional regimes of exception.

EMILIO CRENZEL

The Memories of the Disappeared in Argentina

Military coups and political violence have a long tradition in Argentina. However, the dictatorship which began on 24 March 1976 introduced two substantial changes with respect to the degrees and forms taken in this country by this intense history of violence. First, in contrast to the state repression of political or trade union activists, it instituted in a systematic way the forced disappearance of persons, a political crime which encapsulated a decision by the state to exterminate its opponents. Second, the disappearances involved the exercise of a novel form of death for political reasons, its clandestine practice. This feature distinguished the Argentinean dictatorship from the rest of those which were established in the Southern Cone of Latin America during the 1970s.[1]

The disappearances consisted in the detention or abduction of persons, carried out by military, police or security forces, both uniformed or in plain clothes. The kidnapped persons were taken to illegal places of captivity, the Clandestine Detention Centres located mostly in military or police buildings, where they were tortured and, in most cases, murdered. Their bodies were buried in unmarked graves, incinerated or thrown into the sea. Afterwards, the State denied any responsibility for these events.

How have the disappeared been remembered in Argentina? What representations of this iconic symbol of the political repression have circulated in the country since when the crime was perpetrated up to now?

To answer these questions the following pages start from a number of premises. On the one hand, they take up the theoretical perspective elaborated in the second decade of last century by Maurice Halbwachs,

1 In this respect see L. Roniger & M. Sznajder, *The Legacy of Human Rights Violations in the Southern Cone: Argentina, Chile, and Uruguay*, Oxford, Oxford University Press, 1999.

who founded the sociological study of social memory. Halbwachs held that individuals do not remember in an isolated manner but as members of groups located in space and time which, through specific frameworks, give meaning to their experiences. He also maintained that the past could not be recalled at will and in its entirety, because its evocation implied processes of selection based on the interests and values of the present. As a result of his research, memory began to be conceived of in a plural key, given the multiplicity of social groups; and the sense of the past abandoned its status as an immutable "thing", literally susceptible to apprehension of the private will, and came to be understood as the result of political and cultural dynamics and hence of the struggles to endow it with meaning. On this basis, the possibility was established of historicizing social memory, that is to say, recording and analysing its changes and continuities over time[2]

On the other hand, this article takes up the principles of Georges Didi Huberman, who confronted ideas which postulate the impossibility of thinking about and representing the experiences of extreme violence and its victims. Huberman points out that the perspectives which deny such possibilities make absolute both the idea of irrepresentability and the opacity of horror and are, thus, the prisoner of the latter. He warns, further, that in no case is the representation of an event ever complete or full. On the contrary, he argues, it is always partial, fragmentary and incomplete, but neither these qualities nor the properties of the object have the ability to deny the imagination, the word or thought.[3]

The Argentine case confirms that social memory combines changes and continuities and that these are the result of political struggles between different actors which can be examined historically; it refutes, moreover, the supposedly unthinkable, unspeakable and irrepresentable nature of the horror and its protagonists. In fact, the struggle for the interpretation of the disappearances and of the figure of the disappeared began at the same time as the perpetration of the crime and has gained a renewed momentum

2 M. Halbwachs, *Los marcos sociales de la memoria*, Barcelona, Anthropos, 2004a [1925].

3 G. Didi-Huberman, *Images in Spite of All: Four Photographs from Auschwitz*, Chicago, University of Chicago Press, 2008, pp. 37–57.

since the restoration of democracy in 1983. Since then, moreover, the disappeared have been thought about, represented and evoked by means of a wide variety of vehicles. The *Comisión Nacional sobre la Desaparición de Personas* (CONADEP: National Commission on Disappeared Persons), investigated their fate and the *Nunca Más* report portrayed it. The trial of the military juntas, unprecedented on the continent, culminated in the punishment of the perpetrators with greatest responsibility, and laws were enacted giving reparation to the relatives of disappeared persons and survivors of disappearances. In addition, the investigation of the fate of the disappeared prompted innovations in the field of forensic anthropology and genetics in order to be able to determine affiliations and identities, and in psychology, so as to examine the subjective effects. Likewise, the disappeared were represented in the press, cinema, non-fiction and fiction, on television, through allusive programs and novels of manners, and by means of photography and artistic intervention. Finally, their evocation was incorporated into urban space with the constitution of sites of memory located not only in spaces which symbolize the violence of the state but also in other public spaces such as schools, streets and squares. It was integrated into the school curriculum through the history books used in the middle school. It runs through activist practices and is a recurring motif in media information and the political agenda. In short, it is argued here that, far from any essentialism, the contexts of enunciation and reception have been the result of political confrontations, which modelled the limits and possibilities of the evocation and representation of disappeared persons in the public sphere.

The military discourse and the humanitarian response

The dictatorship combined four strategies for dealing with complaints about the disappeared. Initially, it brandished the denial of every piece of information and responsibility for their fate. Then, the disappearances were justified as the timely or inevitable result of the ongoing war in the country. In parallel, it downplayed the number of disappeared so as to shrug off reports and deny the systematic nature of the disappearances and the national scope and the planned nature of the practice. Finally, it shunted full responsibility for the disappearances onto the constitutional Peronist governments which had preceded it.

After just a year and a half of dictatorship, in December 1977, the official discourse mentioned the disappeared.[4] At a press conference, General Videla said: "In any war there are persons who survive, others who are disabled, some who die and others who disappear [...]. The disappearance of some persons is an unwanted consequence of this war. We understand the pain of that mother or wife who has lost her son or husband, of whom we can not give news, because he passed clandestinely into the ranks of the subversion, because he fell prey to cowardice and because he was unable to maintain his subversive attitude, because he has disappeared as a result of having changed his name and left the country illegally or because in a military encounter his body, having suffered from explosions, fire or projectiles, was severely maimed and could not have been recognized, or because of an excess of repression".[5]

The military discourse thus described the disappeared as guerrillas and explained their disappearances by reference to the state of war, the practices of the "subversion" itself or, as isolated and contingent events, the "excesses" carried out during the process of "repression". The dictatorship thus assumed a dual discourse. In public it presented the disappeared as guerrillas, blamed for their own fate, while its response to family members

4 These statements may respond to the increasingly public nature assumed by the demands in relation to the disappeared. In April 1977 the first demonstration of the Mothers around the Pirámide de Mayo (the May Pyramid in the Plaza de Mayo) took place, and in October 1977 a declaration was published, addressed to the President's Office, the High Command of the Armed Forces, to the military junta, to the ecclesiastical authorities and the *Corte Suprema* (Supreme Court) demanding the truth about the disappeared. See "Madres y esposas de desaparecidos solo pedimos la verdad", *La Prensa*, 5 October 1977, p. 9.

5 *La Prensa*, 15 September 1977. Videla did not quantify every component and did not accept dialogue over any particular case. H. Verbitsky, *El vuelo*, Buenos Aires, Planeta, 1995, p. 78.

in their demands of *habeas corpus* asserted the absence of the crime, issuing them with a certificate of innocence. The truth is that the process of the criminalization and stigmatization of the disappeared, and those who made demands on their behalf, were inscribed within the dictatorial interpretation which attributed to itself the defence of patriotic, moral and normative values. In this context, the rebels were described as violators of the law, hence the association which condensed the label of "subversive criminals". They were portrayed as foreign and alien to the territory, history and national character, as part of the "international subversion".

In a context characterized by the simultaneous exercise of state terror and the passive social consensus about the restoration of "order" and the "war against subversion", the relatives of disappeared asked the State for explanations without questioning the binary pairing of innocence and guilt forged by the dictatorship and the order of values associated with it. Both in the presentations addressed to various bureaucratic agencies of the State in the country and in those directed to international organizations abroad and governmental agencies in other countries, their complaints described their relatives solely in terms of their physical characteristics and basic identity data, highlighting their moral values. That is to say they referred only to their abilities and strengths as children, students, workers, employees or professionals, and omitted, as a complement to this, any reference to their political affiliations, trying in this way to prove their innocence.

It can be postulated that a number of processes intervened in such uses of silence and of the word. First, the strategy of the family formed an intrinsic part of the universe of interpretation amongst the majority of the relatives, for whom their relationship with the deceased was based on ties of kinship.[6] Others ignored the political affiliations of their relatives, while another portion remained silent about them because of the dictatorial persecution of all political commitment, especially armed militancy.

6 E. Jelin, "La política de la memoria: el movimiento de Derechos Humanos y la construcción de la democracia en Argentina", in Carlos Acuña, Adriana Vacchieri, Catalina Smulovitz, Elizabeth Jelin, Inés González Bombal, Luis Alberto Quevedo and Oscar Landi Adriana Vacchieri, *Juicio, castigos y memorias: Derechos Humanos y justicia en la política Argentina*, Buenos Aires, Nueva Visión, 1995, pp. 101–146. J. Filc, *Entre el parentesco y la política: familia y dictadura, 1976–1983*, Buenos Aires, Biblos, 1997.

Second, the main recipient of allegations about disappearances in the country was the judiciary. Tens of thousands of writs of *habeas corpus* were presented to the law by relatives and friends of the disappeared with the aim of establishing their whereabouts. But these claims were also issued to the organizations defending human rights locally and internationally such as the *Asamblea Permanente por los Derechos Humanos* (Permanent Assembly for Human Rights), before which 5,500 complaints were made between 1976 and 1980, the *Comisión Interamericana de Derechos Humanos de la OEA* (Inter-American Commission of Human Rights of the Organization of American States), the International Red Cross, the Human Rights Division of the United Nations, Amnesty International and the organs of various religious confessions. This coincided with a period in which, as Kathryn Sikkink has argued, the transnational networks of international human rights were formed and expanded.[7]

As Vania Markarian has shown in the case of Uruguayan exiles under the dictatorship in that country, the contact of persecuted politicians with these networks resulted in the adaptation of the narratives and interpretive keys for presenting the allegations in accordance with the standards of these organizations and institutions. This involved the appeal to a new rhetoric: that of the humanitarian discourse.[8] This discourse emphasized the violation of the rights of victims, describing in detail the physical suffering endured and omitting the details of their political affiliations and the reasons which had lead to their persecution by the state.

The contact of those who denounced violations of human rights with these organizations, institutions and transnational networks, and with this discourse, resulted in the displacement of the keys of the denunciation from revolutionary militancy, prevalent before the 1976 coup. As a result of this process, the Argentine human rights organizations incorporated

7 K. Sikkink, "The Emergence, Evolution, and Effectiveness of the Latin American Human Rights Network", in Elizabeth Jelin and Eric Hershberg (eds), *Constructing Democracy: Human Rights, Citizenship and Society in Latin America*, Boulder, Westview Press, 1996, pp. 59–84.

8 V. Markarian, *Left in Transformation: Uruguayan Exiles and the Latin American Human Rights Networks, 1967–1984*, New York, Routledge, 2005.

standard models for bringing the complaints and classifying them. In these formulas, factual information was demanded concerning the circumstances of the kidnapping, the torture suffered, the characteristics of the places of detention and the names of other victims and of the perpetrators. It was a question of rebuilding the material aspect of the alleged crimes, in a style similar to that demanded by a technical presentation to the law. To do this, it would be necessary to build a truth based on evidence, which omitted any historicization of the actions and the political affiliations of the victims and the political motives of their victimizers.

On that basis, the families and organizations involved in these networks supplied the basic data about the victims: their age, gender, address, identity, nationality, religious beliefs, occupation and profession, and the circumstances of their abduction or captivity. These were then translated into the presentation of complaints through classifications and groupings based on these variables.[9]

This socio-demographic and socio-occupational presentation of the disappeared enacted a representation which highlighted their denied humanity and suggested a vast and comprehensive picture of the extent of the repression, while at the same time omitting their political commitments. This type of presentation of the disappeared involved a redefinition of their identities and of the keys to explaining the reasons for their disappearance. The "disappeared Spaniards", the "disappeared Jews", the "pregnant disappeared", the "disappeared students" and "disappeared journalists" were different categories constructed by the complainants after the disappearances and omitted any political terms in referring to the identities of the defendants. Rather they occluded political motivations of the crimes in favour of an uncritically formulated corporate, demographic, nationalist or religious presentation which was completely alien to the selective political matrix on which the system of disappearances was based. This type of

9 See, for example: Comisión Interamericana de Derechos Humanos, *Informe sobre la situación de los derechos humanos en Argentina*, Washington, OEA, 1980, pp. 17 and 18; Amnesty International, *Testimonios sobre los campos secretos de detención en Argentina*, Barcelona, Amnesty International, 1980, p. 2.

presentation of the disappeared was also reproduced in reports about the crimes of the dictatorship made in exile by lawyers and political activists, members of the left Peronist and radical Marxist formations.

In late 1977, the *Comisión Argentina de Derechos Humanos* (CADHU: Argentinean Commission on Human Rights), an umbrella organization of lawyers defending political prisoners, produced the report, *Argentina: The process of genocide*. This included specific sections, whose titles, "the persecution of the Jews", "attacks on the Catholic Church", the "repression of the press and journalists" and "education and culture", tried to portray "state terrorism" as a repressive system which pitted the state against civil society as a whole. However, the specific content of these sections did not give evidence of the persecution of Argentina's Jewish community as a whole, nor of an indiscriminate attack on the Church or on the whole of its faithful, but rather of the disappearance of third worldist priests, nor finally of an attack on the media and culture in general but rather of the persecution of oppositional journalists and writers from the Left, both armed and unarmed.[10] Likewise, in another report by CADHU on the testimony of the "genocide survivors", the disappeared are classified and presented according to socio-demographic or occupational variables, or on the basis of family relationships: the "detained-disappeared adolescents", the "disappeared children", the "disappeared conscripts" and "the family as a victim of repression".[11] The masking of the references to the political commitments of the disappeared is also reflected in the testimonies of survivors of disappearances. Detailed descriptions of their kidnapping, the torture suffered, the characteristics of the spaces of captivity and the names of other prisoners and perpetrators identified by them are prioritized.

In these allegations, the use of the word *compañero* (comrade or partner), habitually used by political activists in Argentina to refer to those who shared their militancy, now referred only to the shared captivity linked to attributes outside politics: "the pregnant *compañeras*", "Jewish *compañeros*",

10 Comisión Argentina para la Defensa de los Derechos Humanos (CADHU), *Argentina: proceso al genocidio*. Barcelona: CADHU, 1977, pp 79–90, 116–130.

11 Comisión Argentina para la Defensa de los Derechos Humanos (CADHU), *Testimonios de los sobrevivientes del genocidio en la Argentina*, Barcelona, CADHU, 1979.

"*compañeros* with common crimes" and "the *compañeros* killed because they were witnesses".[12] Among the survivors, the humanitarian discourse was established as a result of the gravity of the extreme experiences suffered, but among them, as among the political exiles, awareness spread of defeat, especially after the failure in 1979 of the Montonero "counteroffensive", and the fracturing of this organization and the PRT-ERP. The *Comisión Interamericana de Derechos Humanos* (CIDH: InterAmerican Commission on Human Rights) had made an inspection visit to the country after receiving thousands of denunciations of disappearances, including the affirmation of the extermination of the majority of the disappeared, highlighting a truth which, though resisted, could no longer be ignored. The diffusion in the same year of its findings had the same effect. In parallel, contact with social democratic and Eurocommunist ideas and the culture of human rights, of increasing importance in the international arena, favoured the review of insurgent practices and their omission of their political commitments from their testimonies.

A couple of years before the end of the dictatorship, the characterization of the disappeared as "innocent victims" and the prevalence of occupational and socio-demographic variables in classifying them had become hegemonic among historic and recent complainants against the crimes of the dictatorship. In late 1981, the winner of the 1980 Nobel Peace Prize, Adolfo Pérez Esquivel, and other intellectuals, including Ernesto Sabato and María Elena Walsh, founders of the *Movimiento para la recuperación de niños desaparecidos* (Movement for the recovery of disappeared children), began to assert that "most of the disappeared were innocents whose only crime was to have been friends or classmates of criminal suspects".[13] This kind of argument was taken up also by political leaders who, a few years earlier, had supported political repression. Arturo Frondizi, a former constitutional president and head of the *Movimiento de Integración y Desarrollo* (MID: Movement for Integration and Development), now condemned the

12 Idem, pp. 1, 9, 13 and 15; Amnesty International, *Testimonios sobre los campos secretos de detención en Argentina*, pp. 1, 2 and 34–39.

13 See *Buenos Aires Herald*, 13 December 1981, cited by M. Novaro & V. Palermo in *La dictadura militar 1976/1983: del golpe de Estado a la restauración democrática*, Buenos Aires, Paidós, 2002, pp. 487–488.

savage murder of "thousands of young people" for their "ideals" and the "indiscriminate" repression which did not distinguish "between oppositionists and true guerrillas".[14] Finally, on the eve of the return of democracy, a political aesthetic intervention popularized as *Siluetazo* which consisted in tracing the empty outline of a life-size body on paper, within which were inscribed the names and ages of disappeared persons and which were pasted on the walls of the city, staged in the public sphere the representation based on the demographic and occupational variables mentioned.[15] Thus, during the dictatorship there operated within the universe of its accusers, both within the country and abroad, a process of cultural and political change, one of the results of which was the constitution of a specific representation of the disappeared and a particular way of evoking and classifying them.

The return of democracy: the narrative of *Nunca Más*

Raúl Alfonsín was elected President on 30 October 1983 and, after assuming the presidency of the Nation on 10 December 1983, signed Decrees 157 and 158 which ordered the prosecution of seven guerrilla leaders and the first three Military Juntas of the dictatorship. The first decree provided for the prosecution of the insurgents. He argued, resuming the military discourse, that their exercise of violence had been instigated by "interests external to the country", but also warned that this had "served as a pretext for disturbing the constitutional peace on the part of a sector of the Armed Forces". In the second, he accused the Juntas, of having "conceived and implemented a plan of operations against subversive and terrorist activity, based on methods and procedures which were manifestly illegal".[16]

14 Idem, p. 488.

15 See, in this respect, A. Longoni & G. Bruzzone, *El Siluetazo*, Buenos Aires, Adriana Hidalgo, 2008.

16 Poder Ejecutivo Nacional, Decretos 157 and 158, 13 December 1983, *Boletín Oficial*, 15 December 1983, p. 5.

The decrees established different time frames. The guerrillas would be the only personification of violence prior to the coup; their actions would be judged to the point of the restoration of democracy but the inquiry into military violence limited to the period 1976–1979. Thus the fourth and final military junta was acquitted, but also excluded from the legal review were the military intervention in the struggle against subversion before the coup, paramilitary violence and the responsibilities of the Peronist government and the rest of political society with respect to this violence. Finally, while subversive illegitimacy and illegality were condemned, even for their actions during the dictatorship, the legitimacy of their struggle of the Armed Forces in combating it was distinguished from the illegality of the methodology which was limited to the dictatorial illegality.

This perspective on the past, translated into judicial volition, was called "*la teoría de los dos demonios*" ("the theory of two demons") for two reasons. On the one hand, because it limited responsibility for political violence to the two above-mentioned leaderships, in such a way as to exculpate the subordinates of these organizations and institutions and, above all, the rest of political and civil society. On the other, because it explained state violence, though not its forms, by reference to guerrilla violence. On the basis of the decrees for the prosecution of the military and the guerrilla leaderships, the "punitive paradigm"[17] was constituted as the dominant form of dealing with past political violence in the country. This approach proposed the courts as the central stage on which to address guilt and innocence in the process of political violence through the above-mentioned prism and, simultaneously, excluded the examination and search for explanations of the political violence in historical-political terms.

The other main initiative of the Alfonsín government was to constitute, on 15 December 1983, the CONADEP, whose objective was to hear the complaints and evidence of disappearances and refer them to the judicial system, investigate the fate of disappeared persons and the location of abducted children, report to the legal system any attempt to conceal or

17 A. Kaufman, "Notas sobre desaparecidos". *Confines* 2, no. 4 (1997), 29–34.

destroy evidence relating to these facts and issue a final report.[18] Although this initiative was contrary to the goal of the human rights organizations of creating a bicameral commission to investigate the complex of practices of State terrorism, it did constitute the disappearances as the object of investigation of the state.

In the literature on transitional justice and Argentina's recent history the CONADEP is presented as a commission composed of recognized personalities through which the state ruled on the disappearances. However, the CONADEP and its public report *Nunca Más* were the result of the formation of a tacit alliance between the majority of the human rights organizations and the leadership of the state which resulted in a reciprocal legitimation process. This involved the Commission, the human rights agencies, the families of the disappeared and the survivors of disappearances. The human rights organizations, in proportion with their strength, provided several members of the national leadership of CONADEP, integrated their delegations, their departments, their professional and support staff within the country, handed over the information they possessed and collected new information; they relinquished their offices so as to be able to form CONADEP delegations inside the country; they used their expertise to guide the investigation; they participated in the dissemination of its findings on the television show *Nunca Más*, which was broadcast on 4 July 1984 and reached an audience of 1,600,000 people, and assisted in drafting the recommendations of its report. For its part, CONADEP gave the human rights organizations, the relatives of the disappeared and the survivors unprecedented public legitimacy, first, by giving them a leading role in the TV program which brought forward its findings, second, by granting them the authority to decide the judicial fate their testimonies would have and, finally, by inviting them to put forward their ideas on the recommendations which should be included in their final report.[19]

18 Poder Ejecutivo Nacional, decree 187, 15 December, in *Boletín Oficial de la República Argentina*, 2, 19 December, p. 2.

19 E. Crenzel, *La historia política del Nunca Más: la memoria de las desapariciones en la Argentina*, Buenos Aires, Siglo XXI, 2008.

This association was also observed in the mode of classifying and presenting the disappeared. The relatives of missing persons and survivors of disappearances and members of the human rights movement presented the disappeared in terms of their basic identifying traits and moral qualities, and their political commitments were ignored. This was the case both in the testimonies given before the Commission, and also on the television program, *Nunca Más*, in which they were the central players. This form of presentation, dominant during the dictatorship as previously noted, was reinforced by two factors. The first of was the decision of the Executive to the put leaderships of the guerrillas on trial. The second was the unstable political context of a newly restored democracy to which the phantoms of a new coup and the dominant social stigma of the "subversive" commitments of the disappeared and their families clung. For its part, the CONADEP, which included in its leadership members of the humanitarian movement, classified the testimony it received in terms of occupational and socio-demographic variables, which the transnational human rights networks had standardized in the complaint forms during the dictatorship. On the TV program which it produced, they were introduced on the basis of these variables, and its president, the writer Ernesto Sabato, proposed before the cameras that the disappeared were young idealists, alien to subversion.

In its report, *Nunca Más*, the mode of presentation of the disappeared maintained this narrative. In its preface the CONADEP introduced the disappeared on the basis of a diverse and inclusive profile, but with boundaries. They included a broad cross-section of society:

> from people who favoured a social revolution to sensitive teens who went to shanty towns to help their residents. Everyone was caught in the haul: union leaders who fought for a simple improvement of wages, youths who had been members of a student centre, journalists who were not supporters of the dictatorship, psychologists and sociologists for belonging to suspicious professions, young pacifists, nuns and priests who had taken the teachings of Christ to the slums. And friends any of them, and friends of those friends, people who had been denounced for motives of personal revenge and by kidnapped people under torture. Everyone, mostly innocent of terrorism or even of belonging to those groups of guerrilla fighters, because the latter had presented themselves in battle and had died in the confrontation or committed suicide rather than surrender, and few arrived alive into the hands of the repressors.

That is, the Commission proposed that the disappeared were those who had fought against injustice, participated in struggles for rights, opposed the dictatorship or revolutionaries who had attempted to change the social order. But, also, "the friends of any of them, and friends of those friends, people who had been denounced for motives of personal revenge and by kidnapped people under torture".[20]

So, the disappeared are presented as an "open crowd", almost without boundaries. Despite this breadth, a restrictive attribute unites them: their distance from the armed struggle excludes them from the universe of the guerrillas. This boundary proposed in the prologue is reconfigured into the *body* of the report which extends the exclusion to all political activities. In most of the fragments included in the testimonial *Nunca Más* (64 per cent), the CONADEP limited itself to making public their names: 16 per cent are described as "persons or human beings'; in a similar proportion they are presented on the basis of the humiliation they suffered as "abducted, detained, disappeared, prisoners or captives" and only 3 per cent of the cases mention their status as activists. Within this small group, their sectoral affiliations are portrayed, and only in a tiny proportion their participation in politics, always outside the armed insurgency.[21]

On the other hand, the report presents an overall figure of disappeared of 8,960, 90 per cent of them kidnapped after the coup of 1976, and it classifies them according to their ages, sexes and "professions or occupations". According to the report, 81 per cent were, when kidnapped, between sixteen and thirty-five years old, and 70 per cent were male, 80 per cent of the disappearances occurred in major cities (27 per cent in Greater Buenos Aires, 26 per cent in the Capital Federal, 9 per cent in the province of Córdoba, 9 per cent in the province of Tucumán, 8 per cent, 3 per cent and 2 per cent in the cities of La Plata, Rosario and Mendoza respectively), 30 per cent of the disappeared were workers, 21 per cent students, 18 per

20 Comisión Nacional sobre la Desaparición de Personas (CONADEP), *Nunca Más. Informe de la Comisión Nacional sobre la Desaparición de Personas*, Buenos Aires, EUDEBA, 1984, pp. 10–11.

21 My own elaboration on the basis of J. Corralini, J. Lobo, E. Di Iorio & J. Pigliapochi, *Políticas de memoria: el Nunca Más*, Buenos Aires, mimeo, 2003.

cent and 11 per cent professional employees.[22] The breadth with which *Nunca Más* presents the disappeared and the restrictions it establishes over their identities are reflected also in its second chapter: "Victims". Its title highlights helplessness as the common attribute of the disappeared and its sections predominantly combine different demographic and socio-occupational variables already mentioned: "Disappeared children and pregnant women", "Adolescents", "The family as a victim", "The repression respects neither the invalid nor the handicapped". Thus, the report endorses the dominant keys for denouncing this crime which had been developed during the dictatorship.

These criteria, now official, reinforce the vast and comprehensive picture of the disappeared and their helplessness and "innocence" and their remoteness from the guerrillas and indeed politics. These keys are not modified when the presenting the disappeared who indeed were members of guerrilla organizations and offered armed resistance to their captors, such as the writer and Montonero activist Rodolfo Walsh.[23] Thus, the CONADEP confronts the crime of disappearance by restoring *humanity* to the disappeared by submitting their names, ages, genders and occupations. This restitution takes the form of an *abstract humanization*, which presents their generic lives, obscuring their condition as concrete historical beings, their political lives, those attributes which record, precisely, the confrontations which divided Argentinean society. The report thus simultaneously performs a double operation. It *re-politicizes* the identity of the disappeared with respect to the dictatorial perspective by presenting them as subjects of rights and *depoliticizes* them by proposing them as innocent victims by excluding their activism.

This portrait of the disappeared spread dramatically in the public sphere. First, *Nunca Más* became a bestseller, selling 185,000 copies between its date of publication in November 1984 and the start of the trial of the

22 Comisión Nacional sobre la Desaparición de Personas (CONADEP), *Nunca Más. Informe de la Comisión Nacional sobre la Desaparición de Personas*, Buenos Aires, EUDEBA, 1984, pp. 294, 296 and 375.

23 Idem, pp. 17, 324, 371 y 372.

military juntas in April 1985 alone. Second, the prosecutor Julio Strassera reproduced its narrative and interpretive key during the Trial of the Juntas by presenting the cases which, from the profile of the disappeared, were distanced from all suspicion of belonging to guerrilla organizations but also from any kind of political activism. This coincided with the decision of the survivors to appear before the court as political or sectoral activists, keeping quiet about their guerrilla activity.[24] For their part, the defence lawyers for the Juntas sought to deny the existence of disappeared persons, although they did recognize the reality of this practice in some way, by diverting responsibility for its exercise onto the Peronist government of Estela Martínez de Perón. They also questioned the integrity of the testimony of witnesses, given their status as "subversives".[25] Thus, while prosecutors and survivors silenced the political affiliations of the disappeared so as to legitimize citizens' rights, the defence lawyers sought to expose them so as to deny the citizenship status of the witnesses. Both strategies illustrate the limits of the notion of citizenship in the early democracy of Argentina. This did not assume the universality of human rights and their independence from any act committed by those who suffered the violation.

Finally, the portrait of the disappeared proposed by *Nunca Más* was reproduced in two films, broadcast on television at the time, which had wide diffusion. *La Historia Oficial (The Official Story)*, directed by Luis Puenzo, was released in 1985 and won the Oscar for best foreign film in 1986. Seen in the cinema by 1,700,000 viewers, it presented the disappeared without any link to the world of politics. *La Noche de los Lápices (The Night of the Pencils)* was released in 1986, directed by Héctor Olivera and seen in the cinema by 500,000 spectators and about three million when broadcast on television in 1988. Based on a book of the same title, it told the story of the disappearance of a group of students from the city of La Plata. It privileged their status as teenagers, their innocence and collective struggle in demand

24 On the decision of the survivors, from the author's interview with Graciela Daleo, Buenos Aires, 17 June 2005.

25 As an example, see the allegations of Dr Tavares, Videla's defence counsel, in *El Diario del Juicio*, 29 October 1985, 1 and 2.

of a "student travel ticket" rather than their political affiliations.[26] Thus, the presentation of the disappeared reflected in *Nunca Más* formalized and disseminated the representation of the identity of the disappeared forged by those who denounced the crime in such a way as to exclude politics and violence. The power of this representation, now official, was reinforced as a result of its legal confirmation in the courts and through the intervention of various actors in civil society.

Reframing an identity

The Amnesty of the military junta dictated by President Menem in December 1990 had a huge moral and political impact among the human rights organizations. The public "mourning" which was called in order to repudiate it, encapsulated the sense that any possibility of justice had been closed.[27] In fact, however, the presence of this past in the public arena decreased in intensity as the rapid and profound economic changes of the period became the focus of public attention. In this context of the privatization of major state enterprises, the dismissal of thousands of public employees and the policies of economic liberalization, the present began to be read as the spectral image of the past without rights. The government of President Menem identified social protest with "subversion," and warned that this could lead to the emergence of new mothers calling for their children in the Plaza de Mayo and, conversely, the *Madres of Plaza de Mayo* visualized in those affected by neoliberal economic policies as the new disappeared.[28]

26 For the numbers of the viewers of these films, see "Cine y Memoria", *Puentes*, August 2003, 13–15.

27 "Protesta y duelo en las plazas", *Página/12*, 30 December 1990, pp. 6 and 7.

28 For Menem's threats, see "Menem: dura advertencia por las marchas", *Clarín*, 10 July 1992, cover, pp. 2 and 3. For Bonafini's declarations, see "Marcha de las Madres", *Clarín*, 9 December 1993, p. 16.

It was not until February 1995, when the former captain Adolfo Scilingo recounted in the print media and television his participation in operations in which the disappeared were thrown alive from Navy aircraft into the sea, that human rights violations returned to the forefront of public debate.[29] It was then that a new hot cycle began in relation to this past in which memory acquired a specific *status*, independent of the punitive goal. This was already in the process of being verified during 1994, when several "memory commissions" were formed in schools, colleges, unions and districts to honour the disappeared, and to reconstruct their names and biographies. In one of these meetings in the city of La Plata, *Hijos contra la impunidad, por la justicia, contra el olvido y el silencio* ("HIJOS": Children against impunity, for justice, and against forgetting and silence) was formed, an organization which brought together the descendants of the disappeared and which, from its establishment, has debated the perspective of *Nunca Más*. It has done so by questioning the state about the absence of justice, but also society for its "obliviousness and silence", by confronting the "theory of the two demons" and rescuing the political activism of their disappeared parents.

In parallel, the evidence gained autonomy from the punitive goal and brought to light activist memories by means of documentaries like *Cazadores de utopías* (David Blaustein, 1995) and feature films like *Garage Olimpo* (Marco Bechis, 1999) and testimonial novels such as *La Voluntad* (Anguita and Caparrós, 1996). These sought to confront the *Nunca Más* report through the understanding that it had hidden, behind a cloak of innocence, the militancy of the disappeared. These memories had maintained, until then, an underground character because of the dictatorial stigmatisation of subversive political commitments, and the prosecution to which members of the guerrilla movement had been subjected before the Amnesties. This new testimonial literature played on the primacy of the witness and the first hand witness, the code of the family and / or romantic tale, those canonical forms which had been made official by *Nunca Más* and adopted by the cinema, theatre and literature after the

29 For the declarations of Scilingo, see H. Verbitsky, *El vuelo*, Buenos Aires, Planeta, 1995.

return of democracy. It lacked an analytical perspective, proposed a new literature of the virtues, emphasizing the ideals of the activists and their commitment to social change but excluding the critique of political violence and reproducing, in other forms, the aura of innocence with which the CONADEP had covered the disappeared. However, these memories restored the political commitments of the disappeared and politics itself as a key to explaining the tensions which permeated those times.[30] Finally, there have been initiatives which have had as their goal the transmission of this past to new generations, through the establishment of archives, museums, monuments, or the preparation of textbooks.[31]

The mass demonstrations and ceremonies that took place in March 1996 to mark the twentieth anniversary of the coup highlighted this new political and cultural climate. It was alien to the constraints of the framework of the judicial treatment of the past and critical of the course the constitutional governments had assumed with respect to violations of human rights and the legacy of profound economic and social inequalities left by the dictatorship and reproduced in a wider form by the Menem government. The activist identity of the disappeared, including their membership

30 On the formation of HIJOS, see "Los hijos se organizan. En el nombre del padre," *Página/12*, 30 April 1995, p. 6. For the most representative book of testimonies, see E. Anguita & M. Caparrós, *La Voluntad: testimonios de la militancia revolucionaria*, Buenos Aires, Norma, 1996. On the intention to confront *Nunca Más*, see the reflections of M. Caparrós, in F. Lorenz, "¿De quien es el 24 de Marzo? Las luchas por la memoria del golpe de 1976" in *Las conmemoraciones: las disputas en las fechas in-felices*, E. Jelin (Ed) 53–100, Madrid, Siglo XXI, 2002, p. 94. For a critique of this testimonial literature, see B. Sarlo, *Tiempo pasado. Cultura de la memoria y giro subjetivo una discusión*, Buenos Aires, Siglo XXI, 2005.

31 On the role of art in the transmission of the past, see, amongst others, E. Van Alphen, *Caught by History: Holocaust Effects in Contemporary Art, Literature, and Theory*, Stanford, Stanford University Press, 1997. On the monuments and parks of memory, see: V. Vecchioli, "Políticas de la memoria y formas de clasificación social ¿Quiénes son las 'víctimas' del Terrorismo de Estado en Argentina?", in *La imposibilidad del olvido: recorridos de la memoria en Argentina, Chile y Uruguay*, ed. Bruno Groppo & Patricia Flier, La Plata, Al Margen, 2001, pp. 83–102; P. Valdez "El parque de la memoria en Buenos Aires", in *Monumentos, memoriales y marcas territoriales*, ed. E. Jelin & V. Langland, Buenos Aires, Siglo XXI, 2003, pp. 97–112.

of political-military organizations was made evident, but without removing the intimate keys and the family-based and private stories of the events which were evident in films directed by children of the disappeared such as *Los Rubios* (Albertina Carri, 2003) or *Papá Iván* (María Inés Roque, 2004). The role of civil society and politics during the dictatorship was questioned and the concept of state terrorism, particularly associated with the imposition of an exclusionary economic order, became generalized in a wide range of representations. In parallel, the denunciation of impunity and the violation of human rights was appropriated with multiple meanings by different actors. This resulted in a double process. The first aspect is its representation as a past which is perpetuated in the present, thereby mimicking the figure of disappeared persons with other othernesses whose existence is denied, persecuted or excluded. The second pertains to the social legitimation of the victims of such disqualifications as the authorized place of enunciation.

The presidency of Néstor Kirchner modified the context of the struggle to make sense of past political violence and of the dictatorship in Argentina, for from his assumption in May 2003, the new president said he would endorse the flags of "Truth, justice and memory" of the humanitarian movement. In fact, his government involved a veritable nationalization of the demands of the human rights movement. On the one hand, following pressure from various local and international actors, he propelled the repeal and annulment of the laws of *Punto Final* (Full Stop) and *Obediencia Debida* (Due Obedience) which in 1986 and 1987 had closed down the trials of those responsible for the disappearances. On the other, he pushed forward the formation of the "Space for Memory and the promotion and defence of human rights" in the grounds of the former School of Naval Mechanics, one of the symbolic sites of the system of disappearances in the country.

Within this framework, on the thirtieth anniversary of the military dictatorship in 2006, a new prologue was added to *Nunca Más*. Signed by the National Secretary for Human Rights, it was written by lawyers, political prisoners and denunciants of the dictatorship in the exile. The new prologue proposed new keys to give a reading of an official nature of a past of political violence. It did so by associating the dictatorial horror with the imposition of a neoliberal economic system in the service of "extra-national interests" which had swept away the social gains of decades. In doing so it assumed thus the perspective which had been proposed by the human rights organizations and other actors in the public arena since 1996, the date of the commemoration of the twentieth anniversary of the coup, a perspective which was reinforced by the economic and political crisis which Argentina had gone through in December 2001.[32]

With a similar intention, although official records accounted for 9334 disappeared, the new prologue presents the emblematic figure of 30,000 disappeared maintained by the human rights organizations. Dismissing the official record, the State itself subordinates its word to the idea of the victims.[33] On the other hand the distinguishing feature of new preface is not translated into the portrait of the disappeared. They are presented as "workers, managers of internal factory committees, trade unionists, journalists, lawyers, psychologists, academics, teachers, students, children, youth, men and women of all ages and social classes". Thus, the new prologue of 2006 reproduces the image, wide and indiscriminate, of the identities proposed by the CONADEP prologue, similarly excluding the guerrilla movements and, moreover, political activism, from that universe.

In a similar vein, recent rulings against the perpetrators of disappearances have framed the extermination of the disappeared under the concept of genocide. Given the restriction of international jurisprudence which excludes political groups as victims of this figure, the disappeared have been

32 Secretaria de Derechos Humanos de la Nación, Prologue to *Nunca Más. Informe de la Comisión Nacional sobre la Desaparición de Personas*, of the Comisión Nacional sobre la Desaparición de Personas, Buenos Aires: EUDEBA, 2006, pp. 7–9.

33 Brisk maintains that the measurement of the number of disappeared is conditioned by the very nature of the crime, the political conditions framing public debate on this topic and the role which given actors play by raising their own accounts in the pubic sphere. See A. Brisk, "The politics of measurement: The contested count of the disappeared in Argentina", *Human Rights Quarterly* 16, no. 4 (1994), 676–692. These arguments can be extended to the study and public presentation of the political commitments of the disappeared. For an investigation into these topics, see I. Izaguirre, *Los desaparecidos, recuperación de una identidad expropiada*, Buenos Aires, Instituto de Investigaciones Gino Germani, Universidad de Buenos Aires, 1992.

characterized as a "national group". This idea picked up on the fundamentals of the ruling of the Spanish judge Baltasar Garzón, on 2 November 1999, in the case against former Marine Adolfo Scilingo, stating that: "an entire plan of 'selective elimination', or elimination in accordance with membership of integral sectors of the Argentinean people, was drawn up in such a way that it can be affirmed that the selection was not so much in terms of real people, since they made them disappear or killed thousands of them without any kind of political or ideological sense, as for their membership of specific collectivities, sectors or groups of the Argentine Nation (the National Group) which in its unbelievable criminal dynamic, it considered to be opponents of the Process". Thus, both the new prologue and recent legal sentences have prolonged, from the start, the humanitarian narrative which structured the classification and presentation of the disappeared during the dictatorship, depoliticizing again the commitments of the disappeared by enrolling them in collectives defined by demographic, national, religious or social-occupational variables.

Thirty-five years since the start of the military dictatorship, the establishment of the quantitative dimension of the disappearances or the study of political commitments, including membership of political–military organizations, await the public agenda and, specifically, academic research, as unresolved topics, just like the study of the local and popular representations and memories of the disappeared. Investigations in certain suburbs of big cities and small towns in the interior of the country have gathered evidence that their representation in these areas assumes phantasmagorical forms, has been integrated into popular religious practices, or is subsumed and renewed within the framework of oral storytelling traditions. The analysis of these regional and class differences is particularly relevant given the deepening, since the dictatorship, of social inequalities and regional fractures in the country.[34]

34 For some exceptions in this respect, see E. Crenzel, *Memorias enfrentadas: el voto a Bussi en Tucumán*. San Miguel de Tucumán: Universidad Nacional de Tucumán, 2001, & L. Da Silva Catela, "Apagón en el Ingenio, escrache en el museo. Tensiones y disputas entre memorias locales y memorias oficiales en torno a un episodio de

Conclusions

These pages have analysed how the disappeared have been remembered from when this crime was perpetrated until the present. This examination allows us to recognize the changes and continuities which the memory of the disappeared has experienced in Argentina in the last thirty-five years, the result of the intervention of different actors and groups struggling to interpret and make sense of the past of political violence in the public arena. The memory of the disappeared has, then, changed over time as a result of various political interventions translated into different narrative keys and specific interpretations. It was the dictatorship itself which founded the first representation of the disappeared when, after having denied their existence and all responsibility for the disappearances, it sought to register their identities in the framework of the discourse of "war against subversion". From this perspective, the disappeared were exclusively a part of the guerrilla ranks and had been shot, were in hiding or had fled abroad as a result of the ongoing war in the country. This configuration of meaning was confronted by those who denounced the dictatorship through the links they had established with the transnational networks of human rights. Their allegations included a representation of the disappeared which favoured the restoration of their humanity by reference to their basic identity data. Simultaneously, it excluded all mention of political commitment, especially to the armed struggle, by highlighting their moral values.

This figure of the innocent victim was institutionalized by the official story of the disappearances, incorporated into one of the centrepieces of the report *Nunca Más*, which confronted and denied the dictatorial denial and relativization of the disappearances. However, this rebuttal did not question the logic of the dictatorial discourse, sustaining the defence of human rights on the moral values of the victims and not on the universal nature of the legal subject. Since the publication of the CONADEP report and the

represión de 1976", in *Luchas locales, comunidades e identidades*, ed. Ponciano Del Pino & Elizabeth Jelin, Madrid, Siglo XXI, 2003, pp. 63–106.

trial of the military juntas which gave this representation of the character of a legal truth, various cultural productions, in cinema and in literature, which reached mass audiences, made this representation hegemonic.

Since the mid-1990s these narrative and interpretative keys have been questioned in the heat of a new political and cultural climate, one which is alien to the constraints of the judicial treatment of the past and critical of the route which the constitutional governments had taken with regard to human rights violations and the legacy of profound economic and social inequalities left by the dictatorship. As well as reproducing the primacy of the witness and the first hand witness, the key of the family and / or the realistic story, canonical forms instituted by the *Nunca Más* and the trial of the juntas, they also incorporated new questions about the past. In particular, they gave an account of political militancy (including armed political militancy) as an element in the commitment of some members of the disappeared, which had been obliterated in the earlier narratives. This new way of evoking the disappeared followed different paths: it was interrogated and reconstructed from the point of view of filial ruptures and the from the perspective of the intimate and private key, especially in the films produced by some of the children of the disappeared, but also on the basis of a renewed literature of the virtues now centred on the figure of the activist.

However, the evocation and representation of the disappeared through a comprehensive but vague image based on the portrayal of occupational and demographic profiles which excludes political commitments, especially to the political-military organizations, is strong. It has survived even in the stories which, like the new prologue added in 2006 to *Nunca Más*, were formally proposed as an antagonistic approach to the canonical tale of the early democracy or recent judgments which have condemned perpetrators of disappearances. The changes taking place in the remembrance of the disappeared in Argentina demonstrate the failure of the dictatorial will in first denying the very existence of their crimes and then imposing a representation of the disappeared in harmony with the discourse of the "war against subversion". As has been highlighted here, different representations and memories have restored, in various ways, the "visibility of the presence" of the disappeared "which the technique of disappearance robbed them of".[35] In parallel, it still prioritizes the presentation of the disappeared on the basis of the raw data of their basic identity and moral qualities, at the expense of registering their political commitments and the conflicts in which they took part. These keys in the history of the memory of the disappeared in Argentina are offered as an eloquent indication that this is not a mere reflection on the past in which the crimes were committed but also warns us that certain keys established in that period remain in many of the initiatives which have been proposed in order to transcend it.

35 N. Richard (ed.), *Políticas y estéticas de la memoria*, Santiago de Chile, Cuarto Propio, 2006.

HUGO VEZZETTI

The Uses of the Past and the Politics of the Present

On 9 December 1985, the ruling passed in the trial of the military juntas was made public. Jorge Rafael Videla and Eduardo Massera were sentenced to life imprisonment, Roberto Viola to seventeen years, Armando Lambruschini to eight years, and Orlando Ramon Agosti to four years. In September 1984, the *Comisión Nacional sobre la Desaparición de Personas* (CONADEP: National Commission on Disappeared Persons) chaired by Ernesto Sabato presented to President Raul Alfonsín the report issued under the title of *Nunca Más*. The trial, a state ceremony which had no parallel in Argentinean history, and the Commission's report were mutually reinforcing and, in their public impact, marked profoundly and lastingly the new meaning acquired by the dictatorship in Argentina society.

Emilio Crenzel has written a documented history of the mass diffusion of *Nunca Más* and the diverse ways in which it has been appropriated. Born of a state initiative, reappropriated by different actors in society, the book had sold over 500,000 copies before November 2007. It "was incorporated into the educational curriculum, published in instalments in newspapers nationwide together with films about the period. Its title was inscribed on many plaques, used as a political slogan and postulated as the name for various museums of memory". The model inaugurated by the CONADEP was replicated in different "truth commissions" throughout Latin America: Brazil (1985), Uruguay (1989), Paraguay (1990), Chile (1991), El Salvador (1993), Guatemala (1996), Colombia (2000) and Peru (2003).[1] Despite the restrictions on its dissemination on television, the trial had widespread public impact through the press over the nine months of its duration. The

1 E. Crenzel, *La historia política del Nunca más*, Buenos Aires, Siglo XXI, 2008, pp. 18–19.

visual narrative came to television in 1998 by which time commercial videos had already been produced which had a wide circulation.[2]

The firmest kernel of the recovery of that sinister past was introduced at the inaugural moment of democracy. In the space of little more than a year between 1984 and 1985 a new vocabulary and new images which characterized the stage which had to be left behind became established: state terror, disappearances, human rights violations, on the one hand, but also *Madres* and *Abuelas de Plaza de Mayo* (Mothers and Grandmothers of the Plaza de Mayo), human rights organizations, and the slogans of truth, memory and justice, on the other. Of course, that past which was thus transformed in social experience had terms which were opened up above all in the period between the defeat in the Malvinas War in June 1982 and the call for elections in the October of the following year. The representation of the years of dictatorship and the story of the "war against subversion" were beginning to change profoundly. Nationalist fervour was collapsing. In a society which had largely supported the war, the dictatorship was condemned in principle by losing it. The public appearance of the victims of the dictatorship was associated with the more recent victims, the soldiers killed in the South Atlantic, and the responsibility lay, in both cases, with the military commanders.

An initial narrative of democracy, which will end up establishing itself with *Nunca más* and the Trial, had as its condition that transition from the images of an order guaranteed by military power against perceived threats of "subversion" to the atrocious scenes of detention and extermination camps and to the protection of the rights of victims, who were turn transformed into the bearers the promise of the ethical and political reconstruction of society. An enduring association between memory, democracy and rights was born there in the world of victims and the persecuted. This political and ethical configuration which rejected forgetting and proposed a course of justice in relation to the dictatorial past was the basis of Alfonsín's triumph and the broad support he received during the first years of his government. As is well known, the sanctioning of the laws of *Obediencia Debida* (Due

2 Claudia Feld, *Del estrado a la pantalla. Las imágenes del Juicio a los ex comandantes en Argentina*, Siglo Veintiuno de Argentina Editores, 2002, pp. 1–5.

Obedience) and *Punto Final* (Full Stop) contributed to discrediting the governance of the first president of the post dictatorship years. And yet, on the occasion of Alfonsín's death in 2009, some of that public approval reappeared, which recovered above all this cornerstone of the new cycle of democracy.

The 1990s

Peronism had another position with respect to the past. It accepted the amnesty which the military regime had sought to impose in 1983, refused to participate in the CONADEP in 1984 and, when Menem came to power, pardoned the military leaders and the guerrillas who were on trial in December 1990. Hardly anyone in the PJ rejected the amnesties, whose aim was the "pacification" of the political and military scene. With the measures taken by Menem, the solution the PJ had pushed seven years prior to his election seemed satisfied, albeit after a period of delay: amnesty and forgetting with respect to the past, reconciliation with respect to the future. Previously, both the *carapintadas* involved in the mutinies against the constitutional government of Alfonsín in 1987 and 1988 and the military leaders convicted of crimes committed during the dictatorship and for negligence during the Malvinas War, had been amnestied.[3] But neither the position of the Peronist candidate in elections 1983, Italo Lúder, nor Menem's decision, can be separated from another part of the political

3 The first series of amnesties granted by Menem's government included 164 of the *carapintadas*, thirty-nine officers condemned for crimes committed during the repression, and the commanding officers of the Malvinas War. The amnesties included the former generals Juan Sasiain, Albano Harguindeguy, Santiago Riveros, Acdel Vilas, Luciano Benjamín Menéndez and Reynaldo Bignone. Only the colonel Seineldín, involved in various mutinees, remained in prison until May 2003, when he was amnestied by the then president, Eduardo Duhalde. At: http://es.wikipedia.org/wiki/Carapintadas.

memory of the recent past: the civil war which broke out within Peronism during the constitutional period led by General Perón and his wife, between 1973 and 1976. The slaughter carried out in Ezeiza, the crimes of the Triple A, the responsibilities of Perón himself in the illegal repression of the "revolutionary tendency", and the actions of the union leaders during the years of dictatorship, are chapters which still today remain obscured from historical or legal investigation.

On the other hand, the political use of the past in the new cycle dominated by the figure of Menem has not confined itself to the question of the recent past. On 30 September 1989, the remains of Juan Manuel de Rosas, presented as "defender of the national sovereignty", arrived in Buenos Aires. Perón himself had, in 1973, promoted the project of repatriation which was now coming to fruition. For that purpose, he appointed as ambassador to England the nationalist leader, Manuel de Anchorena, but the latter was unable to fulfil his commitment. Menem was now giving a signal of continuity with and affiliation to the traditions of Peronism, and Anchorena himself headed the march of 5,000 Gauchos which accompanied the journey of the remains of Rosas to the cemetery of La Recoleta.[4] Menem also had a statue of Rosas erected in Palermo facing that of Sarmiento. The purpose of reconciliation was thus extended into the past, to the civil wars of the nineteenth century (in which Sarmiento and Rosas had represented opposing sides) and the origins of a fractured vision of the nation.

But Menem did not limit himself to intervening in the experience of the past through the amnesties and the integration of Rosas into the national pantheon.[5] Much more important and lasting in its effects on the military issue was the decision to suppress the final *carapintada* mutiny in December 1990. At that point in time, Colonel Seineldin, who had been amnestied a year before, rebelled once more against the authorities. On this occasion loyal army forces crushed the rebellion and a number of officers

4 http://www.elintransigente.com/notas/2010/9/30/menem-hizo-setiembre-1989-llegan-restos-rosas-57364.asp.

5 "Rosas ya tiene su monumento", *Clarín*, 9 November 1999, http://edant.clarin.com/diario/1999/11/09/e-04201d.htm.

died in the fighting. Menem, who amnestied the leaders of the dictatorship, also put a definitive end to sedition within the armed forces. For this he did not rely solely on his own political decisiveness but on having military commanders who were willing for the first time to use weapons against their own comrades. And there were loyal officers (Lieutenant Colonel Pita and Major Pedernera, for example) who gave their lives in defence of the Constitution. Among the conditions which made possible this dramatic change in the position of military was, without doubt, the outright rejection of the spectre of military power on the part of the citizenry, including not just the social and political leaders but a large section of the officer corps. The shift in the understanding of the dictatorship which had occurred with the public impact of the trials finally made it possible for political authority to be imposed on the military commanders.

At the same time, this transformation produced effects which had not been anticipated by those who sought to promote a policy of forgetting. In the early years of the Menemist reign, sustained by a disciplined political party apparatus and supported by big business, the trade unions and the Church, it might have looked as if that first formation of memory associated with the carrying out of justice for the crimes of the past had been cancelled. The present, above all the economy, imposed its demands: hyperinflation had undermined the government of Alfonsín and in the new cycle the omnipresent figure of the market displaced that opening scene of a democracy founded on justice. And yet, although the new economic course was supported by a substantial majority, the marks left by the Trial and *Nunca Más* remained alive in society. The amnesties did not have much social support and the human rights organizations, which continued their struggle, retained their prestige. Furthermore, there continued the trials for the appropriation and suppression of the identity of the children of the disappeared not covered by the amnesty. The Judge María Romilda Servini de Cubría may have been under the thumb of Menemism when it came to the cases of corruption which were being raised within the legal system, but she investigated cases of the appropriation of minors and dictated restitutions in full accordance with the struggle of the *Abuelas de Plaza de*

Mayo (Grandmothers of Plaza de Mayo).[6] Even within the framework of the conservative revolution which prevailed in the economy, politics and society, Menemism encountered limits to its policy of forgetting.

The return of the repressed

By 1995, sinister images of torture, mass killings and the practices of disappearance of the bodies were resurfacing in the public arena.[7] For the first time the revelations did not come from the victims but rather from a member of the armed forces, Captain Scilingo, who recounted how the Navy routinely threw the bodies of the prisoners into the sea.[8] The voices, witnesses and places of enunciation were changing. Other testimonies immediately followed in the Army and eventually the self-critical document of Lieutenant General Balza, Chief of the General Staff of the Army, arrived. It publicly acknowledged the crimes committed. Ten years had passed since the Trial of the Juntas but some of its promises were updated in the new relationship which the leadership of the armed forces wanted to maintain with society.[9] Balza was the commander Alfonsín did not have (and probably could not have had). And yet, within a longer timeframe and in the context of potentials not recognized by politics, a first histori-

6 Marta Dillón, "Todo sobre Servini". *Página 12*, 6 March 2002, http://www.pagina12.com.ar/diario/suplementos/las12/13-94-2002-03-06.html.

7 I partially take up an already published work: H. Vezzetti, "Conflictos de la memoria en la Argentina, 1969–2000. Un estudio histórico de la memoria social", Workshop Historicizing Recent Troubles: Memory in Argentina, Chile and Peru, ILAS (Institute of Latin American Studies), University of London, 16–17 October 2003, http://www.historizarelpasadovivo.cl/es_resultado_textos.php?categoria=Argentina%3A+el+tiempo+largo+de+la+violencia+pol%EDtica&titulo=Conflictos+de+la+memoria+en+la+Argentina.+Un+estudio+hist%F3rico+de+la+memoria+social.

8 See Horacio Verbitsky, *El vuelo*, Buenos Aires, Planeta, 1995.

9 The document can be read at: http://www.bernardoneustadt.org/contenido_88.htm.

cal progression was being organized which stretched from the Trial to the legal repression of the *carapintadas* under the command of Balza himself, and to the self-criticism of the armed forces which, by rejecting the past, initiated a path towards their subordination to democratic order.

General Balza was the army chief appointed by President Menem. In principle, that official discourse (which was later taken up by the heads of the other armed forces) committed the armed forces to the historical narrative built on the basis of the birth of democracy. At the start of his statement Balza took up another beginning, that of *Nunca Más*, in order to refer to the violence of the 1970s: "a decade marked by violence, messianism, and ideology, a violence which began with the terrorism and did not stop even under the democracy we experienced between 1973 and 1976". He reiterated an interpretive matrix which had not been born in 1983 but at least ten years before, a bipolar representation of violence which, before being inserted into the *Nunca más*, had been part of the report produced by the *Comisión Interamericana de los Derechos Humanos* (CIDH: Inter-American Commission of Human Rights) in 1979.[10] The important thing is that he admitted the murder and torture and explicitly rejected the concept of "war against subversion". In the confrontation, he said, force had located itself "above dignity, obtaining, in some cases, this information by unlawful methods, going as far as to suppress life". He also called for the recognition of the responsibilities and referred the blame, a little cryptically, to a "collective unconscious" in which responsibilities were blurred, in keeping with the political decision of the amnesty sanctioned equally for military leaders and guerrillas.

Mario Eduardo Firmenich participated a little later, in May 1995, in the same area of public diffusion (Bernardo Neustadt's television program), in the staging of this ultimately unsuccessful attempt at reconciliation.[11]

10 See H. Vezzetti, *Sobre la violencia revolucionaria. Memorias y olvidos*, Buenos Aires, Siglo XXI, 2009, pp. 117–120.

11 http://www.bernardoneustadt.org/contenido_25.htm. See also Carlos Altamirano, "Pasado presente", in Clara E. Lida, Horacio Crespo and Pablo Yankelevich (eds), *Argentina, 1976: Estudios en torno al golpe de Estado*, Buenos Aires, FCE, 2007, pp. 28–29.

Unlike Balza, Firmenich spoke as a figure from the past: he presented himself as a "soldier of the Montoneros", but he hardly represented any of the many thousands who had joined up under his command. He did not recognize the crimes and, questioned about the murder of Aramburu, responded with the same slogan he had repeated over two decades: "It was an act which we did not decide ourselves, it was decided by the people". He only admitted the error ("ideological" and "militaristic") of the passage into clandestinity and the resumption of armed struggle during the government of Isabel Perón. Otherwise, in a statement lacking in political concepts, Firmenich slid from self-criticism to the Christian confession of sins. In the few paragraphs he read out the evangelical motivations were reiterated: "spiritually, it was the sin of despair", "we were not capable of fighting in compliance with the Christian precept which commands us to love our enemies", "it is not Christian to celebrate the death of even the worst enemy", "we prayed for him" (on the execution of Aramburu).

In this desired scene of reconciliation, the figures and the public statements were quite different. Balza spoke from the perspective of the state and committed the institution he headed to a significant change of position with regard to the actions and responsibilities of the past. At the same time, he did not fail to recognize the difficulties: he admitted that the time for reconciliation had not yet arrived and that it would probably take generations to achieve. The focus of his gaze was on the injuries the repression had had on the bonds of kinship, which were the major topic of the resistance organizations affected: "To wash the blood of the son, father, husband, mother, friend, is a hard exercise of tears, sorrow". And with this painful reality, he offered "silence in the face of pain, and the firm commitment of all my efforts to a future which does not repeat the past". He begged, finally, for "respect for the dead".

Firmenich, by contrast, represented no one and said nothing new, merely repeating the same narrative justifying violence which relegated the responsibilities and decisions to external conditions. The violence came only from the others (who are now called "adversaries") and the people had anointed them with the mission to respond to it. Overplaying his Christian faith and focusing on the sins committed and not on responsibilities and consequences, he ended up offering something more like personal repentance than political self-criticism. Unlike Balza, he did not speak of the dead. In any case the evangelical overflow did not show him to be capable of expressing a word of respect or regret for the killings carried out by the guerrillas who he had commanded.

In the end, these interventions accounted for a certain stage of reactivation of the recent past, but did not have the effect desired by the Peronist leadership. This was so, in the first place, because the army chief's call for pacification and responsibility was unable to break the conspiracy of silence of the officers who had participated in the illegal repression. Balza undertook to receive in confidence any information leading to the reconstruction of the lists of the disappeared. He also appealed to the "individual conscience" of his subordinates (probably because he anticipated that an order would not be met), but obtained no response. Despite the fact that the laws in force prevented criminal prosecution, no one seemed to believe that the path of justice had been closed. Those involved in the repression received legal advice not to speak for the risk of becoming involved in future trials, the representatives of the victims did not cease to seek justice and some judges were still gathering evidence.

Indeed, the law remained active in the cases involving the appropriation and the change of identity of the children of the disappeared. Those crimes, which involved children and family ties, brought into the public realm the figure of the innocent victims who had been consecrated with the diffusion of *Nunca más*. To the moral prestige gained by the action of the *Abuelas de Plaza de Mayo* (Grandmothers of Plaza de Mayo), was added the impact of the trials which had been opened abroad. Between 1997 and 1998 the Spanish Judge Baltasar Garzón revived lawsuits against military personnel who could not be tried in Argentina. These included the former captain Adolfo Scilingo, who volunteered to testify and ended up being prosecuted and convicted. The judge also secured the arrest of the Chilean dictator Augusto Pinochet in London in 1998 and, although the extradition request was unsuccessful, it helped to establish the question of human rights as a live issue globally.

In Argentina, the judicial stage was restored to public awareness as a means of the review and judgment of the past. In March 2001, during the presidency of Fernando de la Rúa, Federal Judge Gabriel Cavallo issued the first annulment of the laws of *Punto Final* (Full Stop) and *Obediencia Debida* (Due Obedience), in a case involving child abduction. In the footsteps of the trials which Judge Garzón continued in Spain, Cavallo co-validated *jurisdicción universal* (universal jurisdiction): crimes which qualified as "crimes against humanity" were subject to international law and were not susceptible to being protected by the amnesty laws.

In those years, the last ones of the Menem cycle, a new generation, that of the children, joined the protests and demands for justice. And an extensive intellectual and aesthetic output (testimonies, essays, drama, film, literature) made it clear that the past was still alive, despite the initiatives undertaken by the ruling party which wanted to leave it behind. Activists' memories emerged. Life stories and a diversity of first person recollections, both celebratory and melancholy, made manifest a new impetus not only of remembrance but of public deliberation about meanings, legacies and responsibilities. A cycle of renewed historical research also began, albeit with less public impact. In the testimony, the essay or historiography, the objects and the problems were amplified. The desire to transmit, to know and to judge extended to the role played by leaders and institutions: the church, the press, intellectuals, political parties, the university and the educational system, the left and the guerrilla organizations. Previously relegated topics or periods were confronted, such as nationalism and Catholicism, the traditions of the left, the 1978 World Cup or the Malvinas War. And the revolutionary enterprise initiated at the start of the 1970s began to be subjected to closer scrutiny.[12]

12 I pick out the most representative works from this varied output: Luis Mattini, *Hombre y mujeres del PRT-ERP. De Tucumán a La Tablada*, La Plata, de la Campana: initially published in 1988, republished with new prologues in 1995 and 2003. *Cazadores de utopías*, 1995, a documentary directed by David Blaustein, with a screenplay by Ernesto Jauretche. Martín Caparrós; Eduardo Anguita, *La voluntad. Una historia de la militancia revolucionaria en la Argentina*, 3 volumes, Buenos Aires, Planeta, 1997–1998. Gabriel Rot, *Los orígenes perdidos de la guerrilla en la Argentina. La historia de Jorge Ricardo Masetti y el Ejercito Guerrillero del Pueblo*, El Cielo por Asalto, 2000. Marcelo Larraquy; *Roberto Caballero, Galimberti, de Perón a Susana, de Montoneros a la CIA*, Buenos Aires, Norma, 2000. Hugo Vezzetti, *Pasado y presente. Guerra, dictadura y sociedad en la Argentina*, Buenos Aires, Siglo XXI editores,

Kirchnerism: trials and memory

In the foregoing I have highlighted the dates, the names and the events which account for some of the conditions which paved the way for the shift in the decisions made from 2003 during the government of President Kirchner. Amongst the background facts, it should be mentioned that as early as March 1998 the Congress had passed a law repealing the laws of *Obediencia Debida* and *Punto Final*.[13] This was done against the wishes of Menem, on the basis of an initiative of the *Alianza* (Alliance) deputies, Juan Pablo Cafiero and Alfredo Bravo, with support from Peronist legislators. The decision had no practical effects on the beneficiaries of those laws but represented a symbolic and political gesture indicating the change of mood in the major parties, above all within Peronism. The invalidity of the laws, with retroactive effect, had been submitted several times by the left and centre-left parties, but had never obtained the support of the majority of the members of the PJ and the UCR. That same initiative, supported now by President Kirchner, was passed in parliament in August 2003 and ratified by the new Court in June 2005. The amnesties issued by Menem were annulled in July 2007.[14]

2002. Gustavo Plis-Sterenberg, *Monte Chingolo*, Buenos Aires, Planeta, 2003. César Tchach (comp.), *La política en consignas. Memorias de los setenta*, Rosario, Homo Sapiens, 2003. Lucas Lanusse, *Montoneros. El Mito de sus 12 Fundadores*, Buenos Aires, Vergara, 2005. Pilar Calveiro, *Política y/o violencia. Una aproximación a la guerrilla de los años 70*, Buenos Aires, Norma, 2005. Marta Diana, *Mujeres guerrilleras*, Buenos Aires, Planeta, 2006. M. Larraquy, *Fuimos soldados. Historia secreta de la contraofensiva montonera*, Buenos Aires, Aguilar, 2006. Roberto Pittaluga; *Alejandra Oberti, Memorias en montaje. Escrituras de la militancia y pensamientos sobre la historia*, Buenos Aires, El Cielo por Asalto, 2006. The magazine *Lucha armada*, directed by Sergio Bufano and Gabriel Rot, commenced publication towards the end of 2004. That year the polemic about the actions of the guerrillas in Salta also began; see *La Intemperie*, Córdoba, Numbers 15 and 16, October and November 2004.

13 *La Nación*, 26 March 1998.

14 *La Nación*, 13 August 2003, 15 June 2005, 13 July 2007.

Kirchner's political decision was crucial, primarily because it forced a change of position in his own party. In addition, the renovation of the Menemist *Corte Suprema* (Supreme Court), which was supported by almost the whole of the opposition, guaranteed the continuation of a favourable legal stance for the prosecution of crimes considered to be crimes against humanity. These early decisions seemed to indicate a long-term policy of retrieving and reviving the judicial stage which had been part of the source of the democratic project. With the reopening of the trials, in practice, a second sequence of the Trial of the Juntas was opened, although it did not have the impact and public mobilization achieved in 1985. On the political front the conditions existed for a new beginning so as to revive this founding scene of democracy and call for a broad agreement between the parties, community leaders and state authorities. But as early as 24 March 2004, in the ceremony at the ESMA, Kirchner displayed a will to negate the experience accumulated by the state and by society in twenty years of civil government. He entered what had been the emblematic stronghold of the illegal repression and extermination as if the dictatorship had ended the previous day. He asked for forgiveness on behalf of the State, in an event organized outside the premises, which lacked the typical features of a ceremony of state, with representatives from neither parliament nor judiciary nor the opposition and almost without governors. In those absences can be seen the virtual veto on the presence of governors promoted by Hebe de Bonafini, who would be assigned an increasingly prominent place in the public discourse of the ruling bloc. In a press release, some of the major provincial bosses of the PJ (Felipe Solá of Buenos Aires, Jorge Obeid of Santa Fe, José Manuel de la Sota, of Córdoba, Jorge Busti of Entre Ríos and Carlos Verna de La Pampa) manifested their opposition to the way in which the government had handled the announcement.[15]

15 *La Nación*, 24 and 25 March 2004. They said: "That day is also ours, in spite of the ideological discrimination which neither Peronism nor its voters deserve", expressed in the press release entitled "Nunca más". They maintain that as Peronist militants they had been "victims of state terrorism" and demanded that "hatreds and resentments" be put aside.

Kirchner's proclamation was primarily an act of militancy. It reviewed and left behind a political position on the past which had been in force in Peronism from Lúder to Menem and Duhalde, a position with which the president had previously agreed. That the party did not easily accommodate itself to this shift was demonstrated at its congress held a few days later. There the governor, Soto, received a standing ovation from most of those present when he condemned the murder of Rucci.[16] The government policies which reopened the road to justice received more support in the Radical opposition and the centre –left than in the Peronist party and unions. This is what was seen when it reopened the case by the crimes of the Triple A in 2007. Immediately there appeared throughout the city of Buenos Aires Peronist trade union posters reading "Do not fuck with Perón". Judge Norberto Oyarbide, who has many close contacts with the government, stalled the case, which remains open.[17]

In recent years, government policies have helped to reopen the action of justice in relation to the past. Although they have limited public impact, the trials now going on remain the most practical support for memory and public awareness. In August 2010 a total of 1,576 people, including civilians and armed forces and security personnel, were involved in cases related to state terrorism, although only eighty-nine were given sentences (81 convictions and eight acquittals). Considering the state of the cases, the delays caused by the accused or by the judicial functionaries and the limited nature of resources, trials might take as long as twenty years.[18] At present, the judicial scene remains a document and a monument, active in the knowledge and the thinking of the past.

At the same time, the actions undertaken in the state politics of memory have been almost exclusively the responsibility of a coalition formed by the

16 *La Nación*, 27 March 2004.

17 *La Nación*, 22 January 2007. In 2010 Oyarbide was warned by the Cámara Federal because of his passivity in the case: see *Perfil*, 15 June 2010.

18 See http://www.cels.org.ar/comunicacion/?info=detalleDoc&ids=4&lang=es&ss=46&idc=1246. CELS, "Adelanto del Informe 2010 sobre la situación de los derechos humanos en Argentina" at http://www.cels.org.ar/common/documentos/juicios_adelanto_IA_2010.pdf.

Executive together with the majority of the human rights organizations. The refusal to admit what had been achieved by the state after 1983, the tendency to take decisions by decree, the relegation of parliamentary action, the absence of agreements with the opposition (which nevertheless mostly supported decisions in this area), the lack of connections with other sectors of the state (in the areas of education, the judiciary, of security or the military, for example), conspired against the participation of other actors and made it difficult to define long-term policies.

The decisions taken in the ESMA complex are illustrative of the weaknesses of a form of state action which has in fact delegated decisions to the organizations of those affected. Towards 1999 the proposal was raised in the legislature of Buenos Aires of situating a Museum of Memory there. In March 2004, the initiative was taken up by the national government, already under the administration of President Kirchner. They announced the creation of the Museum and the Secretary for Human Rights invited proposals. There were a dozen, presented by various entities including CELS, SERPAJ, *Asociación de Ex Detenidos Desaparecidos* (Association of Disappeared Former Detainees), *Secretaria de Cultura del Gobierno de Buenos Aires* (Secretary of Culture of the Government of Buenos Aires), among others. These were never discussed although they were available on the website of the Ministry of Human Rights until 2007 or so. Initially, state action, although limited, had provided the framework for political and historical debate about the project, the objectives and the stories which could organize the space. The initiative of the museum had been taken up with great conviction by *Memoria Abierta* (Open Memory) an organization formed by a coalition of concerned organizations and human rights organizations from 1999.[19]

The design of a space and a mechanism for the education of the historical consciousness which is intended for society required a framework which admitted different, even conflicting, visions, so as to discuss the

19 See H. Vezzetti, *Sobre la violencia revolucionaria. Memorias y olvidos*, Buenos Aires, Siglo XXI, 2009, "Apéndice. Espacios, Monumentos, Memoriales". On the discussion promoted by Memoria Abierta, see http://www.memoriaabierta.org.ar/pdf/museo_de_la_memoria.pdf.

scope and limits of the project, incorporating diverse actors (politicians, intellectuals, academics), in short, building consensuses and defining the recipients of the endeavour. To the extent that it was an initiative committed to building a culture of rights and the democratic project, and could account for a past fraught with conflict, violence and death, it could not be a question of thinking of a single narrative. Public debate and the possibility of involving different social sectors had to be contemplated, in addition to the organizations committed to this cause: parties, social organizations, universities, etc. The process of the intellectual and political construction of the symbolic foundation of that space was just as important as – or perhaps more important than – the material construction of the Museum as such. Such a process, which might be long in duration, could constitute it as a potent symbol of the fundamental relationship which democracy in Argentina has maintained with the development of the past.

The shortcomings are obvious. The Museum project and the discussion of the different proposals were abruptly interrupted in late 2007. Once the site had been vacated by the Navy, the Executive decided to give several buildings in the grounds of the ESMA to various human rights organizations. The place which had been used as a detention and torture centre will be preserved as the museum site, but the proposal of the historical museum and a comprehensive plan for the site have been relegated. It is an internally disorganized space, with little connection to other public state presences (in education, the law or the training of military and security personnel, for example) and criss-crossed by the differences between the various organizations. If they remain absent, the parties and other sectors of civil society run a risk that the older agents of that enterprise (the human rights agencies) will end up as the main recipients. The CELS Report of 2009 says: "there remains the participation of other actors, as well as those from human rights organizations in the institutional framework and decisions on the future of the property". And it highlights "the need to generate actions, so that the spaces of memory transcend the direct victims, their families and human rights organizations".[20] On the other hand, the divi-

20 CELS, 2009Report, pp. 58–59. At http://www.cels.org.ar/common/documentos/ia09.pdf.

sions in the human rights movement are well-known, and are deepened by alignments established by the incorporation of some of their figures into the ruling bloc and by the clashes between different parts of the left. The commemoration of the anniversary of 24 March has become, in this context, a public sphere dominated by discord and mutual recriminations. The inadequacy of state action and the absence of an overall concept for the space of the ESMA were expressed by Hebe de Bonafini (who always opposed the Museum project and rejects the memorial to victims of state terrorism located in the Costanera): "There are many places, everyone can make demands and do what he wants in every place".[21]

Another major development in government administration has been the unexpected inclusion of a new prologue to *Nunca más*, signed by the Secretaría de Derechos Humanos (Ministry of Human Rights) in 2006, the thirtieth anniversary of the coup.[22] It is not a question of a preliminary study or historical presentation of a work which, as previously noted, was instrumental in shaping public awareness of that past. The brief text has the character of a rectifying intervention which, in a paragraph at the beginning of the book, alludes to the historical conditions of state terrorism and reiterates the bipolar representation of political violence (a clash between two terrorisms, left and right) which was very common in the 1970s. This interpretation is ambiguous and insufficient; it deserves to be discussed and in fact has been discussed over twenty years. But this government interference does not propose a debate but rather to eliminate the historical context as a problem in the knowledge and understanding of the events which the book explores. As demonstrated by the research by Emilio Crenzel already cited, *Nunca más* was read, disseminated and imitated; it has been interpreted, rectified and widely discussed for more than twenty years in the society. The decision of the administrative power to establish a doctrine or an official story is comparable to what Paul Ricoeur called

21 *Página 12*, 27 January 2008 http://www.pagina12.com.ar/diario/elpais/1-98071-2008-01-27.html.

22 "Prólogo", *Nunca más*, Edition for the 30th Anniversary of the Coup d'Etat, Buenos Aires, Eudeba, 2006 at: http://www.derhuman.jus.gov.ar/anm/pdfs/Prologo_2006.pdf.

an "imposed memory".[23] That purpose tends to exclude public deliberation about the conditions and responsibilities in the cycle of violence in which the dictatorship intervened, and deprives the various social actors of the ability to narrate and transform that past. Today this can be seen to be doomed to failure, to the same extent as the discussion of violence, and in particular of the guerrilla movement, which had already broken into the public sphere, a discussion which continues and expands.[24]

Memory and the history of the disappeared

Finally, among the outstanding issues for historical research, which is still insufficient, there remains the question of the number of disappeared persons. The issue is not new but came to public notice when, in 2009, Graciela Fernandez Meijide noted the contrast between the figure of 30,000, which has been turned into a banner of human rights bodies and carried forward

23 P. Ricoeur, *La mémoire, l'histoire, l'oubli*, París, Seuil, 2000 p. 580.

24 The debate about guerrilla violence began with the testimony of Héctor Jouvé over the murders carried out by the Ejército Guerrillero del Pueblo (EGP) among its own members in 196 ... and was deepened by the subsequent intervention of Oscar del Barco. See *La Intemperie*, Córdoba, from October 2004 to June 2005; he later continued with various interventions in *El ojo mocho, Confines, Políticas de la memoria y Conjetural*. Part of the dossier can be seen in "No matarás" at: http://laempresadevivir.com.ar/category/debate-no-mataras/. As an example of the present relevance of this discussion, I mention some of the most recent titles: Ceferino Reato, *Operación Primicia*, Buenos Aires, Sudamericana, 2010. Felipe Celesia; Celesia Waisberg, *Firmenich*, Buenos Aires, Aguilar, 2010. Juan Bautista Yofre, *El Escarmiento. La ofensiva de Perón contra Cámpora y los montoneros, 1973–1974*, Buenos Aires, Sudamericana, 2010. Alicia Servetto 73/76. *El gobierno peronista contra las "provincias montoneras"*. Buenos Aires, Siglo Veintiuno Editores, 2010. Hugo Montero; *Ignacio Portela, Rodolfo Walsh, los Años Montoneros*, Buenos Aires, Sudestada, 2010. Ariel Hendler, *La Guerrilla Invisible. Historia de las Fuerzas Argentinas de Liberación (FAL)*, Buenos Aires, Vergara, 2010. Daniel Gutman, *Sangre en el monte*, Buenos Aires, Sudamericana, 2010.

without further ado by the government, and the official data available at the Human Rights Secretariat of the Ministry of Justice of the Nation, which at that time recorded about 8,000 names.[25] Shortly after, the *Archivo Nacional de la Memoria* (National Archive of the Memory) corrected the CONADEP records and provided the figures available: 7,140 missing, 1,336 executed, 2,793 summarily released from secret detention centres; it added to these 1,541 partial and pending complaints.[26] This means that adding all the victims and including the pending complaints, the total comes to 10,017. The new finding was that those released from the clandestine centres equal 28 per cent of total victims and 39 per cent of the registered disappeared.

No doubt there is much yet to be investigated in terms of historical knowledge of the conditions and events, the lives and ideas of the protagonists of this past. The estimated number and the characteristics of the victims is not an insignificant minor detail for this knowledge and the work of collective clarification of a stage which is in many ways still alive and present in social life. In a merely provisional way, we can say, first, that the proportion of the released weakens the thesis of "genocide", when compared with rates of survivors of historical genocides of the twentieth century. Second, from the official figures it is difficult to continue to support the number of 30,000 as a historical fact, while admitting that this group has acquired the force of a symbol of the repression exercised by the state secret. There were thousands and that is enough to characterize this event as a mass murder.

This estimate arose initially in about 1979 on the assumption that the conditions prevailing in the years of dictatorship decreased the number of complaints. But this assumption has not been confirmed. Most of the complaints had already been made to the *Comisión Interamericana de Derechos Humanos* (CIDH: Inter-American Commission on Human Rights), which

25 The question is presented in G. Fernández Meijide, *La historia íntima de los derechos humanos en la Argentina*, Buenos Aires, Sudamericana, 2009. But the public debate unfolded through the medium of the press. See Perfil, 3 August 2009; La Nación, 5 August 2009.

26 Ramón Torres Molina, "Veinticinco años del informe de la CONADEP". *Página12*, 15 September 2009; at http://www.pagina12.com.ar/diario/elpais/1-131783-2009-09-15.html.

in 1979 received 5,580.[27] Years ago, Emilio Mignone estimated the number of missing at about 20,000 and added about 10,000 cases of people abducted and released to reach that already consecrated number, 30,000 victims.[28] If the actual numbers provided by the *Archivo Nacional de la Memoria* (National Archive of the Memory) are compared with those of 1979, it can be seen that allegations of disappearances increased 28 per cent in thirty years. To think that in the course of that time, with all the facilities for making complaints (including the benefit of financial compensation for the families), the names of more than 20,000 people, or twice the actual cases reported, have been lost, is very difficult to sustain.

The known and documented disappeared are people who are almost all political or social activists. They were embedded in society, mostly in urban areas, with ties of friendship and family, politics, work and neighbourhood; they are people who worked and studied, were active in politics, and lived in communities. In short, their absence was generally noted, and not only by family members. In many cases it was their fellow militants, workmates or friends who persuaded the family to make complaints. Is it necessary to conclude that there are more than 20,000 missing persons whose life profile and social inclusion had nothing to do with that of known cases? Can it be argued that the missing names are those of people who lived and died without leaving a trace, who lacked familial, work, political, neighbourhood or friendship environments, that is to say, links to people capable of making the relevant complaint, above all when all the facilities for doing so have been provided? Or that thousands were killed who had nothing in common with the way of life of the known victims, and in this case it would be necessary to explain why the power of the dictatorship came down upon them, given that in general the repression discharged itself against militants and activists? Or, if it is admitted that they were like the known victims, it must be assumed that there were thousands of militants, activists, engaged in or associated with political or social organizations, who

27 See http://www.cidh.oas.org/countryrep/Argentina80sp/ indice.htm and E. Crenzel, *La historia política del Nunca más*, Buenos Aires, Siglo XXI, 2008, p. 41.

28 E. Mignone, *Derechos humanos y sociedad. El caso argentino*, Buenos Aires, CELS & EPN, 1991, pp. 70–71.

were suppressed without leaving the slightest memory, without anyone in their environment noticing or considering that it was worthwhile reporting it. This would imply a sobering critique of the social or political action which they were undertaking (most of them at least) in their communities. There would have been more than 20,000 members of a generation who gave their efforts and their struggles for transformative action in society whose lives and deaths would have been so insignificant that they did not leave even the memory of a name.

This hypothesis also seems inconsistent with what we know about Argentinean society and the process of social mobilization and organization experienced in the years before the dictatorship. Argentina is not (and was even less then) comparable with a confused African region; to assume that thousands of people (activists or not) can be annihilated without leaving a trace or provoking claims is to equate it with the worst examples of disintegrating human conglomerations, precarious and devoid of a minimum share of resources from the state.

To sum up, since the beginning of the democratic cycle in 1983, the past has been subject to various uses, remembered, judged, and transformed on the basis of an event which shook the historical consciousness: state terrorism and the tragedy of the disappeared persons. The greatest symbol of that legacy remains to this day, a rejection and a denial: "Nunca más". Going forward, the positive undertaking in the sense of an affirmation of rights and of justice in society, is not assured and remains a pending legacy which interrogates the fate of the construction democracy. The struggles for meaning and different forms of recuperation and debate, even manipulation, of the past remain open. Public deliberation today appears inclined to a small-minded politicization which reduces and accommodates history to the struggles of the present. There remains a work of investigation and thought which broadens knowledge and nurtures the debate. But its effectiveness and its scope do not rest upon the authority of historians, although they are required, just as the full realization of justice depends not only on the work of judges, lawyers and witnesses. History can be a territory for an endeavour of collective clarification to the extent that it fulfils an intellectual function capable of renewing questions, identifying gaps and contradicting beliefs which sustain frozen visions of past and present.

ALEJANDRO KAUFMAN

History and Memory: Some Theoretical Investigations for the Latin American Context

The present work proposes to review some of the conceptual parameters necessary for framing the problematic of history and memory in the specific Argentinean context in its theoretical and genealogical relations with the social sciences and the doctrinal corpus of human rights. The Argentinean context is understood in turn as part of the Latin American context.

In the first place, it is a question of dealing with the matrix of the human rights, understood as a collection of *social practices*, susceptible of proposing paths of coexistence in contemporary societies organized around a regime of *biopolitical production*. Beyond its politico-philosophical foundations, the discourse of human rights will have to be considered as a *system* capable of delimiting or preventing the emergence of extreme situations.

In the second place, the reference to the social sciences contributes to establishing the relations between the problematics of memory and historiography on the one hand and the polemics of the present on the other. The problem pointed to by the discrepancy between the consideration of the traumatic past and the socio-political problems of the present has become a taken for granted motif. The question about the genealogical articulation between both dimensions examines the question of the regime of biopolitical production as an analytical foundation of the contemporary forms of collective life.

In the third place, trauma and violence are experiences which have been linked to *anthropological transformations* and are heralded as part of the future to come. In the present analysis, the discourse of human rights is not postulated as something which normalizes social life but rather as a genealogical axis of the regime of biopolitical production. The discontinuities created by extreme situations are not exterior to the genealogical line which defines a series between the past and the present, but rather are inseparable from the diachronic timeline, although in contingent forms whose contradictions offer phenomena destined to define the object of analysis.

Our proposal is to examine tentatively some theoretical developments on the basis of the global – and above all European – experiences of the twentieth century, in the light of the specificities of recent Argentinean history. This, in turn, is projected over the problematic needs of the present, more oriented towards consolidating a common framework of coexistence than to examining the past in its own terms. The fluid and elusive character typical of historical events, in terms of the intrinsic difficulty concerning the stories about the past and its memories, is enhanced and overdetermined when the question of extermination is examined. Investigations are then convened which cover the most sensitive dimensions of the problem, beyond that of the problematics of the record (archive) or the reconstruction of the past (history), the representations (collective memory) or the remembrances (amnanetic memory). A pressing problem in relation to extermination is that of the present effects of the conflict, the dispute, or even more directly, the causes which gave rise to it.

I. The way in which we are involved with extermination as subjects does not reside (only) in its historical proximity, nor in that we have (only) a biographical, genealogical or filial proximity to the events which are related to it. The themes usually discussed with respect to the relations between the past and the subjects of the present require specific and unique considerations when we investigate extermination.

Extermination, as established by the paradigmatic experience which gave birth to our time, consists of removing from the human species one part of it, distinguished by some classificatory criterion. The periodization of this paradigmatic experience, the *final solution*, without prejudice to its factual historical dimension – from the Conference of Wansee to the defeat of Nazism in the Second World War – does not account for its *paradigmatic* character. As a paradigmatic experience, the genealogy of the *final solution* is surmounted by the history of *antisemitism*, if we go back, and without this question being the only one to consider with regard to the past.[1] If we consider the aftermath of this event, a series of questions appear to be indicated.

1. The final solution constituted the project of exterminating forever from the face of the earth, and without raising awareness of what was being done, a category of human beings, to whom, in general, a treatment was first applied which determined the cancellation of their human condition. The *cancellation* of the human condition does not refer to a deliberate absence or a lack of resources or to the privation of necessities, understood in the conventional form. The treatment perpetrated on the bodies could also be distinguished from death as a final destination, inasmuch as the victims were made to pass through a specific passage: the in-humanity is not so much related to the exercise of violence over the subjects as to their reduction to a biological state of extra-linguistic subsistence.

2. This project was unprecedented in cultural history, but has inspired in an exemplary way the behaviours of subsequent perpetrators from then on.

3. This project was left unfinished by military defeat. From the categorical point of view, those members of the social collectives destined for extermination can and ought to be considered survivors of a fate from which they were removed by politico-military circumstances. The determinations which led to such occurrences could only be limited by means of the most brutal destructive force.

4. They remain as a survivors of a fate established in history to the extent that this military defeat did not alter the historical causes which lead to the extermination. Extermination is the result of an historico-cultural process, subject to continuation beyond the conditions in which it did in fact take place in the context of the period in which it was actually perpetrated.

1 We understand anti-Semitism as a referential experience in the persecution of otherness in the cultural history of what is known as the "West". The final solution was presented as the mechanism destined to put an end to the "Jewish question". That conclusion would permit the saving of humanity from the conflicts related to the differences between human beings so as to arrive a homogenous and harmonious social world.

5. The fate to which the human beings belonging to the categories distinguished as victims of extermination were subjected remains effective to the extent that it is a question of a *category*, a *qualitative* distinction applicable to human beings in the present and the future.

6. The conditions under which I could imagine a project of extermination taking place might not be repeated in their effective realization, but they remain in force as a threat. It is for this underlying reason, and for no other, that in the countries in which extermination has taken place, it is a crime to deny it. Because there, probably unlike in other countries, it is not a question of an opinion, but rather of the participation of the speaker, even beyond his deliberate intention, in the genealogy of conflict which led to extermination. Those members of the categories destined for extermination are victims of a perpetual threat which belongs to the so-called *final solution*. "That the individual [Individuum] no longer died in the concentration camps, but rather the exemplar, has to affect the dying of those who escaped the administrative measures".[2] It is notable that some of Adorno's most important statements on the subject are not exactly the most quoted. While the denial is attributed to a regulatory intervention in the literature, he was thinking of something else:

> it may have been wrong to say that poetry could not be written after Auschwitz. What is not wrong however is the less cultural question of whether it is even permissible for someone who accidentally escaped and by all rights ought to have been murdered, to go on living after Auschwitz. Their continued existence already necessitates the coldness, of the basic principle of capitalist subjectivity, without which Auschwitz would not have been possible: the drastic guilt of the spared.

This passage anticipates the trauma of survival, not as something which comes from the past in a casual or residual form, but as a current *condition*, one which is in force, which is present. *Having escaped* refers to the members of the categories condemned to extermination. The memory of this survival concerns two antagonistic meanings: it could be anamnetic

2 Theodore W. Adorno, *Negative Dialectics*, trans Denis Redmond, 2001, p. 354: http://members.efn.org/~dredmond/ndtrans.html.

(by revealing the coldness required in order to connect the existential continuity) or could show itself as a threat. The criminalization of the abuse of Nazi emblems and of the denial of the *final solution* protects from this threat the members of the categories destined for extermination.

7. The principal aspect of this threat consists of the fact that something which was unimaginable, impossible to believe, which had never happened before, and with respect to which it ought to be unimaginable that it would ever be repeated – something like that *happened*. Such an event was added to history; this event was established in the series of events which took place in fact. Then *it could happen again*, and there is no argument which can dissuade those who form part of the categories subjected to extermination that they do not run this risk.[3] The danger they run does not reside in the empirically verifiable character of the threat at the present point in time, but rather in the mere fact that the threat was made and was carried out, in such a way that it led to a *radical novelty*, established from then on in the anthropological order, however, in the form of a *crime*.

8. One of the first responses which took place consisted in the creation of specific laws which recognized, in retrospective form, new crimes – crimes against humanity, genocide – and punished them in an exemplary way. A dilemma was created: on the one hand it is necessary to punish the crime of extermination with a regulation which did not exist before the crime, in a way which diverges from the principles of law according to which the norm precedes the crime. But the norm precedes the crime when the crime consists – in conventional terms – in a practice linked with cultural experience, even when it is considered undesirable and forms part of an edge, a margin, an antagonism. On the other hand, extermination assumes a radical change in the available frameworks of experience. "[D]eath has become something which has never yet been so feared. No possibility anymore, that it could enter into the experienced lives of individuals as something somehow concordant with its course".[4]

3 Reyes Mate says that periphrastically anamnetic reason consists "in thinking the unforeseen starting from the fact that the unforeseen has taken place".

4 Adorno, ibid., p. 354.

9. Norm, law, moral, ethics: these are all words whose anthropological dimension refers definitively to established practices, customs, or departures from customs. What we call practices, customs, refers to discursive configurations articulated with stories, myths, histories. What was unprecedented about the *final solution* does not refer only to the fact that we cannot find historical antecedents, but also to the fact that we do not recount any kind of story which prefigures that event and which therefore makes it recognizable or assimilable to experience. In this resides the importance of testimony. The testimony of extreme experiences, with regard to their emergence as a new type of event experienced by human beings, is the only discursive reference which can shed light on the significance of the *final solution*. Without testimony, the descriptions of the events could not take place as such, as mere factual records. Two essential features of the final solution contribute to these circumstances: a) it was jealously concealed, b) the fact that it was not believable that such events could take place.[5]

5 Himmler's discourse directed to the perpetrators is an essential component regarding the final solution. The machinery should not be lent to the corruption of exempting any friends: "I am referring here, with utmost frankness, to a very difficult matter, but it must be discussed now, between us, as we will never do so publicly. As we did not hesitate on 30 June 1934 in the fulfilment of our duty when faced with the comrades who had committed transgressions and ended with them and we never talked about it, nor will we talk about that. It was the tact which, I congratulate myself on this, characterized us, what he did we will never discuss. Each of us shuddered and yet each one of us knew he would do again if he were ordered, if it were necessary. I refer to the purging of the Jews, the extermination of the Jewish people. This is one of those things that is easily said. All party members say, 'The Jewish people will be exterminated'. 'Of course, it is part of our program, elimination of the Jews, annihilation, we will take care of it'. And then they all come, walking with slow steps, 80 million praiseworthy Germans, each with his decent Jew. Sure, the others are pigs, but this is an A-1 Jew. Of everyone who speaks in this way, none has seen it happen, no one has been there. Most of you know what it means to see hundreds of dead bodies lying next to each other, or five hundred or thousands. Having made the move to the front and having remained intact, except for exceptional cases explicable by their human weakness, this is what has made us strong. This is a glorious page in our history which had never been written and will not be written". Himmler's speech, cited by Emil Fackenheim, in *Reparar el mundo*, Sígueme, Salamanca, 2008, p. 223.

10. In order to deal with the paradigmatic character of the *final solution*, it is necessary to understand that its exemplary nature does not consist in the mere adaptation of an event to a conceptual model or ideal. It is a question, rather, of an historical event which new perpetrators read and interpret, and from which they obtain inspiration for the undertaking of their own projects. The perpetrators read history. History is not only of general interest to the public and the academics. Anyone who proposes a project of an ideological, military or political nature, of whatever kind, will inescapably formulate a reading of history. The final solution consolidated a kind of event whose genealogy refers to other previous historical moments from the Inquisition to the wars at the end of the nineteenth century – with their respective and inaugural concentration camps – the First World War, and above all the Armenian genocide. It introduced it into the historical heritage as one more social practice, with respect to which there is still a debate over whether this integration into the order of customs can be prevented in the future ("nunca más": "never again"). "*Nunca más*" refers neither to the violence, nor to the war, nor to the insurrections, but rather to the crime against humanity. Some interpret the term "*nunca más*" in such as way as to make it applicable to undesirable events of a violent, catastrophic or tragic nature. However, far from proposing a utopian concern, what is formulated, under this appearance, is a state of complacency and acceptance of the horrific events. It does so by putting them on an even footing with other events whose absence from the future could only be predicted if modifications were made of such a radical nature that we would not even know empirically what they could be, in as far as we lack the ability to bring about such changes. Such that formulating thus a supposed "nunca más", would only be to offer a euphemism, a trivial equivalence between the events of horror, extermination as an event proper to the twentieth century on the one hand, and the wars and catastrophes which have marked the totality of cultural history from them most remote times on the other. If we have to expect, therefore, that the future will bring us wars, catastrophes, insurrections and conflicts – as social history goes on in conformity with what we know – we will not be willing in the same way, even in tragic or pacifist nonconformity, to be prepared to participate in the perpetration of extermination.

11. In other words: on what basis could we demand "*nunca más*" in the face of a variety of events with respect to which we can only anticipate that they will happen over and over again although they are undesirable in the extreme? Something which is undesirable can only be the object of two attitudes: first, that we must prevent what is preventable, so as to make its occurrence as infrequent as possible, and, second, that we are unable to avoid it, lessen the damage, mitigate the consequences of the harmful or painful event. The method of investigation of these questions resides in establishing a relation between the events which it deals with, their historical antecedents, and the stories with which they have been described in the past. It is in this sense that the extreme situations, of horror, of extermination, have not taken place previously: there are no stories which describe them and even when they have been repeated in our epoch, we *would want* to cherish the hope that they are not repeated, or that the conditions which make them possible are radically modified. When we utter "*nunca más*", what we are saying is that something which had never happened before, and which should never have happened, likewise should never happen again. Nor are we presented with the statement "it should not have happened" in the face of those events which always happen in history, and which we expect will continue to happen. We say that the extermination "should not have happened" because nothing similar had happened before.

What is at stake in these considerations is the status of the human condition, the identity of the species. It is the human condition which is violated and disturbed when a crime is committed against humanity. Again: the crime against humanity is not especially terrible on account of its cruelty, nor its violence, nor the number of victims, but rather is especially terrible *because* it violates and disturbs the human condition and because of *how* it does so. We do not declare crimes against humanity those which for centuries were practiced as part of the order of misfortune and unhappiness and were considered as constitutive of the human condition. The human condition is lamented by those tragic events which recur throughout its history, but does not define them as something alien to the condition of the species. It is to this that the celebrated utterance of Terrence refers which he says that "*nothing human is alien to me*". Auschwitz suspends the force of this utterance and puts it radically into question.[6]

II. One of the difficulties presented in considering the question of extermination resides in its relations to war and violence. In its paradigmatic form, the *final solution*, it is not the violence which defines and makes possible extermination, but rather a combination of industrial methods of torture, induced starvation and coercion, with a consecutive physical elimination under a euphemistic appearance. It is death administered by technical means. The axial aspect of the treatment consists in the expropriation of the human condition of the individuals to the point stated by Primo Levi: *If this is a man*. Every conventional idea capable of being considered as violence is seen as inadequate and insufficient in this case. At the extreme, a detached description of the notion of violence is conceivable, focused more on the consequences and results, as well as on the *meaning* of the actions, rather than on those *physical events* which constitute it.

In this definition of the problem, its complete difference from the conventional notion of war or bilateral conflict is understood. A part of the population is seized by a false covering narrative and is afterwards subjected to a treatment which exempts the victims of every capacity of physical, psychological or moral defence. The individual is reduced to a body limited to the functions essential to its biological survival. It is the inanimate body of the operating table or of intensive therapy. But it has not been reduced to this state in order to procure its health, but rather its total destruction and oblivion. The technical procedures can be up to a certain – horrendous – point comparable, because of the coldness and rational deliberation with which they are conducted. The comparison does not arise from the observer but rather from the perpetrator, who emulates those actions, assigning them a given purpose.

6 However, the above does not cease to be problematic and debatable, even when we hold it as a position. The juridical paradigm tends to extend the category of crimes against humanity to events of the past, amplifying and blurring the limits of the field sketched here.

From the conceptual point of view, the confusion between war, violence and extermination is produced in principle because only the final consequences of each of these phenomena are considered, in terms of "death" or "survival". The distinctions need to be formulated in reverse, through the trajectory followed in the whole process from beginning to end. In every case, survival is a consequence of indeterminate events, but only in the case of extermination do the actions perpetrated have as their aim the definitive physical elimination of the victims, after *treatment*. It is because extermination, to be carried out successfully, and for complex reasons, requires first of all the expulsion of the individual from the species. The individual has to be separated from the species. So it is possible to conjecture a situation in which death was a secondary aspect of the *final solution*. Those expelled from humanity have not even been murdered, but nor can they be properly considered living. The concept on which the notion of "crime against humanity" is based implies this condition of exclusion from the human species. The deprivation of burial is an intrinsic aspect of the event and immediately consequent to it.

III. Anamnetic reason sheds light on one of the forms of memory, one which does not consist in the recorded past but rather in the forgotten past, in *remembrance*. The forgotten is what is forgotten for reasons which are found in the present and refer to the conditions of injustice. Anamnetic reason, as remembrance, brings up to date a meaning which contributes to the comprehension of the present. Every movement or attitude which organizes action around the demand for justice, does so in relation to other demands for justice from the past. To recall that there was injustice and also *struggle* against injustice is what makes it possible time and time again to maintain an ethical political *praxis* in the present. Anamnetic reason is an action which belongs to the tradition of the oppressed, just as the "forgetting" of what anamnesis recalls forms part of the tradition of the oppressors. Anamnesis is always an act of resistance and of opposition, because oppression itself is inseparable from its own oblivion. The naturalization of certain conditions of injustice bases its legitimation on the idea that "*it was always like that*". In the same way, the resistance to oppression bases its legitimation on the idea that although it was always like that, resistance also "*always*" opposed.

But this emergence of resistance is also an event. It is not a permanent condition as what prevails in history is oppression. One should never ask the rebel, the non-conformist, the resister why he protests today if he did not do so yesterday; because if he did not do so yesterday this is related to the reasons why he does do so today. He did not do so yesterday because in that condition of not acting consisted the oppression of which he was a victim, the condition of not knowing, not remembering or not being able to act differently from the mode dictated by power. In this context anamnesis is the act by means of which something happens which resembles an awakening.[7] Suddenly things are seen differently – and as being unacceptable – which previously were admitted as natural. Remembrance permits the association of signs of prosperity, happiness or justice in the present with those of the past which were demanded, and which were not attained in the past either. Remembrance, then, consists in a redefinition of distinctions; it consists in interpreting in a new way that which adopts the character of the undesirable.

A further difficulty in this respect is that none of these processes takes place in a univocal or transparent way, so the belief which is acquired around what we consider to be just in relation to oppression is constituted as a weak expression, however persistent and paradoxically powerful, while nothing of what dominates confirms what is remembered, but denies it. In contrast, the weak expression of remembrance bases its strength on something which, although it is weak, is enough to sustain a conviction which will have to face adversity and overwhelming powers.

Every historical account of the past of the oppressed invokes the appearance of anamnetic reason. Without this it becomes ideology, the story of the victors, oblivion, injustice, in the sense that what is opposed to memory is not oblivion but rather injustice. Oblivion, understood in this way, does not hide the factual record of the past but rather the violence on which the present order is based, the violence which conserves the order of the present, the violence which establishes the validity of law. On the other hand, the movement of the oppressed for their own emancipation

7 The free decision, says Reyes Mate, is like a birth. He thus distinguishes the political dimension of anamnetic reason, which relates politics and memory.

is not exempt from reproducing – depending on the victory which can be gained over the oppressors – the resumption of a new cycle of remembrance and forgetting sustained over the new correlations of power. These processes of emancipation, the object of critical study in terms of the final inversion of the terms, does not, however, deny the presence of a emancipatory legitimacy in its development. In any case violence is present in every social relation, and the consciousness of this presence will not have to give way to an ethico-political decline but rather to the confirmation of the role of remembrance as a critical system in socio-historical relations.

IV. The exercise of anti-establishment, revolutionary or insurrectional violence is not reducible – neither analytically nor normatively – to a free choice adopted from a starting point exempt from the tensions of history. It cannot be understood merely as a "*methodology*". Walter Benjamin distinguishes between the violence which installs and preserves power, and the violence which does not aim to impose anything by force but rather to put an end to the violence of the oppressors. The critical moment of the exercise of violence by the oppressed is historically concomitant with the processes which, in the face of the fall of an institutional framework, is substituted for another which establishes new forms of power and violence legitimated by the myth of the institution. The task of distinguishing between Danton and Robespierre, between Makhno and Trotsky, between Rearte and Galimberti requires – within the framework of the historical narrative – the intervention of anamnetic reason. The first group refers us to the violence which procures justice. It has to be said of this violence that, notwithstanding the rejection which we experience *a priori* with respect to all forms of violence, in ethico-political terms it is assimilable to that exercised in *self defence*. This is what juridical regimes admit as being unfortunately inevitable. It is that violence which is designed only to resist the violence of the oppressors. It is difficult to access the narrative which elucidates it; the paths leading to it are tortuous, because all those experiences, to a greater or lesser extent, usually tend to form part of the "*spoils of the victors*". However, what they have in their hearts as the search for justice remains in shadows. And it is in the cultural battle which takes place between victors and vanquished that the opportunity is established again for the silenced voices to be dimly heard.

The second form of violence, instituting new forms of the conservative violence of power, offers a difficulty which comes about in a form concomitant with it. A factual historical account could dispense with the conceptual tools needed to distinguish them. It will be in the context of the philosophical, literary and artistic practices that the anamnetic experiences can be resumed again which highlight the forgotten voice of the oppressed.

V. Amongst ourselves the current debate finds various meaningful references, in a context in which the general tendency points to the predominance of forgetting, and the appearance of historiographic discourses and analytics which put the emphasis on the general equivalence of all forms of violence, the latter being understood unequivocally and uncritically in its common sense meaning. The conceptual dissolution of the undecidable dimensions of the problem of extermination and of crimes against humanity occurs because studies of memory are limited to the consideration of memory understood as the set of social representations of the past. To express this in an approximate and provisional form: what predominates are the modalities in which the collective and institutional consciousness are embodied and which the historians elaborate as a factual account. At the same time the post-dictatorial institutional framework is adopted as a natural category of socio-historical evolution, instead of being considered as a mythical system of an order of conservation of the existing socio-historical relations. To those who dispense with a critical attitude, the traumatic residue of the dictatorship raises the fear of an abysmal political orphan who seeks to exorcise it with an uncritical adherence to the institutional framework.

On the other hand, we cannot also avoid mentioning the approaches which associate the study of recent history with a relative or complete neglect of the institutional framework, as well as the relative preference which we have for it and with which we coincide in the face of the dictatorial horror and the empirical inaccessibility of ideally emancipatory institutions. Anamnesis is a social practice which runs risks with respect to the references which give guarantees of validation and security. Whoever wants to preserve conceptual security as a priority could not give themselves up to an anamnetic exercise. The truth is that the anamnetic exercise dispenses with every type of guarantee, both for the conservative institutional order and for the values of justice themselves which are pursued: they are put at risk by the very act of remembrance.

VI. If the juridical and institutional order after the Second World War gave rise to the belief that a clear distinction had been established between war and extermination, and although we continue to vindicate this distinction because of its heuristic and anamnetic use, the truth is that it would not only be poetry which could not be written after Auschwitz without falling into barbarism, to return yet again to Adorno's famous expression. It would have to be assumed that after Auschwitz war is no longer the same, even though it had no longer been so for some time, as Walter Benjamin and Ernst Jünger – amongst others – announced in various ways. But even if the problem is delimited around the parading of the *final solution*, one of the questions which has been settled is that we live in a world which follows *that*. That world has included in one way or another the *final solution*. It has been included in such a way that, as we know, it seems trivial and fallacious if it is considered on the terrain of the comparison of events. The challenge is then imposed of undertaking a critical approach towards the hegemonic modes.

The juridico-institutional model conceives of a war comparable to the historical forms of armed violence, in which the classical rules of the art (of war) would have been replaced by current norms of international law. What international law provides us with is a communicative framework of intelligibility which describes the events, but it gives us no help either to understand the genesis of violent practices or to participate in them in such as way as to make possible an effective moral or political intervention; nor, in the end, does it help us to exercise the punishment of the so-called "*war crimes*", always punishable when there is nothing more to be done, not to mention the countless number of reasons relating to the established powers as well as to the classical problematic of the limitations and contradictions of law. The mere existence, production and reproduction of current military technologies, armaments, tactics, military discourses, the demographic and urban conceptions involved – indispensable for a strategic discourse – belies any conviction of hope. Even were it possible to reduce an analysis or an imaginary international order to the "*legal*", while confining ourselves to the law, the contrast between the military pragmatics and the institutional formulations could not be greater nor more delegitimating of every normative discourse, nor safer for any pretence of justice or even fairness. The actually existing armaments cannot be used without consequences little removed from extermination, massacre and genocide. Beyond the criminal character of the war, residing in the fact that it consists in killing, the idea that it is possible to conceive of a war "*crime*" as opposed to a "*non-criminal*" war is one of the most remarkable fantasies which govern in the current hegemonic ideologies. In the exercise of the war of guerrillas against the armed forces of the powers there also emerge spectacular forms of horror and extermination, even when they are made invisible – or highlighted discriminatorily – for "*political*" reasons. For those who nowadays practice guerrilla or minority strategies, in many cases the norms of human rights find their utility as tools of propaganda, a fundamental aspect of war.

Today the criminal and harmful character of the enemy is expressed in the language of human rights. On the other hand, the hegemonic powers, in order to adhere formally to the current normative discourses, try, when they practice war in the way in which it is done currently, to adhere to the norms and the classical narratives of war. In some cases, in the most recent versions, like those of the Second World War. The kind of military violence which came to a head in the Second World War has become impractical from the point of view of propaganda. The death of thousands or millions of people makes combat illegitimate in the eyes of the television viewers. As always happens in war, everyone regrets the losses on their own side, and it is this which eventually stops the combative impulse. To the extent that the lives of individual citizens are valued, civilian deaths provide guidelines for conflicts, even when it takes place in relation to a great number of *mediations*, with the possibility that certain military events concomitant with mass exterminations will not be the theme of media and political agencies for years.

It seems as striking as notable that "*legal*" arms of mass destruction (which on the whole they are not) can be exhibited as technological boasts and narratives without any apparent problem. The humanitarian catastrophes are lamented only because they have taken place. We do not allude here to the question of arms trafficking and its clandestine channels, but rather to the machines of death, inextricably intertwined with the biopolitical frameworks which we inhabit in a constitutive manner and which seem invisible or are represented as innocent. Nowadays it is practical to show off gigantic nuclear aircraft carriers, veritable cities intended solely for mass extermination, as if they were interesting and fascinating cultural phenomena, urban (floating) and technological, worthy of admiration, to give a capricious example which could also have referred to complex rockets, aircraft, satellite cartography and espionage, a paraphernalia of devastation. It should be appreciated that, if the ethics and conflicts which formally exist today are linked to the events of the *final solution* with such apparent triviality and easy approval, it is because the events of the *final solution* do not inhabit us only as memories or recollections of the past, but as limits to what can happen. And while there have not been limited, but rather unlimited evil events, we inhabit a world in which the outbreak of war confronts the shadows of the *final solution* whether from the perspective of justice or of injustice, of the established powers or of the contesting forces from which the military struggle is faced. As long as the languages of peace do not rediscover ethico-political vigour and the powers which they once embodied, there will be no hope of defending the most basic human rights. This is a condition which reduces the possibilities of intervention to a plane comparable with charity. Neither the contempt nor the neglect, neither the illusion nor the promise, should be reserved for such a ground, but rather the reasonable concern which encourages the consciousness of limits.

Index

Hispanic Studies: Culture and Ideas

Edited by
Claudio Canaparo

This series aims to publish studies in the arts, humanities and social sciences, the main focus of which is the Hispanic World. The series invites proposals with interdisciplinary approaches to Hispanic culture in fields such as the history of concepts and ideas, the sociology of culture, the evolution of visual arts, the critique of literature, and the uses of historiography. It is not confined to a particular historical period.

Monographs as well as collected papers are welcome in English or Spanish.

Those interested in contributing to the series are invited to write with either the synopsis of a subject already in typescript or with a detailed project outline to either Professor Claudio Canaparo, Department of Iberian and Latin American Studies, School of Arts, Birkbeck College, 43 Gordon Square, London WC1H 0PD, UK, c.canaparo@sllc.bbk.ac.uk, or Peter Lang Ltd, oxford@peterlang.com.

Vol. 1 Antonio Sánchez
Postmodern Spain. A Cultural Analysis of 1980s–1990s Spanish Culture. 220 pages. 2007.
ISBN 978-3-03910-914-2

Vol. 2 Geneviève Fabry y Claudio Canaparo (eds.)
El enigma de lo real. Las fronteras del realismo en la narrativa del siglo XX. 275 pages. 2007.
ISBN 978-3-03910-893-0

Vol. 3 William Rowlandson
Reading Lezama's *Paradiso*. 290 pages. 2007.
ISBN 978-3-03910-751-3

Vol. 4 Fernanda Peñaloza, Jason Wilson and Claudio Canaparo (eds)
Patagonia. Myths and Realities. 277 pages. 2010.
ISBN 978-3-03910-917-3

Vol. 5 Xon de Ros
Primitivismo y Modernismo. El legado de María Blanchard.
238 pages. 2007.
ISBN 978-3-03910-937-1

Vol. 6 Sergio Plata
Visions of Applied Mathematics. Strategy and Knowledge.
284 pages. 2007.
ISBN 978-3-03910-923-4

Vol. 7 Annick Louis
Borges ante el fascismo. 374 pages. 2007.
ISBN 978-3-03911-005-6

Vol. 8 Helen Oakley
From Revolution to Migration. A Study of Contemporary Cuban and Cuban-American Crime Fiction. 200 pages. 2012.
ISBN 978-3-03911-021-6

Vol. 9 Thea Pitman
Mexican Travel Writing. 209 pages. 2008.
ISBN 978-3-03911-020-9

Vol. 10 Francisco J. Borge
A New World for a New Nation. The Promotion of America in Early Modern England. 240 pages. 2007.
ISBN 978-3-03911-070-4

Vol. 11 Helena Buffery, Stuart Davis and Kirsty Hooper (eds)
Reading Iberia. Theory/History/Identity. 229 pages. 2007.
ISBN 978-3-03911-109-1

Vol. 12 Matías Bruera
Mapping the Tasteland. Explorations in Food and Wine in Argentinean and European Culture. 240 pages. 2014.
ISBN 978-3-03911-345-3

Vol. 13 Angela Romero-Astvaldsson
La obra narrativa de David Viñas. La nueva inflexión de *Prontuario* y *Claudia Conversa*. 300 pages. 2007.
ISBN 978-3-03911-100-8

Vol. 14 Aaron Kahn
The Ambivalence of Imperial Discourse. Cervantes's *La Numancia* within the 'Lost Generation' of Spanish Drama (1570–90).
243 pages. 2008.
ISBN 978-3-03911-098-8

Vol. 15 Turid Hagene
Negotiating Love in Post-Revolutionary Nicaragua. The role of love in the reproduction of gender asymmetry. 341 pages. 2008.
ISBN 978-3-03911-011-7

Vol. 16 Yolanda Rodríguez Pérez
The Dutch Revolt through Spanish Eyes. Self and Other in historical and literary texts of Golden Age Spain (c. 1548–1673). 346 pages. 2008.
ISBN 978-3-03911-136-7

Vol. 17 Stanley Black (ed.)
Juan Goytisolo. Territories of Life and Writing. 202 pages. 2007.
ISBN 978-3-03911-324-8

Vol. 18 María T. Sánchez
The Problems of Literary Translation. A Study of the Theory and Practice of Translation from English into Spanish. 269 pages. 2009.
ISBN 978-3-03911-326-2

Vol. 19 Aino Linda Rinhaug
Fernando Pessoa. A Ludicrous Self. *Forthcoming*.
ISBN 978-3-03911-909-7

Vol. 20 Ana Cruz García
Re(de-)generando identidades. Locura, feminidad y liberalización en Elena Garro, Susana Pagano, Ana Castillo y María Amparo Escandón.
259 pages. 2009.
ISBN 978-3-03911-524-2

Vol. 21 Idoya Puig (ed.)
Tradition and Modernity. Cervantes's Presence in Spanish Contemporary Literature. 221 pages. 2009.
ISBN 978-3-03911-526-6

Vol. 22 Charlotte Lange
Modos de parodia. Guillermo Cabrera Infante, Reinaldo Arenas, Jorge Ibargüengoitia y José Agustín. 252 pages. 2008.
ISBN 978-3-03911-554-9

Vol. 23 Claudio Canaparo
Geo-epistemology. Latin America and the Location of Knowledge. 284 pages. 2009.
ISBN 978-3-03911-573-0

Vol. 24 Jesús López-Peláez Casellas
"Honourable Murderers". El concepto del honor en *Othello* de Shakespeare y en los "dramas de honor" de Calderón. 321 pages. 2009.
ISBN 978-3-03911-825-0

Vol. 25 Marian Womack and Jennifer Wood (eds)
Beyond the Back Room. New Perspectives on Carmen Martín Gaite. 336 pages. 2011.
ISBN 978-3-03911-827-4

Vol. 26 Manuela Palacios and Laura Lojo (eds)
Writing Bonds. Irish and Galician Contemporary Women Poets. 232 pages. 2009.
ISBN 978-3-03911-834-2

Vol. 27 Myriam Osorio
Agencia femenina, agencia narrativa. Una lectura feminista de la obra en prosa de Albalucía Ángel. 180 pages. 2010.
ISBN 978-3-03911-893-3

Vol. 28 *Forthcoming*

Vol. 29 Soledad Pérez-Abadín Barro
Cortázar y Che Guevara. Lectura de *Reunión*. 182 pages. 2010.
ISBN 978-3-03911-919-6

Vol. 30 Gonzalo Pasamar
Apologia and Criticism. Historians and the History of Spain, 1500–2000. 301 pages. 2010.
ISBN 978-3-03911-920-2

Vol. 31 Victoria Carpenter (ed.)
(Re)Collecting the Past. History and Collective Memory in Latin American Narrative. 315 pages. 2010.
ISBN 978-3-03911-928-8

Vol. 32 Geneviève Fabry, Ilse Logie y Pablo Decock (eds.)
Los imaginarios apocalípticos en la literatura hispanoamericana contemporánea. 472 pages. 2010.
ISBN 978-3-03911-937-0

Vol. 33 Julian Vigo
Performative Bodies, Hybrid Tongues. Race, Gender, Sex and Modernity in Latin America and the Maghreb. 391 pages. 2010.
ISBN 978-3-03911-951-6

Vol. 34 Heike Pintor Pirzkall
La cooperación alemana al desarrollo. Factores condicionantes de su transformación en la década de los noventa y su impacto en América Latina. 374 pages. 2010.
ISBN 978-3-0343-0107-7

Vol. 35 Arturo Casas and Ben Bollig (eds)
Resistance and Emancipation. Cultural and Poetic Practices. 419 pages. 2011.
ISBN 978-3-0343-0160-2

Vol. 36 Pablo Decock
Las figuras paradójicas de César Aira. Un estudio semiótico y axiológico de la estereotipia y la autofiguración. 344 pages. 2014.
ISBN 978-3-0343-0169-5

Vol. 37 Guillermo Olivera
Laboratorios de la mediatización. La experimentación con materiales mediáticos, la teoría y la crítica cultural argentina, 1965–1978.
364 pages. 2011.
ISBN 978-3-0343-0201-2

Vol. 38 Guy Baron
Gender in Cuban Cinema. From the Modern to the Postmodern.
334 pages. 2011.
ISBN 978-3-0343-0229-6

Vol. 39 Claudio Canaparo
El imaginario Patagonia. Ensayo acerca de la evolución conceptual del espacio. 576 pages. 2011.
ISBN 978-3-0343-0287-6

Vol. 40 Inmaculada Murcia Serrano
Agua y destino. Introducción a la estética de Ramón Gaya.
220 pages. 2011.
ISBN 978-3-0343-0251-7

Vol. 41 Bill Richardson
Borges and Space. 266 pages. 2012.
ISBN 978-3-0343-0246-3

Vol. 42 *Forthcoming*

Vol. 43 Ann Frost
The Galician Works of Ramón del Valle-Inclán. Patterns of Repetition and Continuity. 241 pages. 2010.
ISBN 978-3-0343-0242-5

Vol. 44 Milagros López-Peláez Casellas
What About the Girls? Estrategias narrativas de resistencia en la primera literatura chicana. 265 pages. 2012.
ISBN 978-3-0343-0264-7

Vol. 45 Bill Richardson and Lorraine Kelly (eds)
Power, Place and Representation. Contested Sites of Dependence and Independence in Latin America. 268 pages. 2012.
ISBN 978-3-0343-0710-9

Vol. 46 Patricia D'Allemand
José María Samper. Nación y cultura en el siglo XIX colombiano. 177 pages. 2012.
ISBN 978-3-0343-0288-3

Vol. 47 *Forthcoming*

Vol. 48 Emilio Rosales
Baroja. La novela como laberinto. 163 pages. 2012.
ISBN 978-3-0343-0774-1

Vol. 49 Kristine Vanden Berghe
Las novelas de la rebelión zapatista. 171 pages. 2012.
ISBN 978-3-0343-0779-6

Vol. 50 William Rowlandson
Borges, Swedenborg and Mysticism. 267 pages. 2013.
ISBN 978-3-0343-0811-3

Vol. 51 Elena Rodríguez-Guridi
Exégesis del "error". Una reinterpretación de la praxis de escritura en *Libro de la vida*, *Novelas ejemplares* y *Desengaños amorosos*.
175 pages. 2013.
ISBN 978-3-0343-0817-5

Vol. 52 Eva Bru-Domínguez
Beyond Containment. Corporeality in Mercè Rodoreda's Literature.
235 pages. 2013
ISBN 978-3-0343-0888-5

Vol. 53 Gabriele Andreozzi (ed.)
Desaparición. Argentina's Human Rights Trials. 355 pages. 2014.
ISBN 978-3-0343-0857-1

Vol. 54 Mel Boland
Displacement in Isabel Allende's Fiction, 1982–2000.
212 pages. 2013.
ISBN 978-3-0343-0932-5

Vol. 55 Eduardo Tasis Moratinos
El exilio en la poesía de Tomás Segovia y Angelina Muñiz Huberman.
234 pages. 2014.
ISBN 978-3-0343-0941-7

Vol. 56 Santiago Pérez Isasi and Ângela Fernandes (eds)
Looking at Iberia. A Comparative European Perspective.
317 pages. 2013.
ISBN 978-3-0343-0934-9

Vol. 57 Daniel de Zubía Fernández
Señas del esplendor ausente. Itinerarios familiares en *Señas de identidad* y en *O Esplendor de Portugal*
373 pages. 2014.
ISBN 978-3-0343-0963-9

Vol. 58 Helena Usandizaga (ed.)
Palimpsestos de la antigua palabra. Inventario de mitos prehispánicos en la literatura latinoamericana
383 pages. 2013.
ISBN 978-3-0343-0967-7

Vol. 59 *Forthcoming*

Vol. 60 Guillermo Laín Corona
Proyecciones de Gabriel Miró en la narrativa del 27.
250 pages. 2013.
ISBN 978-3-0343-0952-3

www.ingramcontent.com/pod-product-compliance
Ingram Content Group UK Ltd.
Pitfield, Milton Keynes, MK11 3LW, UK
UKHW021853100926
8556IPUK00020B/1202

9 783034 308571